IMAG(IN)ING OTHERNESS

AAR

American Academy of Religion
Cultural Criticism Series

Björn Krondorfer
Editor

Number 7

IMAG(IN)ING OTHERNESS
FILMIC VISIONS OF LIVING TOGETHER

edited by
S. Brent Plate
David Jasper

IMAG(IN)ING OTHERNESS
FILMIC VISIONS OF LIVING TOGETHER

edited by
S. Brent Plate
David Jasper

Scholars Press
Atlanta, Georgia

IMAG(IN)ING OTHERNESS
FILMIC VISIONS OF LIVING TOGETHER

edited by
S. Brent Plate
David Jasper

Image for cover and on page one of the text is from the film
Why Has Bodhi-Dharma Left for the East?
Still courtesy of Milestone Film & Video, New York.

Library of Congress Cataloging-in-Publication Data

Imag(in)ing otherness : filmic visions of living together / edited by S. Brent Plate, David Jasper.
    p. cm. -- (American Academy of Religion cultural criticism series ; no. 7)
    Includes bibliographical references and index.
    ISBN 0-7885-0593-9 (alk. paper)
    1. Exoticism in motion pictures. 2. Minorities in motion pictures. I. Plate, S. Brent,
1996– II. Jasper, David. III. Series.

PN1995.9.E95 I46 1999
791.43'655--dc21

                                                   99-045495

Printed in the United States of America
on acid-free paper
∞

Contents

Acknowledgements

For extra help in obtaining film stills, the Editors wish to thank Mary Corliss and Terry Geeskin of the Museum of Modern Art Film Stills Library, NYC; Stacie Smith at Exoskeleton, NYC; Nikolai Amburgey at October Films, NYC; Caitlin Broderick at Miramax, NYC; and Dennis Doros at Milestone Film and Video, NYC. Thank you to Bill Blizek and Ronald Burke, editors of *The Journal of Religion and Film* for permissions to reprint the articles by Tod Linafelt and Kyle Keefer, and Irena Makarushka. Both articles originally appeared in the journal issue 2.1.

Thanks to Michael Bradley of Scholars Press for answering a lot of questions as the manuscript was being prepared.

Brent wishes to thank the following persons for general encouragement and quite a few good discussions over breakfasts in Atlanta: Gabriella Boston, Chris Boesel, and Julie Sexeny. For challenges to the way I see, I would also like to thank Robin Blaetz of Emory University. And finally, many thanks to Edna Melisa Rodríguez-Mangual, for watching all those films with me.

Introduction:
Images and Imaginings

S. Brent Plate

> One exposes oneself to the other—the stranger, the destitute one, the judge—
> not only with one's insights and one's ideas, that they may be contested, but
> one also exposes the nakedness of one's eyes, one's voice and one's silences,
> one's empty hands. For the other, the stranger, turns to one, not only with his
> or her convictions and judgments, but also with his or her frailty,
> susceptibility, mortality. . . . Community forms when one exposes oneself to
> the naked one, the destitute one, the outcast, the dying one. One enters into
> community not by affirming oneself and one's forces but by exposing oneself
> to expenditure at a loss, to sacrifice. Community forms in a movement by
> which one exposes oneself to the other, to forces and powers outside oneself,
> to death and to the others who die.
> -Alphonso Lingis, "The Other Community"[1]

The title of our book can of course be read in two ways: as "imaging otherness"
and as "imagining otherness." Each of these two readings can, in turn, be read
in a multitude of ways. The practice of imag(in)ing otherness is a long and
complicated task. But let's begin with some simple readings. . . .

In the first instance, the dualistic reading of the title exhibits a
relationship between aesthetics and ethics. As "imaging otherness" we mean to
indicate the way the medium of film has invented, produced, and portrayed
otherness in a distinct audio-visual form. Through unique audio-visual qualities,
film has altered given cultural symbols of who "the others" are, what otherness
consists of, and where otherness is to be found (or not found, as is more often
the case). From an aesthetic perspective then, *Imag(in)ing Otherness* analyzes
these visually-constructed symbols. Correlatively, as "imagining otherness" we
mean to take the further positive step of indicating how persons interested in
ethics and religion can think and imagine otherness differently. The book does
not rest content with the analysis of these cultural symbols, but includes
constructive avenues whereby otherness is not simply something "out there" but
makes a demand on us and challenges us to live differently. The ethically
imaginative goal is to offer new forms of living together, new forms of
community. Our contemporary, multicultural social structure needs voices and
images of imagination—not a fanciful imagination of fairy worlds, but a *critical
imagination*. We believe that this book's uniqueness therefore lies in its use of
film as a powerful, unique, and popular medium from which to address
important religious issues, while simultaneously it contributes to the broader
ethical discourses of otherness currently being held in various cultural locations.

The ability to live together with others is a difficult endeavor in a multicultural age and a confrontation with some of the specifically *visual* elements of otherness becomes a necessary response. Scholarly work from an ethically religious perspective has paid increasing attention to issues of otherness over the past two decades, but seldom have the particularities of the visual aspects of otherness been treated within religious studies. Humans live in a world where appearances do make a difference, for better or worse, and where visual images of otherness have helped to promote hatred, intolerance, and violence in various times and places. It is little wonder then that the greatest voices for coming to terms with otherness have come from marginalized groups: from feminism, from gay and lesbian activists, from the liberatory concerns of the two-thirds world. It is also little wonder that these same groups are leading the way toward the analysis and critique of visual images in culture. Quite simply, ethical and religious inquiry must continue to turn toward visual representations of otherness. The goal of this book is to contribute to that shift by analyzing these representations through the visual medium of film. This is not to ignore the essential *audio* component to film, but the essays included here point out the ways in which visual structures of otherness supplement linguistic structures of otherness and, most importantly, what happens when, as with the medium of film, the word and image are brought together to form *new* symbols and structures. The juxtapositioning of the words and images of film is a point of continual reference for the essays that follow.

This, That, and the Other

The term "otherness" is initially used here to denote that which resides outside the margins of the dominant cultural representations, outside the social-symbolic order. In what are by now oft-quoted identity categories in the West this has typically meant persons of color, gays and lesbians, the poor, and women, while the dominant order has been constructed and reigned over by caucasian, heterosexual, wealthy men. Otherness also functions globally in that many northern countries (those of the G-7 and/or NATO) construct the world order by which the others (those of the two-thirds world) must abide. If we are interested in the ethical and critical practice of imag(in)ing otherness, we must undertake a search for that which has been forgotten, pushed aside, and otherwise exiled from the realm of visual-social representation.

Still, there remains a problem with these notions of otherness. As I have described it so far, the "other" is seemingly only able to be defined in relation to the "same," in relation to the dominant social-symbolic order. As Simone de Beauvoir protested 50 years ago, woman "finds herself living in a world where men compel her to assume the status of the Other."[2] Woman, de Beauvoir argued, has been assigned the position of "the second sex," an *object* only understood in a context where man is the primary *subject*. Heeding this critique, an ethical concern with otherness must invert the typical phenomenological direction from self to other, moving instead, as Emmanuel Levinas has rephrased it, from the other to the self. That is, the other precedes and constitutes the self: ethics—responsibility to the other—precedes subjectivity. I am nothing without the other.

Within this reconfiguration some difference must still be maintained; everything cannot collapse into a seamless whole, for then all dynamic tension is eliminated. The aim is not to turn all "others" into the "same." However, difference must become non-hierarchical difference. Jacques Derrida thereby re-inscribes Levinas's writing when he claims "*tout autre es tout autre*" (every other is wholly other[3]); indeed, each subject is an other to her or his self. The practice of imag(in)ing otherness envisions relationships *between others*, not between a primary subject and secondary object. Only in such an open, relational structure can hierarchy be eliminated. Difference is maintained, the other remains other, but none can take the primary, dominant position of *subject* looking at an *object* because the so-called subject is always already preceded by the so-called object. Before the subject can even *look*, to put it in Lacan's visual registers, she or he is already being *looked at* and is caught up in a *gaze* that structures her or his own being. John Caputo nicely paraphrases these ethical concerns and sets out a certain imperative for those of us contributing to this book:

> To surrender to the other, to love the other, means to go over to the other without passing the threshold of the other, without trespassing on the other's threshold. To love is to respect the invisibility of the other, to keep the other *safe*, to surrender one's arms to the other but without defeat . . . To love is to give oneself to the other in such a way that this would really be giving and not taking, a gift, a way of letting the other remain other, that is, be loved, rather than a stratagem, a ruse of jealousy, a way of winning[.][4]

However we may fail, however impossible it is to achieve this, the practice of imag(in)ing otherness nevertheless holds up such a guiding *ethos*.

In coming to terms with this term otherness, therefore, we mean to differentiate it from a term such as "outsiders," for otherness carries with it the connotation of changing what it comes into contact with. Thus the practice of imag(in)ing otherness entails more than mere tolerance; it entails being changed by the other and having to rearrange given structures and established communities. This makes the responsibility of "living together with others" a difficult demand, and raises the stakes of this current book. *Imag(in)ing Otherness* attempts the admittedly difficult (nay, impossible) feat of speaking for the other while not allowing otherness to be subsumed into conventional categories of representation. If we could simply re-present the other within conventional forms (for example, within commercial Hollywood cinema) then otherness would cease to exist and nothing would be changed. To the contrary, if we are truly able to imagine the image of the other we will have to learn to *see differently*. This entails both a difference in the images that are being looked at and a difference in the way they are looked at—a difference, again, of images and imaginings. A cinema of otherness would be one in which the structure of production and the style of a finished film would necessarily be different than what we are expecting to see, indeed, what we have been trained to see. For those of us raised on Hollywood cinema, a cinema of otherness would be unrecognizable, and it certainly would not be found playing in the shopping mall multiplex.

That is, it is not simply enough, for example, for African Americans to be given more roles in Hollywood films when the formal and technical structure of film production itself is oriented around—indeed designed by and profited from by—white men.[5] (One logical consequence of this, as we saw thirty years ago, is a cinema of "blaxploitation," which, while it remains controversial as to whether it was a positive or negative step for African Americans, certainly did little to change the deep structures of film production.[6]) Images of the other cannot simply become commodities, warns bell hooks, critical of certain trends in popular culture that attempt to "image the other": "Certainly from the standpoint of white supremacist capitalist patriarchy, the hope is that desires for the 'primitive' or fantasies about the Other can be continually exploited, and that such exploitation will occur in a manner that reinscribes and maintains the *status quo*."[7] The other can be represented *ad infinitum*, but as long as these images remain structured by and under the control of the dominant order, the *status quo* is merely bolstered. We still have yet to see the other.

Early cinema visionaries like Eisenstein and Chaplin saw a great potential for film to change the way humans perceived and understood each other, and therefore to change the way they lived together. Optimistic, even utopic, these early filmmaker's universalizing hopes and dreams were fairly quickly subsumed by the capitalization of the film industry which chose only to portray that which could make money. As a result, a homogeneous cinema has been instituted and the average film-goer in the average multiplex (or Blockbuster video rental store) is subjected to the same images of the same types of people, over and over again. Thus, in his study of African Americans in film, Ed Guerrero critiques the film industry's narrow-mindedness, stating at the beginning of his study:

> Instead of efforts to construct a truly universal system of communication that builds egalitarian understandings between diverse groups and cultures, what we have seen arise in commercial cinema is a monopolistic, capital-intensive film business. And in spite of some narrative innovation, dissenting artistic exploration, and political countercurrents, the industry has been formula bound and conservative in its vision in order to deliver commodified visual entertainments to the broadest possible consumer market. Instead of inspiring aesthetic, cultural, and political masterworks aimed at liberating the human potential, Hollywood, for the most part, has tended to focus narrowly its

increasingly shallow product on escapism, sentiment, glamour, romance, and, more recently, spectacular orgies of violence and sexploitation, all in the service of feeding the dulled cravings and fantasies of the dominant social order.[8]

Every other must approach every other with caution and respect. Every other must be careful not to simply turn the other into "one of us." Every other must be careful not to objectify the other for one's own entertainment, instead, every other must imagine the image of relations *between others*. And this is a role that religious studies scholars might play, as Margaret Miles argues:

> Americans [i.e., North Americans] need images that help us picture religious, racial, and cultural diversity not merely as tolerable but as irreducible and delightful. Media images could help all Americans imagine difference that is neither overcome nor transcended, difference that is evenly distributed rather than posited of anyone who diverges from a repetitiously reiterated norm. . . . By analyzing and criticizing public images, religious studies can serve religious institutions that seek to propose images representing values alternative to those of a culture based on entertainment and consumption.[9]

Scholars of religion have a task set before them in a multi-media, multicultural age. The task that Miles points out is the task we have here called Imag(in)ing Otherness. The essays in this book do not have metaphors of melting pots as their goal, but contribute to an ethics of otherness by pointing out communities of difference rather than communities of unity—where living together does not end in a harmonizing homogeneity, but where the lines of difference perpetually show through.

Before turning to introduce the contents of this book, let me attempt to rephrase the paradox entailed with regard to imag(in)ing otherness. The other, by definition, cannot be defined. If the other can be discussed and thereby brought into the symbolic order, it ceases being other. To simply re-present the other would make the other one more recognizable object put in circulation in the symbolic order. To commodify the other is not to *see* the other. Any "discourse of otherness" itself must be questioned, for otherness in its strictest sense cannot be discussed. The other, then, is (the) impossible.

At the same time, if "every other is wholly other," then we must also question certain tendencies in theoretical discourse that continue to set up "otherness" exclusively as problems of race, class, gender, or sexuality (the four current dominant identity categories). To do so is to categorize and objectify otherness itself. This is not to eliminate such categories, but to intensify them and make the categories of otherness more diverse. As the following essays help make clear, one encounters otherness even within one's own religious tradition, even within one's own culture, even within one's own family. Again, this does not deny the crucial difference that race, for example, plays in social structures but it is to take the further critical step and ask *who* is creating and maintaining these categories, and to what end?

The challenge of *Imag(in)ing Otherness* is thus two-fold, and is represented by the following two sets of questions: 1) How is it possible (or not) to represent otherness (i.e., to "image otherness") given the fact that film is a symbolic structure situated within a dominant social order? What otherness has this order repressed and forgotten? What would a cinema of otherness look like? 2) How can others "live together"? If difference is omnipresent, how can we "imagine otherness" and thereby help to form, in the words of Alphonso Lingis, "a community for those who have nothing in common"?[10] How can we exist between the homogenizing forces of a "global community" and the brutality of a local tribalism? We may define new languages for our local communities, but what happens when these local communities have to communicate with each other? Some of the essays that follow lean toward the challenge of the first set of questions, some lean toward the second, and others move between the two.

Imag(in)ings

Given several of the concerns stated above it is clear that a careful and thoroughgoing critique of commercial cinema needs to be enacted, but it may also be the case that too much emphasis (critical or not) on commercial cinema finally only serves to continue to prop up the homogeneous industry. Criticism *is* a form of advertisement. So instead, as Fredric Jameson strategically considers with regard commercial television, perhaps "Thinking anything adequate about commercial television may well involve ignoring it and thinking about something else."[11] A similar strategy may be usefully (un)applied to commercial cinema. In this light, the present book hopes to serve as a supplement to many of the recent publications that have appeared under the guise of "religion and film," publications that show a decided trend toward analysis of "popular" and "Hollywood" film.[12] Each of these publications contain some very excellent critical work (indeed, several of the contributors to those volumes are also contributors to this book), but what we hope to achieve with the present book is both an advertisement for alternative cinema and a related "ethics of vision"[13] that may be enacted through the *practice* of viewing alternative films. By "alternative" we mean quite simply those films produced outside of the industrial production companies of Hollywood. Many of the films discussed in the following were produced outside of the United States—in Denmark, Korea, India, Britain, Canada—or in the United States with independent producers. At the same time, it must quickly be noted, this book continues to show an interest in popular cinema, and several of the essays focus on some popular films, including *You Can't Take It With You* and *A Passage to India*, as well as marginally popular films like *Breaking the Waves* and

Babette's Feast, and even B-films like *The Giant Behemoth* and *Leviathan*. We certainly do not imagine that popular cinema can be ignored, but we do feel that too much interest (critical or not) serves to continue its negative cultural effects.

Again, the practice of imag(in)ing otherness is caught up in the relationship between aesthetics and ethics, and between what *has been* imaged and what *can be* imagined. With an eye for both past and future orientations, this collection of essays takes a variety of films from differing locations and times and from a variety of religious perspectives—including Chan Buddhism, Hinduism, Native American religion, Christianity, and Judaism—to examine the particular problems of "living together" when faced with the tensions brought out through the otherness of differing sexualities, ethnicities, genders, religions, cultures, and families. Films analyzed come from various places and range in time from the 1938 *You Can't Take it With You* and 1956 *Aparajito* to the 1996 films *Dead Man* and *Breaking the Waves*. The book is organized through five themes that examine from different perspectives the theme of otherness, and how to live with otherness in community. Each of the five themes is comprised of a pair of essays.

The first section includes essays by Gregory Salyer and Jennifer Koosed and sets up issues related to "Surviving Community." Salyer and Koosed push the readers toward the survival of communities, asking how religiously and culturally inherited stories can contribute to the establishment of life together in the wake of catastrophe. Salyer's examination of *Dead Man* and Koosed's examination of *The Quarrel* highlight a unique ability for film to tell stories— stories of the dead, stories of the past, stories that work to bring others together for the future. Salyer and Koosed implicitly and explicitly point out how verbal narratives remain as a vital component of film production but also how this verbal tradition is enabled to survive through its adaptation into the audio-visual medium of film. Salyer particularly implies that surviving catastrophe may itself depend on such reimag(in)ings, such shifts in the medium of our storytelling, and directors like Jim Jarmusch (the director of *Dead Man*) point out ways in which this may be done. Similarly, if the post-Holocaust imperative to "never forget" is practiced, then it also becomes necessary to think about the medium through which one might not forget. This is perhaps part of what director Eli Cohen has accomplished by filming the post-Holocaust story, *The Quarrel*.

In "Desiring Community," two essays on the film *Breaking the Waves* take up the theme of *desire* and its relation to otherness, a relation that goes to the heart of the paradox of analyzing otherness mentioned above. Danish director Lars von Trier has triggered a number of responses within religious and feminist circles with his 1996 film *Breaking the Waves*, and the two essays included here continue and, I believe, critically enlarge the issues raised by the film. Each of the essays focuses on the vital force of desire that propels the action of the film, and by the end of the two essays a substantial discourse surrounding desire's relation to the other is enacted. In this discourse we find that desire is not a simple "wanting" (as in wanting ice cream, or a new car), but desire for an other is a dangerous force that, as with the previous section's emphasis on storytelling, is bound up with loss and with death. Irena Makarushka articulates the risk of desiring the other via feminist film and literary critics, as well as by putting the scenes of the film itself under careful scrutiny. Tod Linafelt and Kyle Keefer compare the film with The Song of Songs, using Georges Bataille's theories of eros to link the ancient book and contemporary film. In both essays we see quite clearly that desire, whether desire for God or for another human, is a risk. To desire an other means that one's own self is risked.

In the third section, the economics of living together in the household are highlighted, especially when they are centered around the dinner table. We thus have given the title "Eating Community" to this section. Maria Maisto interprets Gabriel Axel's *Babette's Feast* through one of the earliest critical works in religion and film, Paul Schrader's *Transcendental Style in Film*. Patrick Caruso and I recall Frank Capra's somewhat forgotten 1938 film, *You Can't Take It With You*. Each essay sees the household table as the site of transformation, the site where otherness is brought together in communion. At the same time, this site/sight of communion is the space where transgression, a mixing and confusion of boundaries, takes place, and where difference continues to show through. Maisto examines *Babette's Feast* from the theoretical middle ground of the interdisciplinary divide between religious studies and film studies. In so doing she comes to the conclusion that interpretive conclusions of the film itself will depend on the interpretive standpoint—whether one approaches it from film studies or from religious studies. Real transformation must come about through a mixing of two sides, two othernesses. Caruso and I pay attention to the otherness found in familial structures. Using the psychological theories of contextual therapy, a dialectic of freedom and obligation is found at the crux of the family, so that the family becomes estranged, and the stranger becomes family. Again, transformation occurs, but it is not a transformation that leads to a nice-and-neat conclusive communion, for otherness haunts all such homogeneity.

"Colonizing Community" brings us to postcolonial perspectives on India and to competing images/imaginings of culture, religion, and nationality. As Diana Eck has stated, in words which echo many of our concerns in this volume,

> The medium of film is especially important for the student of Hinduism, for it provides a way of entering the visual world, the world of sense and image, which is so important for the Hindu tradition. . . . In India's own terms, seeing is knowing. And India must be seen to be known.[14]

This section thus leads readers to the "knowledge" of India in a new way. David Jasper compares the British version of India through British director David Lean's *Passage to India* with the Indian version of India through Indian director Satyajit Ray's *Aparajito* (the second part of Ray's "Apu trilogy"). Lean's film depicts an "other" world, defined here in the negative terms highlighted above whereby British culture represents the subjective position from which India and Indians are objectified. Ray's film, by contrast, shows us an India where the joys and struggles are indeed "exotic" to western eyes (because westerners do not know how to see them), but where the joys and struggles of Apu and his family are in fact simple, quotidian, and therefore quite possibly also universal. At the heart of each film, as Jasper hints, is the impossibility of the "passage to India," the impossibility to translate between cultures, religions, and languages, an impossibility that again goes to our paradox of understanding and representing the other. While Jasper's focus is on an India set in the first half of the twentieth century, and therefore still a British colony, Ira Bhaskar brings us to a similar tension in the contemporary postcolonial setting through British dramatist Peter Brook's version of *The Mahabharata*. Bhaskar acknowledges the possible benefits of the multicultural attempts of the postmodern-inspired Brook, but questions the eclecticism and the pastiche mode of representing the other found in many postmodernisms. Representation of the other here again verges on the border of fascination, which quickly leads to the objectification and finally the commodification of the other.

Finally, to remind us that otherness is generally too-quickly consumed by the reigning symbolic structures, we conclude with two essays that challenge the theoretical issues of otherness and community themselves. In "Ending Community" we find two completely different—though nonetheless related—critiques of the very concepts that this book struggles to discuss. Taking up the Korean-Buddhist film *Why has the Bodhi-dharma left for the East?*, Francisca Cho asks whether otherness itself is located within a specifically western religious climate and may not translate universally. Otherness implicitly entails a western dualistic structure of thought, a mode of organizing the world that Chan Buddhism does not necessarily share. By playing with the concept of otherness in a Buddhist setting she is able to draw out a proposed new method of religiously viewing film. She labels this the "cultic mode," whereby signification is highlighted by a certain cinematic ritual. From another angle, Timothy Beal once again takes up the fundamental paradox of this book by questioning whether the other can indeed be represented in film. Utilizing the genre of horror film and specifically Eugene Lourie's 1958 eco-horror classic *The Giant Behemoth*, Beal suggests that the monster in monster movies is only truly horrible when it is not *imaged* on screen, but rather when it is left to the viewer's *imagination*. Perhaps film is finally only effective when cinema viewers, like Moses in the cleft of a rock (Exodus 33), are only allowed to see the "backside" of the "wholly other." This other may be divine, monstrous, or some combination of the two, and in this way, Beal considers, Rudolph Otto's *Mysterium tremendum et fascinans* becomes *Monstrum tremendum et fascinans*—with the monster functioning as an envoy of sacred terror.

In our contemporary postmodern climate we have been exposed to the image of the face of the other as never before, and in this exposure we are given the opportunity to respond in new and imaginative ways, or to go on objectifying the other for our own profit. We hope these contributions will be seen to rest firmly on the side of imaginative response. In this way we might enter into a new community.

the necessity tO find new forms
of liVing
nEw
foRms of living together
to stoP the estrangement between us
tO overcome
the Patriarchal thinking
the aUthoritarian structures
and the coLdness
humAn
noT togetherness
the necessIty
tO develop a culture
that coNsciously opposes the ruling culture
A culture which we create
we determiNe which overcomes the passive
attitu Dues
And
which is not Ruled
by profiTeering

-John Cage, from "Overpopulation and Art"[15]

Endnotes

1. Lingis, *The Community of Those Who Have Nothing in Common* (Bloomington: Indiana University Press, 1994), pp. 11-12.

2. Simone de Beauvoir, *The Second Sex*, trans. H.M. Parshley (New York: Vintage Books, 1980), p. xxxv.

3. Jacques Derrida, *On the Name* (Stanford: Stanford University Press, 1995), p. 74.

4. John Caputo, *The Prayers and Tears of Jacques Derrida* (Bloomington: Indiana University Press, 1997), p. 49.

5. A simple example of this—though not the only one—has to do with the choice of lighting and film stock that a filmmaker uses when filming persons with varying shades of skin color. With certain film stocks and lighting a light-skinned person's features come out very sharply and nicely defined while a dark-skinned person's features will blur together (Spielberg used this to dramatic effect in the opening scene of *Amistad*, 1996). Filmmakers have always had to choose which film stocks to use when simultaneously casting dark and light skinned people. A vast majority of filmmaker's choices should be quite predictable. For more on the ideologies behind film stock see Richard Dyer, *White* (London: Routledge, 1997), chapter three; and Brian Winston, *Technologies of Seeing*, esp. ch. 2: "White Skin and Colour Film: The Ideology of the Apparatus" (London: British Film Institute, 1996).

6. On the films and controversies of blaxploitation, see A. L. Woll and R. M. Miller, *Ethnic and Racial Images in American Film and Television* (New York: Garland Publishing, 1987), and Catherine Silk and John Silk, *Racism and Anti-racism in American Popular Culture* (Manchester and New York: Manchester University Press, 1990).

7. *Black Looks: Race and Representation* (Boston: South End Press, 1992), p. 22.

8. *Framing Blackness: The African American Image in Film* (Philadelphia: Temple University Press, 1992), p. 2.

9. Miles, "Image," in *Critical Terms for Religious Studies*, Mark C. Taylor, ed. (Chicago: University of Chicago Press, 1998), pp. 170-171.

10. This is the title of his book from which I have taken the epigraph found at the beginning of this introduction.

11. *Postmodernism, or The Cultural Logic of Late Capitalism* (Durham: Duke University Press, 1992), p. 71.

12. E.g., Martin and Ostwalt, eds., *Screening the Sacred* (Boulder: Westview Press, 1995); Margaret Miles, *Seeing and Believing* (Boston: Beacon Press, 1996); *Semeia 74* (1996); Marsh and Ortiz, eds., *Explorations in Theology and Film* (Oxford: Blackwell, 1997).

13. This is a phrase used by Mieke Bal in her review of Kaja Silverman's recent book *The Threshold of the Visible World* (New York: Routledge, 1996). See Bal, "Looking at Love: An Ethics of Vision," in *diacritics* 27.1 (1997).

14. Diana Eck, *Darśan: Seeing the Divine Image in India*, 3rd ed. (New York: Columbia University Press, 1998), p. 11.

15. Published in *John Cage: Composed in America*, edited by Marjorie Perloff and Charles Junkerman (Chicago: University of Chicago Press, 1994), pp. 23-24.

Part One: Surviving Community

Poetry Written with Blood:
Creating Death in *Dead Man*

Gregory Salyer

"Drive your cart and your plow over the bones of the dead."
-William Blake

"Stupid fucking white man."
-Nobody

Fade In
Train sounds. The following line in white letters against a black background:
"It is preferable not to travel with a dead man." Henri Michaux
Fade to Black

Fade In
Starkly beautiful black and white image of a train's drive mechanism stroking the wheels. An electric guitar plays over the scene adding to the metal-to-metal imagery.
Fade to Black

Fade In
A young man dressed in a plaid suit and bow tie with a black hat. He appears to be uneasy in the company of the strangers on the train who are dressed better and appear to be more comfortable with this mode of travel. A metal lantern creaks overhead.
Fade to Black
The theater pulses with light and darkness as these fadings continue throughout the film. They suggest a succession of days and nights as the train moves west, passing through forests, plains, and Indian country and by abandoned wagons and teepees. Passengers change from properly dressed easterners to homesteaders to—as the Rocky Mountains appear in the window—hunters and trappers carrying guns (also, no more women are seen on the train). The young man and the passengers exchange glances—some knowing, some compassionate, some threatening. The fireman, having stoked the fire that fuels the nineteenth-century steam engine, sits by the young man and offers the first spoken words of the film: "Look out the window." He goes on to speak as if he knows this young man intimately: "Doesn't this remind you of when you were in the boat, and then later that night you were lying looking up at the ceiling, and the water in your head was not dissimilar from the landscape. And you think to yourself, 'Why is it that the landscape is moving, but the boat is still?'"

The fireman begins to ask the young man questions, such as where he is from (the answer is Cleveland, specifically, Lake Erie) and learns that the young man's parents recently died. When asked if he has a wife in Erie, the young man replies that he had a fiancée but "she changed her mind." The fireman corrects him with, "She found herself somebody else." "No," he replies. "Yes, she did," says the fireman with a sad look and tone. The fireman says that the young man's story does not explain why he has "come all the way out here, all the way out here to hell." When the young man explains that he is moving west because he has a job as an accountant in the town of Machine, the fireman is clearly troubled and explains that Machine is "the end of the line." After the young man shows the fireman a letter from a Mr. Dickinson, owner of Dickinson's metal works, assuring him of a job, the fireman explains that he does not read but that he "wouldn't trust no words written down on no piece of paper, especially from no Dickinson out in the town of Machine." He continues, "You're just as likely to find your own grave." Immediately after the word grave is spoken, gunfire erupts on the train. The hunters wake up and fire their rifles out the window. The young man is terribly frightened, clutching his suitcase to him as he ducks his head and looks around. The fireman explains that the men are shooting buffalo, and "the government says it killed a million of them last year alone."
Fade to Black
Opening Credits

Introduction

I have taken time to describe the opening scenes of *Dead Man* for a number of reasons.[1] Besides being a striking series of scenes, it also provides a symbolic and structural frame for the film itself. We know from the opening, for example, that this is a journey film; the young man is traveling in unfamiliar territory. The black-and-white cinematography sets the story in a distant time and place by making even familiar elements strange. These alienating elements contribute to the perception that the film involves transgressions into unknown and perhaps dangerous territory. The journey west is a primal American myth that conjures imaginary "uninhabited" landscapes and freedoms and dangers to be found there. The western, whether it be film or literature, embodies this mythology by emphasizing the transgressions of boundaries in the pursuit of otherness, even if it seeks to make that otherness no longer other, as colonizers do. The first words of the film, "Look out the window," signal that the characters in this western are viewing the landscape at some remove as the train speeds through it. The passengers travel in the comfort of nineteenth-century technology, which is easier and safer than moving west in a covered wagon, as the abandoned wagon in the opening scene shows. As we will see, the film explores these new technologies involving metal and how they turn upon their creators, a theme explored frequently in science fiction. The advantages of train travel, print, and guns are gained in a kind of Faustian exchange that results in a loss of connection to the landscape, the promulgation of lies, and death. There is, then, a terror embedded in these technologies that the characters seem to be unaware of, or perhaps resigned to, because they are operating with a nineteenth-century point of view. Their naïveté is at times tragic and humorous, but it also seduces us into believing that we are not so naïve. Yet another theme that runs through the film is that of capitalism as the engine of technology and thus the producer of death. It is greed in one form or another that situates most of the characters in the film, from the hired killers to the young man who is assured of a job and is willing to cross the country for it. Capitalism is not simply depicted as a kind of collective greed in *Dead Man*; rather, it is represented as an American incarnation of Christianity. Christianity and commerce, so often wedded in colonialisms around the world, are the driving forces that propel the characters in *Dead Man* toward violent death. *Dead Man* is richly provocative in its commentary upon American culture in the last two centuries, and as such engages many different aspects of American life. In this essay I examine *Dead Man* in light of the following three themes: mythology, technology, and capitalism. I will use these themes as lenses for seeing what *Dead Man* contributes to the imagination and imaging of otherness and the negotiations necessary for living together in America.

In a recent essay Brent Plate warns of the dangers of over-using popular film as a vehicle for the analysis of culture and argues that "art-house" films ought to be valued for their ability to offer deep interrogations of cultural values that popular films by their very nature reinforce. He writes:

> In contrast to the emphasis on popular film, I suggest that we pay attention to non-Hollywood, non-commercial films. I do not say this to suggest this is the only worthwhile approach in religion and film, but to suggest that we might be going too far with the current trend of analyzing popular film. I want to suggest that certain avant-garde, experimental, and independent films challenge us to see differently. They challenge our notions of spectatorship and help develop resistance to oppressive images by drawing our attention to representations of persons via camera angles, varieties in lighting, how a narrative may be constructed or deconstructed visually, etc. . . . In the popular cinema, viewers know what to expect and are already trained to watch in a particular way. "Art-house" films (and avant-garde and experimental) themselves often serve as a point of critique and offer "comment" on the ways we see. Rarely does popular film challenge the way we see, and thus offers little help in developing an ethics in a visual culture.[2]

While it is arguable that any Miramax film these days is "non-Hollywood" and "non-commercial," *Dead Man* does anything but reinforce the way we typically understand what passes for American values. My own sampling among people who have seen the film reveals that most people, to use their own words, "don't get it." This conclusion is affirmed in the newsgroup discussions on the internet where comments about the film include sentiments of appreciation, apathy, confusion, and hostility, but the majority reflect confusion or hostility. I suspect this is exactly the reaction that writer and director Jim Jarmusch desired and expected. Such ambivalence regarding a cultural product by no means assures that it is offering a cultural critique, but I would argue that films that do challenge us to examine more closely our assumptions and beliefs about "what goes without saying" (good always wins over evil, America is a good place, capitalism is necessary and natural, death is to be feared, etc.) are in fact going to be received with ambivalence or outright hostility, if they are seen at all. *Dead Man* is such a film.

Some of the difficulty involved in understanding *Dead Man* no doubt has to do with the plot, which blends Native American understandings of death and the afterlife with a traditional Western mythological journey. But in this journey the hero's final destination is, instead of deeper understanding or victory in battle, a meaningless death. From the perspective of the Native American character in the film, death means to slip—or more literally float—into the world of the spirits, a journey that calls for both understanding and courage. Seen through the lenses of American mythology and history, however, the plot is a nihilistic inversion of the Horatio Alger story that involves a working man's attempt to die a good death in spite of bad luck and the forces arrayed against him. In this light *Dead Man* can be viewed as a kind of *Death of A Salesman* without the optimism.

Set in the nineteenth-century American west, *Dead Man* is the story of William Blake (Johnny Depp), an accountant from Cleveland who travels west to work for a notorious industrialist named Dickinson (Robert Mitchum) in the town of Machine. Blake runs into trouble at Machine. After he sleeps with a woman named Thel (Mili Avital), her fiancé, Dickinson's son Charles (Gabriel Byrne), returns to find them in bed. Dickinson shoots Thel, but the bullet passes through her heart and into Blake's. After Blake returns fire and kills Dickinson, he escapes to the desert. Lost and alone in the wilderness, Blake is "rescued" by a Native American named Nobody (Gary Farmer), who asks, "Did you kill the white man who killed you?" Blake is dying. Nobody thinks that Blake is the poet and painter he read with great interest when he was being educated by the whites, and he sets himself to the task of taking care of Blake so that he can "go back to where he came from." During his prolonged death, Blake becomes a feared and wanted outlaw whose poetry is now "written with blood." The search for Blake, undertaken by every person in the southwest who is willing to kill for money, becomes a metaphor for the ideologies of the nineteenth-century American west and, by implication, for the twentieth-century's ideologies that can be traced back there.

Postmodern Storytelling and Film

Postmodern storytelling, such as is found in *Dead Man,* is laced with a kind of serious irony that plays with ideologies of mass destruction, ennui, and humor all in the same imaginative space. Such ominous concerns arise from the ashes of Western culture in the late twentieth-century as capitalism flattens all meaning into exchange value and technology offers us the chance to annihilate the planet in a maelstrom of scientific and political frenzy. Humor, especially the dark kind, allows us some measure of hermeneutic play in the face of mass-produced meaning lapped up in great gulps by Americans too tired—or too afraid—to think. Postmodern storytelling assaults these productions by reserving meaninglessness as a viable hermeneutic option. As such, all cultural productions, historical artifacts, and political ideologies are fair game for postmodernism's nihilistic agenda. As Peter Brooker has written: "Postmodernism splices high with low culture, it raids and parodies past art, it questions all absolutes, it swamps reality in a culture of recycled images, it has to do with deconstruction, with consumerism, with television and the information society, with the end of communism."[3] While those of us who read and write about postmodern literature tend to look to that genre for such constructions, it is in film that the majority of Americans and probably Europeans encounter and negotiate our postmodern condition. Conrad Ostwalt writes in *Screening the Sacred*:

> Whereas in the nineteenth century popular novels and presses held the imagination of the American public, it seems that for contemporary Americans images are replacing texts in the ability to capture the imagination and to shape worldviews. . . . Perhaps this is a comment on the postmodern context of our age: Visual images are replacing written texts as the conveyors of information and meaning.[4]

Film is a cultural medium that serves to generate ideologies, shape values, and inform practice, and it does so via a unique combination of imagistic storytelling or narrativized image-making. We should not be surprised, then, to find in postmodern storytelling and film the opportunity to reflect upon our unconscious assumptions about the world, our social constructions of it, and our deepest fears and greatest hopes about the future.

Gerald Vizenor, an Anishinaabe writer and critic, seems to have been the first to remark upon the relation between storytelling, postmodernism, and "survivance." His description of Native American storytelling is uniquely tribal and distinctly postmodern:

> Native American Indian stories are told and heard in motion, imagined and read over and over on a landscape that is never seen at once; words are heard in winter rivers, crows are written on the poplars, last words are never the end.[5]

Vizenor, better quoted than paraphrased, sees in postmodernism opportunities for "postindian warriors" to oppose the intrusions of Western culture with stories of survivance that not only reject colonial nationalisms but also offer ways of imagining a future in which life continues:

> Manifest Destiny would cause the death of millions of tribal people from massacres, diseases, and the loneliness of reservations. Entire cultures have been terminated in the course of nationalism. These histories are now the simulations of dominance, and the causes of the conditions that have become manifest manners in literature. The postindian simulations are the core of survivance, the new stories of tribal courage. The simulations of manifest manners are the continuance of the surveillance and domination of the tribes in literature. Simulations are the absence of the tribal real; the postindian conversions are in the new stories of suvivance over dominance. The natural reason of the tribes anteceded by thousands of generations the invention of the Indian. The postindian outs the inventions with humor, new stories, and the simulations of survivance.[6]

We need not imagine how a trickster figure would function in contemporary American culture. We have one in Gerald Vizenor, a postindian warrior of survivance and a postmodern storyteller.

Robert Detweiler has also connected poststructuralism and postmodern storytelling to survival. He writes: "Survival is, indeed, not the subtext but the supertext of poststructuralism."[7] The very appearance of myths and stories of immortality in postmodern literature and poststructuralist exercises on the survival of texts indicates an interest—sometimes an obsession—with human survival. Such an interest, such an obsession, according to Detweiler, is indicative of a desire for something sacred.

> Sacred language expresses survival and in that very expression establishes its sacredness. Interpretation becomes an act of survival, and interpretation of the sacred texts ensures their survival and our own. Certain cultures beat the drums to make the eclipse go away—scare off the monster threatening to eat the sun—and maintain the order of things. We b/eat the text.[8]

Detweiler and Vizenor offer perspectives on postmodern storytelling that face the horrors of twentieth-century life and yet open to religious possibilities. Such analysis frees us from the dichotomy of a "manifest manners" approach to traditional storytelling where noble savages sit around campfires and tell coyote stories and a consumer culture approach where "image is everything" and story is obsolete. On the contrary, we can read postmodern storytelling in film in such a way that we are able both to critique manifest manners and hear/see iconoclastic stories without freezing them into new versions of surveillance and domination. In fact, they may even bring us to the sacred space and time set apart for the encounter with otherness.

Like postmodern literature, postmodern film rehistoricizes the past while subtracting its claim to truth and adding irony. Jedidiah Purdy, in an essay titled "Terminal Irony," explains the use of irony in postmodern culture as a way of passing judgment without committing to the dialectical opposite of what is being judged:

> Irony does not stand alone. It is a way of passing judgment—or placing bets—on what kinds of hope the world will support. . . . We surely mistrust our own capacity to bear disappointment. So far as we are ironists, we are determined not to be made suckers. . . . Still, the wish to escape irony is probably mistaken—though hope of enriching it is not. Just as we cannot live in the flatness of irony, we cannot breathe the cloying air of anti-irony. The human reserves of pompousness, self-seriousness, and the leaden earnestness that always threatens to run molten are unlikely ever to be exhausted. Among our most trustworthy weapons against them is an intelligent and resourceful irony.[9]

When irony is used in the medium of film, the powers and possibilities of judgment are heightened. Film, at least in the culture of film viewers in the United States, demands a response because it, like sports and music, is one of the few ways we live together imaginatively. Unlike reading a book, which is usually done at different times and is solitary, watching a film is an exercise in communal interpretation. Most of us go to the cinema with others, and even if we do not, others are there. Whether I go alone or with friends, I am always having conversations about films with those around me. We are reviewers as well, often listening to or reading the reviews of film critics, but even more often critiquing the critics themselves because we feel that we have a right to and a stake in the interpretation of film. Film has a different dialogical relationship with the "reader" than literature does by virtue of its use of image, sound, and motion in a ritualistic, that is, communal, space. In addition to providing communal space, the cinema generates sacred time, a time that vibrates with mythic and ritualistic rhythms. The hermeneutic possibilities open to new dimensions and the capacity for cultural critique and alternative meaning-making are strengthened.

Jim Jarmusch's *Dead Man* is just such an ironic rumination upon sacrality, meaning, and the future in light of mythology, technology, and capitalism. Even before we get to the narrative content of the film, we are exposed to postmodern elements in the very medium of the film itself. For example, it is clear that Jarmusch is using technology, in particular a certain kind of cinematography, to invoke the presence of the past. In describing his use of black and white film, he notes:

> Since the late 1950s and early 60s, stories using the "western" genre seem to be filmed in the same dusty color palette over and over again. Whether in a film by Leone or Eastwood, or even a TV episode of *Bonanza,* the colors always seem the same to me. If these color values operate on a sub- or semi-

conscious level for the audience, I would prefer that the black-and-white of
Dead Man recalls the atmosphere of American films from the 40s and early
50s, or even of the historical films of Kurosawa or Mizoguchi, than the overly
familiar palette of more recent "westerns." Last but not the least, I wanted to
work again in black-and-white with Robby Müller. Robby, as always, did
amazing work photographing *Dead Man,* and working with the negative to
include all possible gray tones while keeping the black and whites very strong,
almost as though color film hadn't been invented yet.[10]

Perhaps the very first interpretive act the viewer performs is to make sense of
the black and white imagery. We understand it semiotically to invoke not only
the past but also the seriousness of the past. It is the medium of historical
documentary where weighty issues of history and culture are displayed
unironically. It is also the medium of film noir and Kurosawa. Jarmusch is
setting us up for ironic parody from the very beginning, and we can see from
his comment that he is invoking "intertextually" the history of film itself and is,
as Brent Plate points out, offering "comment" on the way we see.

Jarmusch's use of William Blake and Native American thought converge
in postmodern fashion to reinvent a history where Blake comes to America and
meets a Native American who has read his poetry. Of course Blake does not
remember his poetry, but he does live it out. When accosted by two marshals
who ask if he is William Blake, he affirms this and asks them if they know his
poetry. He then shoots one, and this one accidentally wounds the other as his
rifle fires wildly. As Blake puts a fatal bullet into the wounded marshal, he
recites a Blakean line: "Some are born to sweet delight/Some are born to
endless night." In fact, Nobody is especially fond of quoting William Blake's
"Proverbs of Hell," often to the consternation of the William Blake he is
traveling with.

Jarmusch is adept at orchestrating distance and immediacy in terms of the
audience's ability to relate to the characters. This orchestration is in the service
of connecting us with various elements of the film and disconnecting us with
others in order to tell a story that is both at a safe distance and yet penetrating in
its critique of our lives and culture. Thus we can laugh at Conway Twill as he
babbles incessantly about nothing to the point that his companion Cole Wilson,
known as "the finest killer of men and injuns in this here half of the world" as
well as a rapist and cannibal, kills him and eats him. But we are chilled by the
realization, especially at the end of the film, that Cole, Conway, and all the
other "stupid fucking white men" are not just strange characters who are
laughable because they are so bizarre but are representative of the spectrum of
American culture and its inevitable drive toward unnatural death through the
same myths, rituals, and magic that are employed in the late twentieth century.
We are tricked, in good postmodern fashion, into a plot that is in the end a
mirror of our own susceptibility to believing in plots. *Dead Man* is a story that
warns us of the danger of believing in stories because the stories that inform,
shape, and maintain America, regardless of the century, are deadly.

Mythology: Telling Li(v)es

Jim Jarmusch is as much a mythologist as George Lucas. *Dead Man,* however, is no *Star Wars*; I can say with great confidence that there will be no merchandising tie-ins for *Dead Man* (although the tobacco industry may have some interest). While Jarmusch is as adept as George Lucas at playing seriously with mythological structures and elements, the use Jarmusch puts them to is practically the opposite. Rather than affirming our notions of heroes and heroines, the forces of good and evil, and the possibility of meaning, *Dead Man* questions these notions by ironic parody, humor, and historiography. When Blake escapes death from a group of trappers that includes an Italian transvestite who regales his friends with stories from Roman history and the Bible, a British expatriate who loves to play with knives, and a hillbilly who claims that he cleans up real good, the viewer is left laughing and troubled at the same time. The humor of the situation is in the service of a larger commentary upon the "America" constructed out of the confluence of capitalism, colonization, and Christianity.

Dead Man is a postmodern western where stories fly like bullets and people drop like flies. The combination of rail travel and print has allowed stories to flourish, but the same technology has produced guns and bullets and made all life expendable. In *Dead Man* all plots move deathward, all plots lead to plots in the ground. Death is all around, and so are stories. The most meaningful stories, or at least the stories that move people to action or travel, are false. John Dickinson tells a story about the death of his son that brings out every killer in the west to search for William Blake. The story is false because it has Blake killing Thel as well as Dickinson's son. This story gets disseminated through printed flyers that Blake finds on trees and at a trading post. Nobody believes that Bill Blake the accountant from Cleveland is William Blake the romantic poet in spite of the fact that Blake does not seem to know his own poetry when Nobody quotes it to him. Nobody tells him that from now on his poetry will be written with blood and that he will be a killer of white men. Afterwards, when two marshals come to kill him, Blake asks them if they know his poetry just before he kills them. While the movement of the characters proceeds via "false" stories, those same stories keep people oriented in a world that is spinning toward death. Blake lives only to die, but the story keeps him alive long enough to die well, under the care of Nobody, who sends him to his death in a canoe floating out to sea.

After Blake kills his second man, he is willing and able to kill again. The second killing (of a trapper named Ben) has been a kind of initiation for him (Nobody calls it a test), and he is born again as William Blake the killer. Not surprisingly, Nobody leaves him for a while afterwards. Nobody functions as the mythical helper who leads the hero into tests and helps him through them. True to mythological form, the helper leaves and Blake functions on his own for a while before his final test when Nobody will return to help him cross the final barrier. One of the most poignant scenes during Blake's isolation shows him coming upon a fawn that has been shot in the neck and left in the woods. Blake ponders the blood that has formed on a leaf, smells it, mixes it with his own blood, and then paints his face with it. He then lies down beside the fawn and sleeps for a while. The camera shot here is from above, and the image of Blake curled up next to the dead fawn is powerful and disturbing. Clearly, they are alike: innocents in a world dominated by the experience of death, a death that comes from metal. In the identification with the fawn Blake finds sufficient meaning to continue the journey while he writes his poetry in blood. He must kill the white men who have killed him.

The fireman is especially important mythologically, as he provides the warning that Machine is the end of the line and a place where one is likely to find his own grave. He also offers the cryptic lines about "remembering" something that has yet to happen to the young man. Too easily dismissed at the beginning as a raving, illiterate train worker, the fireman at the end shows himself to be speaking from the timeless world of the sacred where remembering the future is not only possible but necessary. Like most myths, the myth of Blake the dying poet-killer must be acted out ritually. Blake catches glimpses of his ritual when he remembers the message that the fireman gave him on the way out. These prophecies, easily lost in the first viewing, describe Blake's particular fate. The fireman asks him to remember when the water was in his head and the landscape moved by. When Nobody places Blake in the canoe that will take him to Nobody's village, Blake remembers the saying about the landscape and the water. There are other echoes of this initial prophecy. When Blake looks up into a tree and sees it spinning as he stands motionless, he almost "recalls" his death as prophesied by the fireman. This phenomenon of the landscape moving while Blake stands still speaks metaphorically of the disconnectedness from the landscape that is produced by the technologies of death. When Nobody finally places Blake in his coffin, which is a canoe prepared with cedar boughs, and tells him that it is time for him to go back to where he came from, Blake replies, "You mean Cleveland?" As Blake drifts out into the river that will carry him to the ocean, to where the sky meets the water, he looks up long enough to see Cole and Nobody shoot each other. Death is a presence that has traveled with him from Cleveland to the Pacific northwest, but now he moves beyond it into the mirror of the sky and water, back to where all the spirits are from, and his story and ceremony—his life—is complete, or perhaps completely finished. For Nobody William Blake has completed the circle back to where the spirits reside. For Blake the adoption of the myth and the performance of the ritual have given him a death different from those around him. In living out what is factually a lie but mythologically true, William Blake finds a good way to die, or at least a different way.

Technology: White Man's Metal

The characters in *Dead Man* survive for a while by not becoming "bullet magnets" and living to tell their stories. While the film tells many of these stories, most of them are incapable of adequately reflecting the land and culture that the characters inhabit. The stories drift aimlessly like clouds, unconnected to land or people, cut loose by the technologies of metallurgy, print, and rail travel. Ironically, the one person who has a story that makes sense to Blake is Nobody, who must keep him alive by telling Blake's story to him, but that story is, in Western terms, "false." This sense of falseness, of inauthenticity, is at the heart of *Dead Man*. It strikes the chord that many Americans fear most—the thought that in our myths and rituals we are lying to ourselves and that we will die recognizing that we have spent our lives in pursuit of false hopes and manufactured dreams. The film offers no consolation for these fears; on the contrary, it dramatizes them.

In *Dead Man* technology is the machine that produces inauthenticity or falseness. It also generates death. The most immediate image of technology is that of metal. The sound of the train is the very beginning of the film and occurs even before we see any images. The very first scene after the epigraph ends with William Blake staring at the creaking lantern overhead, and we wonder why the director has drawn our attention to it. By the end of the film it is clear that the production of "white man's metal" is the dominant enterprise in the film and the technological source of death. The possessive is correctly placed— this metal is produced, used, and valued by white culture first and foremost. While Nobody is happy to use the white man's metal, whether it is a knife or a gun, he understands its provenance and accepts that it is necessary for life in America. This sentiment is first expressed by Thel (also a character in William Blake's poetry), the woman Blake has sex with in Machine and the fiancée of Mr. Dickinson's son. When William Blake pulls a gun from underneath the pillow and asks why she has it, Thel replies incredulously, "Because this is America." After Nobody understands that the man who has white man's metal next to his heart is the poet and painter William Blake, he realizes that the Blake of the nineteenth century will use a gun instead of poetry and painting: "You were a poet and a painter, and now you are a killer of white men." And later he declares: "That weapon will replace your tongue; you will learn to speak through it, and your poetry will now be written with blood." The pervasiveness and perniciousness of the white man's metal can be seen in William Blake's death walk through Nobody's Makah village in the Pacific northwest where among the representations of death there is, half-buried in the ground, a metal sewing machine.

Mr. Dickinson, the owner of Dickinson's Metal Works, is by his own admission a killer who makes his living by producing metal. His factory dominates the aptly named town of Machine and belches black smoke into the air as the towns-people engage in various occupations that produce death. When he first arrives in Machine, William Blake must walk a kind of gauntlet through hunters, coffin makers, and other strange and threatening people. He loses his sense of orientation when he enters the factory itself. He completely misses the sign pointing to the office, and when he leaves, he cannot find his way out and runs into the workers who are moving quickly through the narrow passages. In fact Blake is lost the moment he enters the factory, and he does not find his way again until he realizes that he is William Blake the killer and must go to the mirror of water to die.

William Blake's encounter with the producer of white man's metal is frightening and unproductive. Having learned that his job has been taken by a Mr. Olafsen, Blake insists on speaking to Mr. Dickinson himself. This demand produces laughter among the accountants in the office, but Blake is steadfast. Upon entering the office of the notorious industrialist, Blake sees an open safe, a lit cigar, and a stuffed bear but no Dickinson. After looking around the room, he turns back to the desk to find Dickinson pointing a shotgun at him. Completely ignoring Blake's attempt to explain that his letter assures him of a job, Dickinson threatens to kill Blake right there in his office. In fact, Dickinson does the same thing when he hires the three killers to murder Blake and says that if they do not follow his demands, he is "prepared to do a little killing" of his own. The portrayal of Dickinson as a crazed, wealthy killer is one of the hinges upon which turns the critique of technology and capitalism in the film.

Metal is used to produce many things—bullets, guns, knives, pens. Perhaps the most complex and influential use of metal in the film, and by implication in the nineteenth century, is in the creation of the railroad. As we saw in the opening scenes, train travel is what moves William Blake and nameless others west. The fadings help us to imagine days of travel where people sit and stare blankly for hours or else sleep. The reaction is found even today in subways and passenger trains, whether in the United States or Europe. There is a kind of blankness in people on a train, especially when they are alone. Traveling under the power of a technology that most of us do not really understand and under the direction of people mostly unseen and almost certainly unknown, we are drained of any engagement with the landscape as it flies by or with the other people as they retreat into their own worlds. It is as if we trade our engagement with place for the achievement of destination. Moreover, innovations in travel allow us to span great distances without ever experiencing anything other than the cabin between our departure and arrival. In flying past or over the landscape we fly past or over stories and cultures, over people and places that are meaningful in ways that we can never know. The alienation that this kind of travel produces is symptomatic of the way technology uses us. It offers us a way to be together without living together or even knowing each other. William Blake speaks to no one and rarely even makes eye contact as he travels thousands of miles. The only person he does speak to is the fireman, who utters ominous comments about the journey itself. He makes it clear that William Blake is riding a metal carriage on metal rails to the "end of the line." We are not surprised when that journey ends in death.

The combination of white man's metal with train travel and other technologies produces the dramatic sense of lostness that the characters display in *Dead Man*. One of these other technologies is writing, especially in the form of print. Throughout the film we encounter characters, such as the fireman and Conway Twill, who cannot read. Their illiteracy places them at an obvious disadvantage, but it also provides them with certain advantages. Specifically, the fireman is not subject to the false hopes that define William Blake, who not only reads but holds the same occupation as the first writers in Sumeria in 2000 BCE—accountant. The fireman proclaims, in regard to Blake's letter "assuring" him of a job, that writing is untrustworthy and dangerous, a sentiment that can be found in non-writers when the writing is introduced to the culture (Plato is most notable in this regard).

The fireman's point has been made by theoreticians as well. Walter Ong's seminal observations on the nature of orality and literacy show that writing isolates while speech tends toward community. The work of Marshall McLuhan is relevant here too. He argues in *The Gutenberg Galaxy* that with the advent of print the human sensory field became dominated by vision to the degree that culture was hypnotized by print in the same way that an individual is hypnotized—by the exclusion of other senses due to the dominance of one. This divisive process also helped create and sustain the subject-object dichotomy that ascended with the rise of the sciences, since language, with writing and especially print, became encapsulated in an object instead of a subject.[11] Regarding objectivity and writing, Ong notes:

> Writing separates the knower from the known and thus sets up conditions for "objectivity," in the sense of personal disengagement or distancing. The "objectivity" which Homer and other oral performers do have is that enforced by formulaic expression: the individual's reaction is not expressed as simply individual or "subjective" but rather as encased in the communal reaction, the communal "soul." Under the influence of writing, despite his protest against it, Plato had excluded the poets from his Republic, for studying them was essentially learning to react with "soul," to feel oneself identified with Achilles or Odysseus.[12]

This psychic and material separation represents a rupture in communication that is not unlike the rupture in our relationship to landscape that train travel produces. We trade personal engagement and community for objectivity and efficiency. One of the ramifications of this rupture and this trade off is that in writing and print we find new and more powerful ways to lie.

In *Dead Man* writing is the primary medium for disseminating lies. When William Blake and Nobody come upon the wanted posters that Dickinson has printed and displayed all over the region, Blake is upset because the flyers claim that he murdered Thel, when in fact the murderer was Dickinson's son, Charlie. Blake begins tearing down the posters, but Nobody points out that his actions are useless. Nobody knows that more are being printed and displayed even as they speak. Lies move even faster than trains in *Dead Man*, and they are just as unstoppable. Writing, like the other technologies represented in the film, leads to alienation and death.

Capitalism, Christianity, and the Ideology of the West

Two of the most powerful ideologies at work in America (and around the world) are Christianity and capitalism. In fact we might go so far as to say that these two are in fact one, each supplementing the other to form a perfectly suitable myth for late twentieth-century American culture. In popular Christian myth, salvation comes from acceding to a set of doctrines and is manifest in the accumulation of wealth, property, or other items that signify God's blessing. Of course heaven awaits the one who believes, but the way to heaven is paved with economic success here on earth. Studies show that most wealthy Americans believe that God is responsible in some way for their economic privilege. Such beliefs are propagated in mainline churches, the most crass televangelism, and even in "secular" popular culture, but its roots lie in fifteenth-century notions of a land to the west where Christianity and commerce can thrive. The diary of Cristóbal Colón (Christopher Columbus) is telling in this regard and lays the foundation for contemporary notions of religious and economic exploitation. Here are his first impressions of native people in this hemisphere:

> They should be good servants and very intelligent, for I have observed that they soon repeat anything that is said to them, and I believe that they would easily be made Christians, for they appear to me to have no religion. God willing, when I make my departure I will bring half a dozen of them back to their Majesties so that they can learn to speak.[13]

The merging of Christianity and the need for cheap labor (the foundation of capitalism) flows easily and even naturally from his pen. Colón set the stage for future enterprises in Christianity and commerce. In *The White Man's Indian*, Robert Berkhofer makes it clear how these interests merged in the formulation of official government policy toward American Indians from contact to the nineteenth century:

> Ideals and interests of settlers and missionaries, of policy makers and private profit seekers were touted as compatible, even intertwined, in official statement and public propaganda—if not in practice, as all were to discover in actual settlement. Religion subdued the natives for economic advantage and paved the way for national expansion through peaceful conquest at the same time that it saved souls from eternal damnation. Trade and agriculture were presumed to extend national power and glory while they also converted the

Fig. 1.1 "In *Dead Man* one scene in particular engages Christianity, capitalism, and the ideology of the west ..." (From the film *Dead Man*. Photo by Christine Parry. © 1995 12-Gauge Productions/Miramax Films)

heathen to Christianity and European civilization through the social
interaction of the commercial nexus. Thus propagandists for the missionary
enterprise presented arguments for the increase of trade, while proponents of
the commercial advantages of colonies mentioned the desirability of spreading
Christianity.[14]

As this enterprise was carried out successfully, the notion of the west as a place
open to economic and religious colonization, already in place in the time of
European contact, took on new dimensions. Whites began to push for the sea on
both fronts, to claim all the resources available for capitalism and all the people
available for conversion to Christianity. It was Frederick Jackson Turner in
1893 who distilled these ideas and others into his so-called Frontier Thesis.
Essentially, the thesis depicts Native Americans as the obstacle to the social and
economic progress evident in Euro-American civilization and places the frontier
experience at the center of American ideology. Turner's thesis is still taught as
a viable explanation of American identity and success. This trinity of ideologies
formed and continues to inform American mythology to this day.

In *Dead Man* one scene in particular engages Christianity, capitalism,
and the ideology of the west. Nobody and Blake have traveled from the
southwest to the Pacific northwest where they come upon a trading post on the
bank of a river. Nobody explains that Indians get diseases from the blankets
sold at the post (an all-too-common event across the country—the blankets
were infected with smallpox and other diseases). Needing ammunition and a
canoe, Nobody and Blake walk to the trading post. Outside are wanted posters
depicting Blake and listing the people he has killed (Fig. 1.1). Blake is no
longer upset by the printed flyers; in fact, he gives one to Nobody as a gift.
Blake enters the post first and begins to look at the ammunition. The proprietor
is a Catholic missionary/huckster who promotes the ammunition by telling
Blake that it has been blessed personally by the Archbishop of Detroit. At this
point Nobody enters the post, and the missionary, thinking that Nobody does
not speak English, utters an oath that calls upon God to wipe the earth clean of
savages and Philistines. Nobody responds with a line from William Blake's
"The Everlasting Gospel": "The vision of Christ which thou dost see is my
vision's greatest enemy." Nobody then asks if he has any tobacco, and the
missionary replies that he does not, despite the fact that there are tins of tobacco
on the shelf behind him. He offers Nobody a blanket instead. At this point
William Blake comes to the counter and asks for tobacco, which the missionary
produces. As they are paying him, the missionary recognizes William Blake
from the flyers and asks for his autograph. While Blake is signing the flyer, the
missionary pulls a gun. Blake is quicker than he is and stabs his hand with the
pen. Blake then draws his own gun on the missionary, who damns him to hell
with a curse. Blake replies that God has already damned him so, and shoots the
missionary in the heart. A man flings open the front door and fires at Blake and

Nobody. Blake returns fire and kills the gunman, who falls through the door. On the door is a sign reading "Work out your own salvation" (Phil. 2:12).

The trading post is a contested site for the ideologies of the west and the practices that follow from them in the American west. The missionary's easy blend of Christianity and capitalism seems humorous until we experience or see others experience the effects of this merger. Among these effects are the debasement of Christianity, the elevation of greed to virtue (or at least nature), and the channeling of all meaning into exchange value. The film suggests that those of us who live this way are already "dead men," even though we may be alive. When William Blake adopts Nobody's interpretation of his role in the world, he understands that he is a part of a death culture where meaning is found only in the acquisition of goods and wealth (especially tobacco) and creativity serves the interests of extermination not survival. We can see this ideology at work when Cole Wilson comes upon a marshal that Blake has killed. The marshal has fallen into the campfire in such a way that there appear to be rays of light surrounding his head. Cole Wilson's response is to note that the image "Looks like a goddamn religious icon" and to crush the marshal's head with his boot. The scene is the most horrific in the film, but it serves a clear purpose: the sacred, or any image of it that does not accommodate capitalism, is to be exterminated or erased. Even Conway Twill seems disturbed by Cole's act, but it accords perfectly with the culture of Christianity, capitalism, and the west, where technological and ideological progress hurls westward without any thought for its victims.

Conclusion

A pivotal scene in *Dead Man* engages survivance and irony, myth and lies, technology and terror, Christianity and capitalism, and life and death. Around the campfire, while the beans made with possum cook, stories are told to explain the world. They are full of innocence and experience and come from everywhere, including Roman history, children's fables, and the Bible. The characters are trappers and include a southern hillbilly named Big George (Billy Bob Thornton), a transvestite Italian cook named Salvadore but better known as Sally (Iggy Pop), and a British expatriate. The conversation introduces the word Philistine, which means "a real dirty person" and has important echoes later in the film. As Blake and Nobody observe from a hill above, we can hear Sally telling Big George and Ben the story of Goldilocks and the Three Bears. The scene is an ironic portrayal of a family having dinner with the "mother" cooking, telling stories, and reading from the Bible. Nobody's comment is, as usual, "Stupid white man." He tells Blake to go to them, but Blake makes it clear that he does not want to encounter these people. Nobody insists that he must go because "It is a test." As Blake makes his way down to the men, we are treated to a story about Nero told by Sally: "Tonight we are reminded of the evil emperor Nero Augustus. He was the scourge of all the Christians." When Big George asks him what a scourge is, Sally responds by saying, "It's like when something real bad happens. Like when everybody gets killed, and you can't do anything about it. Like a swarm of locusts." This is an apt description of the world the characters inhabit. In fact when Big George asks Sally to say grace before they eat their beans, Sally offers a grace that is both biblical and violent: "This day will the Lord deliver thee into mine hand, and I will smite thee, and take thine head from thee, and I will give the carcasses of the host of the Philistines this day unto the fowls of the air and to the wild beasts of the earth" (I Sam. 17:46). The other men respond with a resounding "Amen."

After Blake joins the men, they gather around him and inspect him as if he is a beaver who can offer them a fine pelt. They comment upon his hair, clothes, and eyeglasses and show him how sharp their knife is. Blake himself hopes they will offer him something to eat since Nobody believes that he must fast in order to prepare for the return to the spirit world, but their designs seem to be on his material worth. In fact their greed creates an argument between Big George and Ben; each one says that "it" belongs to him. Ben ends up shooting Big George, and Big George responds by declaring: "I'm going to have to kill somebody now." As he points the gun at William Blake, he says prophetically: "Well goddamn it, I guess nobody gets you." At that moment Nobody appears and cuts Big George's throat.

As I mentioned earlier, this scene is a turning point in William Blake's journey, for it confirms his willingness to become William Blake, the killer of white men. At the same time, it encompasses all the themes that I have explored in this essay. Sally's mythologizing is cut loose from any particular landscape and draws from biblical, historical, and children's texts. The only element of the stories that makes sense to the men is the killing, and even though they agree that it is terrible (or horrible), they also understand that death is a scourge, "like when everybody gets killed, and you can't do anything about it." Their lives are shaped and driven by these stories, which is why they, like everyone else, make their living by killing. They are entranced by the technologies of killing, such as how sharp a machine can make a knife, and by the acquisition of goods, such as eyeglasses, suits, and hats. In the midst of their rituals is a Christian grace that gives biblical sanction to their creation of death as they roam the open spaces of the American west. They are, in these senses and others, typical Americans trying to get by and relatively oblivious to the forces that are arrayed to define their lives and their deaths.

The first words of the film are "Look out the window." They seem now to serve as a fitting metaphor for viewing the film itself. As the landscape flashes by like frames of film, we speed over stories and land toward our own deaths. *Dead Man* asks us to look at the film and our world the way William Blake looks out the window of the train. It asks us to recognize the forces that drive us and otherwise inform us and to understand the impossibility of living

Fig. 1.2 "Nobody's last words to William Blake before he is sent out to the mirror of waters to die: 'This world will no longer concern you.'"

(From the film *Dead Man*. Photo by Christine Parry. © 1995 12-Gauge Productions/Miramax Films)

together when we do not know what we are living for other than what has been manufactured and sold to us as true, meaningful, or profitable. This way of seeing involves great struggle and pain, and it is with great relief that we hear Nobody's last words to William Blake before he is sent out to the mirror of waters to die (Fig. 1.2): "This world will no longer concern you." Why, then, should we watch such a film, so full of darkness and death? Perhaps many people should not watch *Dead Man*. Those who are too tired or too afraid to encounter otherness by finding the edges of America and going beyond them will do better watching a film like *Deep Impact* or *Armageddon*. But we should at least be aware that in rejecting otherness we reject the sacred, which comes to us in images that are awesome and fearful. And in rejecting otherness we reject interpretation, the opportunity to beat the drums and scare away the monster threatening to eat the sun. If, as Robert Detweiler says, interpretation is an act of survival, then we need more films like *Dead Man*, which demands interpretation and allows us no refuge in the shelters of mass-produced meaning and technology. In making those demands upon us, *Dead Man* forces us to face the ultimate otherness of death. It is only then, after the encounter with death, that we can say that this world will no longer concern us.

Endnotes

1. *Dead Man*. Written and Directed by Jim Jarmusch. Miramax Films. 1995.

2. S. Brent Plate, "Religion/Literature/Film: Toward A Religious Visuality of Film," in *Literature & Theology* 12.1 (March 1998): pp. 23-24.

3. Peter Brooker, ed. *Modernism/Postmodernism* (New York: Longman, 1992), p. 3.

4. Joel M. Martin and Conrad E. Ostwalt, Jr., eds. *Screening the Sacred: Religion, Myth, and Ideology in Popular American Film* (Boulder, CO: Westview Press, 1995), p. 153.

5. Gerald Vizenor, ed. *Narrative Chance: Postmodern Discourse on Native American Indian Literatures* (Albuquerque: University of New Mexico Press, 1989), p. xiii.

6. Gerald Vizenor, *Manifest Manners: Postindian Warriors of Survivance* (Hanover, NH: Wesleyan University Press, 1994), pp. 4-5.

7. Robert Detweiler, "Overliving," *Semeia* 54 (1991): p. 240.

8. Ibid., p. 241.

9. Jedidiah Purdy, "Terminal Irony," *The Utne Reader* 89 (October 1998): pp. 26-29.9.

10. *New York Trash* (http://www.nytrash.com/deadman/deadjj.html)

11. Marshall McLuhan, *The Gutenberg Galaxy: The Making of Typographic Man* (Toronto: University of Toronto Press, 1962).

12. Walter Ong, *Orality and Literacy: The Technologizing of the Word* (London and New York: Methuen, 1982), p. 46.

13. Sam Gill, *Native American Traditions* (Belmont, CA: Wadsworth, 1983), p. 3.

14. Robert Berkhofer, *The White Man's Indian: Images of the American Indian from Columbus to the Present* (New York: Vintage, 1978), p. 117.

Joseph and His Brothers:
Quarreling After the Holocaust*

Jennifer L. Koosed

I talked to you about the difficulty of being Jewish, which is the same as the difficulty of writing. For Judaism and writing are but the same waiting, the same hope, the same depletion.

-Edmond Jabès

The film *The Quarrel*, based upon a short story by Chaim Grade,[1] recounts the chance meeting of two Holocaust survivors: Chaim and Hersh. They had been best friends in their youth, yet they had quarreled and parted before the war. When they meet in a park in Montreal on Rosh Hashanah, the quarrel continues and is shaped anew by their experiences of destruction and exile. As their conversation enfolds it is interwoven with the memories of their youthful life together, and the past after they had parted. The unveiling of memory is painful and slow, yet it lies at the heart of their quarrel about God, Torah, and the world.

The film is loosely structured around three biblical allusions to the Joseph story: one at the beginning of their meeting, one in the middle, and one at the end. There is a powerful ambiguity in the Joseph saga, for it begins and ends in slavery. Through the enslaving of Joseph, the descendants of Jacob were saved. Yet, their salvation led to the enslavement of future generations. Not until God remembered them hundreds of years later were they liberated from their oppression. Through biblical allusion, the film plays with these poles of family betrayal and family loyalty, God's abandonment and God's rescue.

The Quarrel

The year is 1948. Chaim is in Montreal to give a book reading. He is a secular Yiddish writer of some repute. While in the park, he sees a group of Orthodox Jews moving toward him. One figure arrests Chaim's attention. He is older than the rest, obviously their rebbe. Chaim thinks he recognizes him and he approaches. They stand face to face.

"Chaim, you're still alive?" This question opens their conversation. Chaim compares the scene of meeting to the first time that Joseph reveals himself to his brothers. In the same breath that Joseph unveils his identity, he asks about their father: "I am Joseph your brother, is our father still alive?" (Gen 45:3 as quoted in the film). Chaim and Hersh ask each other to recount the dead and alive of the war. Hersh had been with Chaim's parents in the ghetto, and told him how they had been murdered. Chaim knows the story already, but is compelled to hear it again. They already know, as did Joseph for he had asked the question about his father earlier in the narrative when his identity was still unknown to his brothers (Gen 43:27). They already know, yet, like a ritual action, they must hear it again, the names must be repeated, their fates retold. However, Joseph asks of one and receives the comforting answer of yes, he is still alive; Chaim and Hersh ask about many and all except one are dead.

Like Joseph and his brothers, they draw each other near, they ask each other for forgiveness. Then they begin to recount their stories, and in the process they revive the quarrel that forced them apart many years ago, this time with a new fervor. The two men had been boys together in Bialystok before the war. Yet, Chaim had felt the draw of the world outside of the yeshiva. He began to read and then to write secular literature. Writing is regarded as the holiest act and Chaim understands himself as honoring God through his writings, but honoring God in his own unique way. For Hersh, all that one needs to know can be found in the book of the Torah. His concern is not that Chaim writes; it is *what* he writes. Chaim has been seduced by the world by adopting the manner and dress of the outsider, and by writing for a general public. Because of this he has betrayed his family, his community, and he has even betrayed God. Since the time of the destruction of the Second Temple, when the rabbis converged at Yavneh to resuscitate the Jewish people through language, the Book and its interpretation have become bound to Jewish identity.

The argument quickly moves from how it began in their youth, to how it is configured now after the destruction of one-third of the Jewish community. Their questions of theodicy are intimately bound to the questions of writing and identity. In their argument, God's responsibility for the Holocaust hinges on the people's responsibility for maintaining Jewish identity against the pressures of Gentile society. Jewish identity is always configured in exile.

Exile is the experience of rupture in the world, the never-ending quest and questioning, the search for God and for oneself. Exile is the continual and continuing state of all people, but it has been a particularly relevant theme in Jewish history and writing. The film connects all of these themes by placing Chaim and Hersh in the park. They wander through the park as their words wander through their lives. While Chaim first is sitting in the park alone watching a distant group of Jews, he begins to remember: "My mind wandered and there was Bialystok before me. . . ." The process of remembering is linked to wandering at this early moment in the film. The park is the scene of their wandering/remembering. It is a liminal space between the city and the country, civilization and wilderness. It negotiates between what is constrained and what is wild. It is only within this place of the meeting of boundaries where Chaim and Hersh can come together. And they must physically walk as they verbally wander. Wandering is the act of the exiled ones, the ones who are compelled to remember.

This walking through the park is the only cinematic image during their meeting. Chaim calls his memories "powerful images." Yet, even though the film is a visual representation of the story, it does not recreate these memories for the viewers. Instead, the words of the two men fill the screen and the viewers are required to create the images in their own minds. The viewers are not allowed to passively take in the images; rather, they must be active participants in image-making, and in remembrance. In the Tanak, to remember (*zakhor*) is an existential imperative which is intimately linked to covenant. Over and over again, the Israelites are commanded to remember their history, to repeat it to their children, and to study it themselves. The verbal retelling of biblical survivals are ritual acts performed in worship to this day (in the Shema and the Passover seder, particularly). This memory constitutes their identity as a people, and their relationship to their God. The Holocaust is another event of tragedy and survival that demands ritual retelling and remembrance. This film is an enactment, a command to remember, and the people who view the film must actively participate in this.

Covenant

The question of the covenant is central to the understanding of theodicy and history. During one of many heated moments during their meeting, the covenant is highlighted. Chaim accuses God of being a liar:

> C: At Sinai God made a covenant with the Jewish people. At Auschwitz he broke it.
> H: . . . The Germans are entirely guilty. But we Jews, we are not entirely innocent. The Jews wanted to become like other nations so we broke our covenant with the God of Israel. . . .
> C: Since when is punishment for assimilation death by gas?

Hersh believes that, since all Jews are responsible for all others, even the Jews who maintained their traditions were punished for those who assimilated. He was punished for not turning Chaim back to God.

> C: You still see me as someone who betrayed you, you and God.
> H: No we betrayed each other and God abandoned us. . . .
> C: God abandoned us. No, he humiliated us. . . . The children did not abandon God, Hersh. How can we ever forgive him for not saving the children?
> H: If I knew God, I'd be God.
> C: If I knew God, I would put him on trial.

The Sinai covenant is established after the great redeeming work of God, the Exodus. God is understood as a God who is experienced through history, especially through the history of this particular people. The covenant is the promise between two, God and Israel, who have chosen each other for their very own. After the destruction of six million Jews, ninety percent of the

Eastern European Jewish community,[2] how can this covenant be understood? In the words of Irving Greenberg, "there can be no covenant without the covenant people."[3] How then can the events of World War II be interpreted? Did God break God's covenant, or did the people break the covenant? Who betrayed whom? And in what way?

The covenant between God and the people began with Abraham when God said, "Go from your country and your kindred and your father's house to the land that I will show you" (Gen 12:1).[4] The first covenant begins with an exile. The exile is continued through the story of Joseph—thrown into a pit by his family, sold into slavery, and taken to live as a slave in a foreign land—the exile continues and intensifies. Yet, Joseph triumphs in the end. He rises from the depths of a prison, to the highest position in Pharaoh's court.

Joseph in the court of Pharaoh acquiesces to the dominant culture. He wears Egyptian clothing and jewelry (Gen 41:42). His name is changed, and he marries Aseneth, a daughter of a priest of On (Gen 41:45). There are two tendencies in the narrative: one that constantly emphasizes Joseph's ethnic identity by repeatedly referring to him as "the Hebrew"; the other a drive toward Egyptianization manifest in his interaction with Egyptian people and culture. Joseph is caught in this tension—his desire to forget his origins and be satisfied in his new position, and his inability to do so. This is exemplified in the names he gives his two sons: Manasseh means "for God has made me forget all my hardship and all my father's house" (Gen 41:51); and Ephraim "for God has made me fruitful in the land of my misfortunes" (Gen 41:52). In Egypt, he forgets—yet, he remembers precisely what he forgets. He is fruitful—yet, he is still living within his misfortunes.

And it is through this position of power in the dominant culture, through his at least partial assimilation, that he was able to save his family. He was able to save his people. But this rescue, orchestrated by God through the betrayal of brother by brother, through the exile and assimilation of the favorite son, leads to another enslavement and threatens genocide. The roots of the hundreds of years of slavery and oppression before the Exodus lay in the story of Joseph. Throughout these stories, God appears and disappears, rescues and abandons.

The quarrel between Chaim and Hersh separates them; but it also binds them together. They cannot let each other go. Chaim calls Hersh his dearest friend and his bitterest enemy. They adamantly disagree but they are compelled to continue the meeting because of their childhood connection with one another—they are the only family either of them has left. The second allusion to the Joseph narrative is spoken by Hersh and it comes after another climax in their argument. Chaim breaks from him and walks off in anger. Hersh follows:

> H: Chaim, wait. . . . We deserve better from each other.
> C: What's the point?
> H: The point is that we are family. If Joseph and his brothers can make peace, then, Chaim, so can we. Let's promise each other not to walk away again. . . .

C: I'll listen.
H: Don't just listen. Stay and be with me.
C: And if I do?
H: I promise to stay too.

They continue to walk through the park together. Not only does walking represent the process of remembering and the state of exile, but it is also the medium of their companionship.

With this second reference to the Genesis narrative, the film again uses an allusion from near the end of the story of Joseph. But the beginning of the story is in this end, and in order to see the full impact of these words, we must begin at the beginning. In Genesis 37, Joseph is not the innocent victim of his brothers' hatred. While it is true that he had no control over his father's preference for him, Joseph's own actions aggravate the situation. First of all, Joseph brings "bad reports" concerning his brothers to his father (Gen 37:2). Joseph is a tattle-tale. But even worse than this, Joseph is hated because he has two dreams which depict his family bowing down to him, two dreams which he immediately relates to his family. The portrait painted of Joseph in chapter 37 is not very flattering. He is proud and self-righteous, though perhaps naïvely so. There are hints of this pride in both Chaim and Hersh's characters—both are convinced of the rightness of their position, both could be accused of arrogant moments.

As boys, Chaim was the favorite of the two brothers. Hersh's father used to criticize his own son, comparing him to Chaim. Yet, this favorite son left the yeshiva to pursue worldly interests. He attempted to take Hersh with him and in the process almost destroyed his faith; Hersh was broken when his best friend turned from Torah. This is Chaim's betrayal of Hersh: he abandoned Hersh, he abandoned Torah, and threw them both into the pit of despair. Hersh, in turn, walked out on Chaim, and then turned Chaim's family against him, as Joseph's brothers told his father that he was dead. By turning Chaim's family against him, Hersh betrayed their friendship and pushed Chaim out of the community. He is exiled and never returns. Both Chaim and Hersh are Joseph, both are the brothers that betray. As Hersh says in the scene cited above, "We betrayed each other. . . ."

For Hersh, the Jewish people broke the covenant with God by wanting to be like other nations. But what is assimilation? Where is the boundary that can be drawn and maintained between the insider and the outsider? Joseph carries within him the pull toward the dominant culture as well as the reminder of his heritage, and it is these two tendencies held in tension that leads to the redemption of his family. Both Chaim and Hersh shape their identities within the tension of these two tendencies—the one toward the foreign outside world, and the other that never lets them forget their family and the home from which they both come. Despite the fact that Hersh wears tzitzit and studies Torah, he is still shaped by the dominant culture. He is still a product of exile and assimilation. As Chaim points out, he lives in a city with a cross in the center. Despite the fact that Chaim smokes on Rosh Hashanah and writes secular literature, he is still a son of Israel in exile.

Hersh's complaint against Chaim was that he had been seduced by the secular world; consequently, he had abandoned God and tradition. Yet Chaim was immersed in Jewish culture, Yiddish writing, and Jewish community. He had not abandoned Judaism; his life was still suffused with the stories and traditions of his childhood; he was still living as a product of Jewish history. He had, however, abandoned the traditional religious aspect of Judaism. And this is all that Hersh could see. But he also sees that Chaim's reliance on reason, and his belief in humanity's ultimate goodness, is mistaken. Reason alone is amoral, argues Hersh. Without God, morality is a matter of opinion. The events of the Holocaust ended the enlightenment fiction of human progress.

Chaim counters that Hersh is clinging to a God that did nothing to prevent the mass murder of God's people, and that he is teaching a narrow interpretation of Torah, one that is cruel and fosters hatred. Toward the end of the film, Chaim meets one of Hersh's students. Although the viewer does feel sympathetic toward Hersh's position, the student is irredeemable. Hersh's student spews ugly accusations at Chaim about his abandonment of Judaism and family. Chaim dismisses Hersh's student and when Hersh defends him—he is young, he does not know what he is talking about, forgive him—Chaim turns on Hersh. It is not the student but the teacher who is cruel and full of hatred. Their argument continues thus:

> H: Wake up. Chaim, look around you. We are living in a broken world. In Bialystok maybe I could have taught them that the Torah has seventy faces of truth; each face a different reality, but not now.
> C: Yes, now! We are a devastated people. This is precisely why we should be taught to treasure each other like you treasure a rare jewel. Be tolerant!

For Hersh, the Holocaust made it even more important for the Torah to be saved. But his Torah manifests Jewish unity through the suppression of intra-Jewish difference. There is only one interpretation of Torah for Hersh and only one way to retain Jewish identity. For Chaim the Holocaust makes it even more imperative that all Jews, even Jews like himself, be accepted within the Jewish community. The Torah has seventy faces, each one uniquely enriches the whole.

Writing and Faith

The film pulls the viewer back and forth between Chaim and Hersh's positions. Irving Greenberg, in his article "Cloud of Smoke, Pillar of Fire," discusses how an easy faith is no longer possible after the Holocaust.[5] We can no longer approach God like dependent children. Also, the easy dichotomy between religious and secular, theist and atheist is no longer viable. The God who rescues and the God who abandons is not clear—children die while others less innocent or less worthy escape. Chance and not providence seems to rule the day. The Holocaust clearly demonstrated that professed faith in God had nothing to do with people's ethical behavior. Chaim expressed this well. He tells a story about an atheist in France who saved Jewish books and religious items. She risked her life, not because she loved God, but because she loved humanity. Yet the Holocaust also demonstrated that human progress through civilization is a fiction, and this is Hersh's point. There is a dialectic between the atheist and the theist, even within one person. Greenberg calls this "moment faith." Together, Chaim and Hersh equal the wrestling with God found in post-Holocaust theologies—it is a wrestling that can never be resolved.

Chaim as the modern Jew continues the process of writing and interpretation. Both Hersh and Chaim have chosen the world of the book—but Hersh's book is the religious book, defined traditionally as Oral and Written Torah. Chaim's book is the secular book. But as Greenberg points out, the easy dichotomy between religious and secular is no longer viable, and this applies to Chaim's and Hersh's writings as well. Writing and identity are forged together in the first destruction: from the destruction of the Temple to the ovens of Auschwitz, each new destruction configures the relationship between writing and identity differently. Books become a homeland for the wanderer, but the text is not a restful home. Exile has not ended simply because the Jewish people have found a home in words. The very nature of language forbids any comfortable and stable relationship for words themselves wander in and out of texts. And because words as signifiers are not synonymous with the signified, language perpetually exiles us from meaning even as we use it to create meaning. Chaim and Hersh are in exile from their home, driven out by death and destruction. Both now live within language, a language that they share.

Joseph in exile was a reader and an interpreter as well, though not of Bible or Talmud. Rather, Joseph was an interpreter of dreams. He built his home on the foundations of this interpretive talent. Chaim and Hersh are both Joseph, both live as Hebrews in a foreign court, both betray and are betrayed. But the betrayals go deeper than the betrayal of brother by brother. As the afternoon unfolds, as the wandering of the friends continues, they reveal to each other the greater betrayals and abandonments of their lives, the ones that haunt them even more than the abandonment and betrayal of one another.

Survival ("Living On")

Hersh's father had always been a critical voice in his son's life, first by negatively comparing him to Chaim, then by rejecting the woman Hersh chose to marry. He refused to perform the marriage ceremony, and he ignored Hersh's wife whenever he came to visit. But one day, the day before Yom Kippur,

Hersh's father came to beg forgiveness. Rather than accept his father's repentance, Hersh turned away. As he watched his father slowly walk out, he felt the power of being able to inflict pain, a small portion of the pain he had experienced at his father's hand. Tomorrow, he thought to himself, tomorrow I will forgive him. But tomorrow morning was never for Hersh and his father. That next morning the Nazis began their deportations, killing Hersh's father before Hersh could get to him. He had spent his last night on earth unforgiven by his son.

This story of family betrayal elicits Chaim's own. He had married as well, and had two children. As the Nazis approached, the rumor circulated that they only wanted the men to work in the camps. Believing this to be true, Chaim's wife begged him to escape to the East. He agreed, and left his home. A day into his journey, he found out the horrifying truth of Nazi intent. They did not want only the men; they did not want only workers. He decided to turn back and return to his young wife and children. But a friend grabbed him and compelled him to continue his escape—you can't save them now, you can only save yourself, he said. Chaim allowed himself to be persuaded. His wife and children were murdered by the Nazis.

It is these two experiences that lay at the core of their pain. They not only betrayed each other in their youth, but they betrayed their families on the eve of the Holocaust. And unlike Joseph and his brothers, unlike Chaim and Hersh themselves, they can never ask for their families' forgiveness. Their families are dead, and they inhabit no known grave. In the inverted world of Europe in the late 30s and early 40s there was no such thing as a free and moral choice between viable alternatives. They lived in a world of "choiceless choices."[6] Yet these "choices" continue to haunt them, shaping and informing all of their after-lives, a "living on" haunted by nightmares and despair and pain. Chaim and Hersh did not need the Nazis to physically kill them. The guilt and shame of the survivor kills them everyday.

Chaim and Hersh are not alone in the park. While Hersh and Chaim recount to each other their most painful memories of betraying their own families, little boys play ball in the background. Their joyous shouts mix with the chirping of birds, thereby providing the audial background of the men's confessions. There is a marked contrast between their memories of murder and betrayal and the ordinary serenity of the park. There is a particular dissonance between their words and the images of children playing. The boys, active and alive, contrast to the dead children of the Holocaust, especially to the dead children of Chaim and Hersh. The boys playing also remind the viewer of Chaim and Hersh's own past. Before the war, and before their quarrel, they were simply boys together.

The last reference to the Joseph saga is the very last line of the film. The sun is setting and Hersh must recite the afternoon prayers before Rosh Hashanah comes to an end. They promise to meet again, but there is a sense of parting that goes beyond a temporary separation. Once they leave the confines of the park, the viewer doubts they will ever see each other again. As Chaim walks away from the praying Hersh, he says, "When Joseph lived in Egypt he was great and powerful. He saved the kingdom and rose from slave to prince. Only the mighty Pharaoh was above him. Joseph had friends, disciples, wealth, and slaves—he had everything. But until his brothers came, Joseph was alone." Both are alone in the world—all family and friends have died, and they are exiled from their homeland. God is an elusive presence and absence. But more importantly, both live in private hells of shame and regret. "Egypt" is the dominant culture, the place of fleshpots, a foreign land. But Egypt also contains the prisons of oppression, external ones and the ones that we create for ourselves. This more than anything else makes them alone and makes it impossible for either of them to save the other. Hersh refused his father's apology not knowing that it was his last night on earth. Chaim left his wife and child behind to the Nazis as he fled to the east. They forgive each other for these choices, telling each other that their families are at peace because they have survived. Yet, Chaim and Hersh forgive each other only in the form of a question and their raised voices at the end of their sentence undermine the substance of that sentence: Chaim's last words to Hersh, the words that close their conversation, are "We have survived, haven't we?"

Rosh Hashanah is ending and Yom Kippur approaches. The days that lie between these two High Holy Days are days of seeking forgiveness, days of reconciling oneself with God and humanity. But does humanity have to ask for God's forgiveness this year, or does God have to be forgiven? As Chaim said, the covenant that was made at Sinai was broken at Auschwitz. Broken and fragmented, but not ended. As the quarrel between Chaim and Hersh brings them together even as it pulls them apart; as Hersh endlessly defers but does not deny accepting his father's apology; as Joseph and his brothers save each other by abandoning each other, so it is with the covenant. We continue living on in this post-Holocaust world—a world of wandering through the wilderness, a world of inversions and ambiguity, a world where God needs to ask for forgiveness. So we too can only continue to question God, forgiving perhaps, but always deferring and ending that forgiveness with the inflection of a question.

Endnotes

* No paper is written in isolation, and this is particularly true of papers about films. I would like to thank Jay Geller for introducing me to this film and for his comments on and encouragement of this essay's initial form.

1. Chaim Grade, "My Quarrel with Hersh Rasseyner," in Irving Howe and Eliezer Greenberg, eds. *A Treasury of Yiddish Stories* (New York: Schocken Books, 1973), pp. 579-606.

2. These numbers are from Irving Greenberg, "Cloud of Smoke, Pillar of Fire," in John K. Roth and Michael Berenbaum, eds. *Holocaust: Religious and Philosophical Implications* (St. Paul, Minnesota: Paragon House, 1989), p. 306.

3. Ibid.

4. All biblical quotations are from the NRSV.

5. Greenberg, "Cloud of Smoke, Pillar of Fire," p. 319.

6. Lawrence L. Langer, "The Dilemma of Choice in the Deathcamps," in Roth and Berenbaum, eds. *Holocaust*, p. 224.

Part Two: Desiring Community

The End of Desire:
Theologies of Eros in the Song of Songs
and *Breaking the Waves*

Kyle Keefer
Tod Linafelt

If, as Wallace Stevens has written, "not to have is the beginning of desire," then "to have" would be its end. If Eros arises from separation, lack, a felt absence, then union, plenitude, and presence represent its *telos*. This is, of course, a *telos* in both senses of that word: *telos* as the goal or objective, that which is sought; and *telos* as cessation or termination, the quitting of seeking. Thus, fear of contentment is the beginning and end of desire. Desire begins when one is torn out of contentment, and it reaches its end with a return to that contentment. Eros exists, then, only as a denial of its beginning and as a deferral of its end.

Yet how long can its beginning be gainsaid and its end cheated? Desire is as precarious as it is overwhelming. Recognizing the threat of contentment for desire, Georges Bataille has written that "happiness is the most demanding test of all for lovers."[1] And though one may learn this seeming truism by watching any soap opera, Bataille has explored its implications and paradoxes in a striking way. He writes:

> Compared to the person I love, the universe seems poor and empty. This universe isn't "risked" since it's not "perishable." . . . Carnal love, because not "sheltered from thieves" or vicissitudes, is greater than divine love. It "risks" me and the one I love.[2]

Affirming that it is the very precariousness of desire—the fact that it is not sheltered—that constitutes its desirability, Bataille nevertheless complicates the truism by introducing two other propositions: first, that carnal love not only is at risk itself but also puts those in its thrall at risk; and second, that precisely this double-edged risk makes carnal love superior to divine love.

The first of these propositions may once again seem to repeat what any melodrama or soap opera knows about desire—"star-crossed lovers" and all that—but Bataille pursues it in unexpected ways. In the volume *Erotism*, he begins by emphasizing that we exist as "discontinuous beings." While individuals may interact, affect each other, and even experience an intense solidarity with each other, each being is nonetheless separate and distinct from all others. "Between one being and another," Bataille writes, "there is a gulf, a discontinuity."[3] Birth is the starting point for this discontinuity, as *a* being emerges out of the continuity of *being-in-general* and into a self-contained

49

existence. Death is the return to continuity, a dissolution of individual existence back into being-in-general. Eroticism arises when "we yearn for lost continuity." The promise of Eros is the promise of "a total blending of two beings, a continuity between discontinuous beings."[4] Bataille himself cannot seem to decide whether or not the promise is ever kept. Indeed, who among us can tell if desire is simply a quest for the impossible or if there is in carnal love a moment—"precarious yet profound"—of genuine dissolution of individual existence. In any case, it is this promise of continuity by which Bataille links sexuality to death: both represent ways of overcoming the discontinuity of being—an overcoming that is, in each case, both promise and threat.

The second of these propositions—that carnal love is superior to divine love—is based on Bataille's insistence that "God by definition isn't risked." "However far the lovers of God go with their passion," he writes, "they conceive of it as outside the play of risk. . . . In carnal love we ought to love excesses of suffering. Without them no risk would exist. In divine love the limitation of suffering is given in divine perfection."[5] Returning to the etymological roots of "passion" (coming as it does from the Latin *passus*), one is reminded that the meaning of the word has progressed from "suffering" to "the state of being affected by an external agent" to "desire." For Bataille, these three meanings are bound up with one another still. Passion in relation to an external agent exists as suffering both because the promise of unity may well turn out to be a fraud, and because of the threat that this promise may *not* be a fraud. That is, to experience, even for the briefest of moments, continuity with another is to experience what Bataille calls "the abrupt wrench[ing] out of discontinuity." To take seriously the fact that we exist as discontinuous beings is to take equally seriously the fact that "the domain of eroticism is the domain of violence."[6] The commingling of selves exists only in the violation of borders, only in the state of being affected by an external agent, which, though we may know such violation as an experience of ecstasy, is no less an experience of anguish.

In this chapter we intend to use Bataille's reflections on Eros, death, and God as a basis for a comparison between the biblical book the Song of Songs (or the Song of Solomon) and the film *Breaking the Waves*. Both the biblical book and the film manifest desire as the commingling of separate realms and separate bodies in the service of a longed-for continuity, even while both acknowledge that such a commingling is never far from the domain of violence, and that continuity of being is never far from death. But what a consideration of the Song of Songs and *Breaking the Waves* introduces that is missing from Bataille's analysis is a more complex understanding of the implications of desire for the divine. That is, what if God were not "by definition" immune to risk? What if God were not above the fray of passion? What if the divine were not understood to be perfection, but also bound to the vicissitudes of desire, with all the anguish and ecstasy that it implies?

The Song of Songs

As the only example of erotic literature in the Bible, the poetry of the Song of Songs stands out for its unabashedly voluptuous character. It is, as Robert Alter has aptly put it, "the great love poem of commingling—of different realms, different senses, of the male and female bodies."[7] In alternating voices, two young and obviously unmarried lovers take great delight in describing each other's bodies and their desire for one another. In these descriptions, all borders become fluid and begin to dissolve: as the voluptuousness of the body fades into the voluptuousness of nature and back again, as the five senses of these bodies become intertwined, as the bodies themselves are intermingled. Consider the following exchange between the male and female voices (4:11-5:1):[8]

(*The man begins*)
Your lips are honey, honey and milk
are under your tongue,
your clothes hold the scent of Lebanon.

An enclosed garden is my sister, my bride,[9]
a hidden well, a sealed spring.

Your branches are an orchard
of pomegranate trees heavy with fruit,
flowering henna and spikenard,
spikenard and saffron, cane and cinnamon,
with every tree of frankincense,
myrrh and aloes,
all the rare spices.

You are a fountain in the garden,
a well of living waters
that stream from Lebanon.

(*The woman responds*)
Awake, north wind! O south wind, come,
breathe upon my garden,
let its spices stream out.
Let my lover come into his garden
and taste its fruit.

(*Reverting to the man*)
I have come into my garden
my sister, my bride,
I have gathered my myrrh and my spices,
I have eaten from the honeycomb,
I have drunk the milk and the wine.

As elsewhere in the Song of Songs, nature and landscape provide the poetic metaphors for the lovers' imaginings. Sometimes the surrounding landscape is presented as the place of the couple's lovemaking ("Wherever we lie our bed is green./ Our roofbeams are cedars, our rafters firs" [1:16-17]), but at other times the bodies of the lovers *become* the landscape, as in the above quoted passage where the woman's body is described as an impossibly rich garden bursting with a superabundance of sights and scents, a babbling brook, and the taste of milk and honey. The mingling of the senses and the poetic identification of the lovers' bodies with the surrounding landscape provide the metaphorical means of imagining a union between these two discontinuous beings. Bataille's language of discontinuity and continuity is quite appropriate here: the woman is described as "an enclosed garden, a sealed spring"; yet she invites her lover to come into the garden, which, we are told, he does. Now, the Song of Songs is full of double entendres, and on one level the garden most certainly represents the woman's sexuality, with her invitation being to the pleasures of carnal love. Yet the garden is also *more* than the woman's sexuality, it is the woman *herself*, and the invitation is more than to the act of consummation, it is an invitation for her lover to become one with her, an invitation to, in the words of Bataille, "substitute for their discontinuity a miraculous continuity between two beings."[10]

This longing for continuity is of course what drives the Song of Songs, and it is expressed in both subtle and overt ways. For example, an implicit expression of continuity may be seen in the essential mutuality between the lovers that persists even in the choice of descriptive metaphor. Each of the lovers is described in terms of beauty and tenderness: thus, both are said to have eyes like doves, both are associated with lilies, both evoke the grace of fawns and gazelles, and both have pretty hair and a sweet smell. But likewise, each is described in terms of power and strength: the woman is compared to towers and ramparts and said to be as daunting as a bannered army, while the man is said to be as strong as a cedar tree and to have thighs like marble pillars. One also finds more explicit expressions of this longing for continuity, as in the woman's account of her desire in the first of two "night scenes" (3:1-4):

> Night after night, in my bed,
> I have desired the one I love.
> I sought him, but did not find him.
>
> I must rise and go about the city, through the streets and squares,
> till I find the one I love.
> I sought him everywhere, but I could not find him.
>
> Then the watchmen found me, as they went about the city.
> "Have you seen him? Have you seen the one I love?"
>
> I had just passed them when I found the one I love.
> I held him, I would not let him go

until I brought him to my mother's house,
the chamber of her who conceived me.

Night after night the woman in her bed longs for her lover. Her longing drives her out of her house in the middle of the night to search incessantly for the object of her desire. When he is found she brings him into the place of ultimate safety and, it must be noted, ultimate identification: "I brought him to my mother's house/ the chamber of her who conceived me." This image of the lovers as having existed in the same womb of continuous being before being wrested apart into discontinuity, and of their desire to return to this state of continuity, is reinforced by the woman's statement in another passage, that "If only you were a brother who nursed at my mother's breast!/ I would kiss you in the streets and no one would scorn me" (8:1).

All is not, however, milk and honey and desire fulfilled in the Song of Songs, though many modern interpreters have portrayed it so. But the Song of Songs, long before Bataille, recognized "the anguish of desire,"[11] the precariousness wherein it exists, never quite fulfilled yet never quite denied. Thus, in one of the most striking passages of the book (5:2-8), one finds the counterpart to the woman's first night-time search for her lover:

I was asleep but my heart stayed awake.
Listen! My lover knocking:

"Open, my sister, my love,
my dove, my perfect one!
My hair is wet, drenched with the dew of the night."

But I have taken off my clothes, should I dress again?
I have bathed my feet, must I dirty them?

My love reached in for the latch
and my heart beat wild.

I rose to open to my love,
my fingers wet with myrrh,
sweet flowing myrrh on the doorbolt.

I opened to my love
but he had slipped away.
How I wanted him when he spoke!

My desire went out to him, but could not find him.
I called his name, but he did not answer.

Then the watchmen found me, as they went about the city.
They beat me, they bruised me, they tore the shawl from my shoulders—
those watchmen of the walls.

As confident in the undeniability of Eros as the earlier passage seemed, with its culmination in fulfillment and union, the book refuses to pretend that this is the end of desire, it refrains from telling us that this *telos* is inevitable. So now instead of the presence of the lover there is stark absence, and instead of consummation with the lover there is a beating at the hands of the watchmen (it is no accident that they are called "the watchmen of the walls," they who guard boundaries and refuse Eros its power to overcome the discontinuity over which they stand guard).

Perhaps even more striking, though, is that the Song of Songs, again in anticipation of Bataille, recognizes that not only is desire at risk from the vicissitudes of the world (in this case the watchmen and, in chapter 8, the woman's brothers), but that desire *itself* entails risk. Not only is there the risk that borders may be rigorously policed, there is the equal if opposite threat that borders may well be violated. As Bataille puts it, "What does physical eroticism signify if not a violation of the very being of its practitioners?—a violation bordering on death, bordering on murder?"[12] Or, as the woman in the Song of Songs puts it (8:6):

> Stamp me as a seal upon your heart,
> sear me upon your arm,
>
> for love is as fierce as death,
> its passion harsh as the grave.
> Even its sparks are a raging fire,
> a devouring blaze.

Though thoroughly rooted in the body, Eros transcends the confines of the body and takes on near-cosmic dimensions. The risk to discontinuity is enormous, as a mere spark of desire threatens to become an uncontrollable blaze. The language of the body, elsewhere in the Song of Songs so positive, teeters here on the brink of obsession, as one lover demands to be stamped into the very being of the other and tattooed upon the other's skin. *This* is serious continuity. And it should perhaps come as no surprise that here, at the poetry's most intense moment of continuity and dissolution of borders, that love is equated with death.

One needs reminding that this is in the Bible. Given that fact, the character that is most conspicuously absent from all this is God. The Song of Songs fails to mention God even in passing, and this absence of the divine has vexed pious interpreters no end, causing them to expend great interpretive energy in the service of allegorical interpretations whereby the body-to-body business of the Song of Songs is transposed into the relationship between God and humanity. Thus, in traditional Jewish interpretation, Israel is cast as the female lover and God as the male lover. Collections of midrashic interpretations become virtual compendiums of homoeroticism, as the male heroes of Israel's faith become the objects of God's desire. One such interpretation of Song of

Songs 4:7, "Every part of you is fair, my darling; there is no blemish in you," reads: "This refers to our ancestor Jacob for his bed was blameless before God and no flaw was found in it" (*Shir ha-Shirim Rabbah* 4:7,1). When the biblical book has the male lover state that "your breasts are like two fawns/ twins of a gazelle" (4:5), the midrash explains (from its thoroughly masculine perspective), "These are Moses and Aaron. Just as the breasts are the pride and beauty of a woman, so Moses and Aaron are the pride and beauty of Israel" (4:5,1). Christian interpreters are no less imaginative as the human lovers of the biblical book become ciphers for God and the church, or Christ and the individual soul, or even God and the Virgin Mary.[13]

Modern biblical scholars have tended to dismiss these allegorical interpretations, since they so obviously do violence to the literal sense of the text. But while it is true that such a mode of interpretation *spiritualizes* the Song of Songs, and thus tames its potentially subversive role in a Bible that has so often been taken as shoring up borders and fencing in sexuality, it is no less true (as Howard Eilberg-Schwartz has pointed out) that such interpretation *eroticizes* theological discourse, with potentially very radical results.[14] With the stroke of an allegory, God becomes both an object and a subject of desire. The world becomes the result of "an explosion of erotic energy, the ecstasy of a God who, in his act of creating, stands outside himself, perhaps literally 'beside himself' with Eros."[15] By way of the allegorical interpretation, God is introduced into the vicissitudes of erotic existence and is no longer "by definition" un-risked. "It risks me and the one I love," writes Bataille; and while the traditional allegorical interpretation will sometimes try to delimit the flow of Eros so that God remains unmoved by human desire, the effort seems ultimately vain. God desires the world; *and* God desires the world's desire.

Breaking the Waves

The portrayal of Eros in *Breaking the Waves* is in many ways strikingly similar to its portrayal in the Song of Songs. Most obviously, and not surprisingly given the fundamental dynamic of the erotic, there is the breaching of borders, the commingling of bodies and of different realms. The very first line of the film succinctly introduces those bodies and realms that will be caught up with one another. "His name is Jan," spoken by Bess before the elders in the church, places Bess, Jan, and God as the foci of the story. When asked if she knows what matrimony is, Bess replies with a seemingly innocuous answer, but one that will have dangerous consequences later: "The joining together of two people, under God."

The coming together of Bess and Jan physically both mirrors and depends upon the overcoming of the communal borders set up by Bess's church and embodied by the elders. Jan and his friends from the oil rig are patently presented as outsiders, whom Bess is introducing into this place in which they seem so foreign. The character of Bess embodies the erotic impulse toward border-crossing and the mixing of realms. (She also breaks down the divide between viewer and characters by directly looking at the camera/film-viewer.) It is a bit more complicated, however, than just introducing the "outsiders" into the provincial world of this Calvinist village, for as the film makes clear, the world represented by the village is not so very different from the world found on the oil rig, despite their seeming polarity. Thus the humorous scene at the wedding celebration—when Jan's friend chugs a beer and crushes the can only to be matched by an elder from Bess's church chugging his lemonade and crushing the glass—illustrates the intrinsic similarity of these worlds: each is an entirely homosocial realm in which male subjectivity is imagined as paramount and autonomous. The superficial contrast of the workers' cavorting in the shower room and smoking a joint with the dour meetings of the church elders only serves to heighten their similarity as stereotypically all-male realms. Into both these realms, however, Bess intrudes. And her desire, both for God and for Jan, exceeds the strictures of both.

This larger tendency toward the transgression of borders is of course, as in the Song of Songs, rooted in the experience of carnal love. Consequently, the bodies of the lovers in each are of primary importance. In the biblical book this importance takes the form of literary set pieces in which the man and the woman take turns articulating a sort of erotic inventory of each other's bodies. In chapter five, the woman begins at her lover's hair and playfully yet methodically works her way down the man's body, describing his eyes, his cheeks, his lips, and his arms, and allowing her gaze to come to rest on his stomach "like hard ivory," and his thighs "like marble pillars" (5:14). In chapter seven, the man indulges his gaze in reverse order, beginning with the woman's feet, and moving up to her thighs, her navel, her stomach, her breasts, her neck, her eyes, and culminating in her hair, imagined as a thicket in which he finds himself caught. These literary set-pieces—the most strikingly visual of this love poetry that otherwise privileges touch and smell—have their counterpart in *Breaking the Waves* in the filmic set-pieces where Bess and Jan also stand naked before each other, delighting in a similar erotic inventory of their respective bodies.

"Stripping naked is the decisive action," writes Bataille. "Nakedness offers a contrast to self-possession, to discontinuous existence."[16] The act of stripping naked means that there is physically one less layer of separation between one discontinuous being and another, or between a discontinuous being and being-in-general. It presages the dissolution of the individual—on the one hand as a prelude to erotic union, but on the other hand as a symbol of vulnerability, as a reminder that the violation of borders inherent to sexuality is but a step removed from the violation of borders inherent to violence and culminating in death. Thus, also like the Song of Songs, the film refuses the lovers an idyllic existence free from threat. It is perhaps here, in the "risk" of

Eros, that *Breaking the Waves* most closely resembles the biblical book: first of all, in the inevitable existence of desire at the intersection of presence and absence, of longing and consummation, of "not having" and "having." Bess and Jan's physical consummation, though representing a *telos* of desire (in the sense of its goal), nevertheless takes place at the *beginning* of the film and gives way to an absence, while Jan is on the oil rig, that only intensifies desire. So also must the first of the "night scenes" we looked at above from the Song of Songs, ending as it did in a union in the mother's house, give way to the second night scene, ending as it does in absence and violence. This parallel is reinforced by the pointed barring of Bess from her "mother's house" after her excommunication by the elders, a scene that comes immediately on the heels of the "watchmen" (here represented by the male children of the village) stoning Bess and chanting "Who's the tart?"

Breaking the Waves, however, takes the risk associated with Eros and the connection of sexuality with death much further than the Song of Songs, takes them in fact to their deeply disturbing conclusion. "Bess is sacrificed on the altar of patriarchy," said one reviewer.[17] This reviewer is, we think, correct, but fails to recognize that the distance from eroticism to sacrifice is never so far as it might seem. "Paradoxically, intimacy is violence, and it is destruction, because it is not compatible with the positing of the separate individual."[18] We are back to Bataille, who explores not only the interrelatedness of death and sexuality, but more particularly between sacrifice and sexuality. "The [sacrificial] victim dies and the spectators share in what [t]his death reveals .... the revelation of continuity through the death of a discontinuous being to those who watch it as a solemn rite."[19] We cite Bataille here neither to defend the practice of sacrifice in general nor to justify the sacrifice of Bess in particular; for there are at least two caveats to this theory of sacrifice. First, because the sacrificial victim must be something or someone from within the community that is carrying out the sacrifice and must be of value to that community, the act of sacrifice becomes for Bataille an act of recklessness, an act that depletes the life of the community. He writes:

> Such an intense movement of consumption responds to a movement of malaise by creating a greater malaise. It is not the apogee of a religious system, but rather the moment when it condemns itself: when the old forms have lost part of their virtue, it can maintain itself only through excesses, through innovations that are too onerous.[20]

The sacrifice of Bess on the altar of patriarchy, represented both by Jan and the elders of the church, serves not as a reinforcement of its order but rather as a condemnation of it. The second caveat to this theory of sacrifice arises from the filmic medium itself. If sacrifice so clearly depends on "those who watch it as a solemn rite," then the sacrifice of Bess complicates this theory, for it occurs off-camera. As Brent Plate points out to us, this is quite significant, for

Fig. 3.1 "As human sexuality and theology mingle in the allegorical commentaries on the Song of Songs, so do Bess's desire for God and her desire for Jan come together." (From the film *Breaking the Waves*. © 1996 Trust Films Svenska AB, Zentropa Productions. All Rights Reserved Still courtesy of October Films.)

by its intriguing treatment of point of view (the hand-held camera that gives almost a home video feel to it; Bess's direct looks at the camera) the viewer has already been brought into the film almost as another character. The fact that we as viewers are allowed access to the most intimate scenes of Bess's and Jan's lovemaking only underscores the fact that we are denied access to the scene of Bess's sacrifice. This refusal of voyeurism challenges not only traditional filmic notions of point of view as neutral, but also challenges the notion of sacrifice as "a solemn rite" that can be absorbed into a system of religious meaning by those who watch it.

Sacrifice, like Eros, is about excess—that which exceeds boundaries, systems, societies, individual bodies. The moment of death, like the moment of erotic fulfillment, is finally no moment at all, but rather the difference between two moments: the final moment of "not having" and the initial moment of "having," the moment of absence and the moment of presence. Eros is the threshold, the link between two things that cannot be linked. This brings us, finally, back to God. Just as the concept of Eros functioned to link the divine and the human in the allegorical interpretation of the Song of Songs, so does the embodiment of Eros in the character of Bess serve to link the divine and human in *Breaking the Waves*. As human sexuality and theology mingle in the allegorical commentaries on the Song of Songs, so do Bess's desire for God and her desire for Jan come together. This commingling of bodily desire with spiritual desire is made explicit in the wedding scene, when the minister interrupts the ceremony to praise Bess's "love for God in heaven," and it is reinforced when Bess, while making love to Jan looks heavenward and utters a thank-you, which she then repeats to Jan.

We have no desire to defend Bess's God, who is after all thoroughly shaped by the authoritarian, patriarchal religious community of which she is a part. Likewise, we have no desire to defend the twisted relationship that develops between Bess and Jan after his accident, a relationship no less shaped by an authoritarian patriarchy. (And it is worth noting in this regard that the third, mediating option—represented by the well-meaning doctor who refuses to collude either with the church or with Jan—also presents one more version of a controlling patriarchal perspective.) Bess, and her desire, finally exceed all of these. This desire is not "good," in the same way that it is not "bad." It is, rather, *excessive*; and such excessiveness is required if one is to overcome discontinuity. Bess's desire, in its excess, unites good and bad, her church and the outside world, sexuality and theology, the audience and the film. To paraphrase Bataille,[21] what Bess desires is to bring into a world founded on discontinuity all the continuity such a world can sustain. The shame is that we can finally sustain very little . . . the wonder is that we can sustain any at all.

Endnotes

1. Georges Bataille, "Love," in *The Bataille Reader*, Fred Botting and Scott Wilson, eds. (Oxford: Blackwell, 1997), p. 95.

2. Ibid.

3. Georges Bataille, *Erotism: Death and Sensuality*, trans. Mary Dalwood (San Francisco: City Lights, 1986), p. 12.

4. Ibid., p. 20.

5. Bataille, "Love," pp. 95-6.

6. Bataille, *Erotism*, p. 16.

7. Robert Alter, afterword to Ariel Bloch and Chana Bloch, *The Song of Songs: A New Translation with an Introduction and Commentary* (New York: Random House, 1995), p. 121.

8. Quotations from the Song of Songs are, for the most part, taken from Bloch and Bloch, *The Song of Songs* (1995), though we have occasionally modified them in reference to the Hebrew text or borrow a phrase from Marcia Falk *The Song of Songs: A New Translation and Interpretation* (San Francisco: HarperCollins, 1993).

9. It should be noted that although the male voice refers to the woman as "sister" or as "bride" throughout the poetry, it is clear that she is neither. Rather this is part of the role-playing that the two unmarried lovers engage in throughout the book. Thus the woman also refers to the man playfully as a "king" and as a "shepherd," neither of which is to be taken literally.

10. Bataille, *Erotism*, p. 19.

11. Ibid.

12. Ibid., p. 17.

13. For surveys of the allegorical interpretation of the Song of Songs in Jewish and Christian commentary-writing, see C. D. Ginsburg, *The Song of Songs and Coheleth* (New York: Ktav, 1970); Ann Matter, *The Voice of My Beloved: The Song of Songs in Western Medieval Christianity* (Philadelphia: University of Pennsylvania, 1990); and Roland Murphy, *The Song of Songs* (Minneapolis: Fortress, 1990).

14. See Howard Eilberg-Schwartz, *God's Phallus and other Problems for Men and Monotheism* (Boston: Beacon, 1994), pp.163-96.

15. Denys Turner, *Eros and Allegory: Medieval Exegesis of the Song of Songs* (Kalamazoo, MI: Cistercian Publications, 1995), p. 47.

16. Bataille, *Erotism*, p. 17.

17. Linda Lopez McAlister on *The Women's Show*, WMNF Radio (Tampa, FL, February 8, 1997).

18. Bataille, "Love," p. 214.

19. Bataille, *Erotism*, p. 22.

20. Bataille, "Love," p. 219.

21. Bataille, *Erotism*, p. 19.

Transgressing Goodness in *Breaking the Waves*

Irena S. M. Makarushka

> For a woman . . . to explore and express the fullness of her sexuality, her
> ambitions, her emotional and intellectual capacities, her social duties, her
> tender virtues, would entail who knows what risks and who knows what truly
> revolutionary alteration to the social conditions that demean and constrain her.
> Or she may go on trying to fit herself into the order of the world and thereby
> consign herself forever to the bondage of some stereotype of normal
> femininity—a perversion, if you will.
> -Louise J. Kaplan, *Female Perversions*[1]

Introduction

It is tempting, as many critics have done, to read the character of Bess (Emily
Watson) in *Breaking the Waves*,[2] a film written and directed by Lars von Trier,
as yet one more Christ-figure, Mary Magdalene, or Joan of Arc.[3] Fitting Bess
neatly into these Christian literary conventions provides a replay of familiar
paradigms and guarantees that the "natural" order of things will not be
disrupted. It is equally tempting to dismiss Bess, as others have,[4] as a woman
with a history of mental illness, who, like so many other heroines in women's
films,[5] behaves irrationally because she refuses to accept reality. To give into
either of these temptations, I suggest, is to reduce this complex film to its least
significant common denominators.

I see Bess as neither a tragic nor saintly heroine. Rather, like most
women, she is caught between the two culturally constructed paradigms that
reflect traditional patriarchal assumptions about women: the virgin and the
whore. On the surface, the story is deceptively simple. Bess, a young
inexperienced woman living on an island off the northern coast of Scotland,
falls in love and marries Jan (Stellan Skarsgård), an older and more experienced
man who works on the off-shore oil rig. Their love and passion for one another
transforms them both. An accident on the rig leaves Jan paralyzed from the
neck down, irrevocably altering their expectations of sexual intimacy. Bess
feels responsible for the accident because she had prayed for Jan's return. Either
out of concern for her loss of sexual pleasure, or under the influence of strong
pain medication, or both, Jan asks Bess to have sex with other men. He believes
that they can reclaim some vestige of their sexual intimacy if Bess tells him
about these encounters. At first she is horrified but later begins to believe that
Jan needs to hear these stories in order to heal his physical and psychological
brokenness. In spite of attempts to intervene by Dodo, her sister-in-law, and Dr.
Richardson, Jan's physician, and in spite of being cast out by her religious

61

community, Bess prostitutes herself because she believes that she can prevent Jan from dying. As his condition worsens, Bess places herself more at risk by returning to a boat where her life had previously been threatened. After she dies of slash wounds inflicted by her "client," Jan's recovery accelerates. Masked by the simplicity of the story, the troubling and complex question remains: is Bess "good?" Furthermore, whose values constitute the norm by which the "good" is defined?

I am not convinced that there is one adequate way of interpreting her choice to prostitute herself. Nor, for that matter, is there one adequate way of approaching the question of competing notions of the "good." Rather, I see her choice as profoundly conflicted. On one hand, it underscores the paucity of culturally sanctioned positive paradigms available to women. On the other, it surfaces one of the core issues that concern women: is it possible to be good outside of the culturally constructed paradigms that, as Kaplan writes, demean and constrain them? In other words, is it possible to interpret Bess's choice as a transgression of culturally convenient and patriarchally over-determined categories of goodness? Is it possible to see her not as a victim of patriarchy but as a woman who chooses out of her own desire to be good and to live for the other on her own terms? My analysis of *Breaking the Waves* focuses on this dilemma.

Although my reading of *Breaking the Waves* is informed by feminist film criticism,[6] nevertheless it differs from that of some feminist critics who have argued that von Trier, like the sadistic, misogynist deity with whom Bess speaks, creates a failed religious fable of woman as sacrificial victim.[7] I can see why feminists could find fault with von Trier's creation of Bess. Encoded in the beginning of this story is its tragic end: fairy-tale weddings do not have happy endings. In both narrative and real time the princess dies. The recent death of Diana, Princess of Wales, and the unprecedented out-pouring of grief were sad reminders of the fate that invariably awaits women. Even today the dominant cultural paradigm seems to pertain: the good woman is the dead woman who can be safely mourned when she can no longer disrupt the "natural" order of things.[8] Therefore, given women's history, it seems appropriate to suspect von Trier of rehearsing the same old story in *Breaking the Waves*.

As tempting as it may be to leave it at that and as hard as it may be to create a compelling argument to the contrary, I believe that von Trier is interested in more than merely creating one more film to titillate viewers with violence against women. I am not attributing to von Trier a conscious intentionality, rather, following Bordwell's description of symptomatic meaning, I suggest that embedded in von Trier's filmic narrative are current cultural and ideological concerns, including that of gender.[9] An argument can be made that von Trier does play with traditional representations of woman-as-sinner/woman-as-martyr which have provided some critics the opportunity to see Mary Magdalene and Joan of Arc as antecedents to Bess. However, I would argue that it is possible to interpret his use of these paradigms as critique. If one allows for this possibility, then von Trier can be seen as less of a misogynist, less of a proponent of repressive attitudes toward women and more of a critic of the religious and cultural attitudes that, as Kaplan argues, condemn women to "the bondage of some stereotype of normal femininity. . . ."

Furthermore, I suggest that von Trier's use of a hand-held camera, the insertion of postcard-like images with musical accompaniment to mark the "chapters" of Bess's life, not to mention the ending that verges on kitsch, conspire to suggest both irony and parody. In the instance of chapter breaks, there is the sense of visual and temporal distanciation, a kind of commentary on the unfolding narrative that, along with the 70s songs, puts the events into a critical, if not comic, relief. These visual devices make it possible to see *Breaking the Waves* not only as a painful representation of the life of a woman in a culture over-determined by a rigid patriarchal religious tradition, but also as a condemnation of that culture and of its destructive effects. Furthermore, they help to focus the viewers' attention on the film's fundamental questions: Is Bess, in the end, the good girl she desires to become? If she is "good," what is the moral of von Trier's story?

My analysis of *Breaking the Waves* falls into two sections: (1) the "good," and (2) transgressing goodness. The focus is Bess, her status as woman in a patriarchal culture and her struggle to be good. In the introduction that accompanies his screenplay, "Director's Note - This Film is About 'Good,'" von Trier states that he tried to represent the complex nature of goodness.[10] The reading that I propose explores von Trier's meditation on competing notions of goodness and the cultural assumptions that inform them. In the first section, I explore how Bess negotiates the moral landscape within which she lives as daughter, sister-in-law, member of a religious community, and wife. The church elders and Bess represent von Trier's vision of the two extremes of the contested notion of the good. At one end is unambiguous, uncompromising, immutable and eternally true definition of the good, on the other is the desire to be good. In the second section, I consider how the tension between a static and a dynamic understanding of the good is experienced. What choices are available to Bess as she struggles to make sense of her life in the aftermath of Jan's accident? How does she reimagine her desire to be a "good girl" under the circumstances?

As already noted, goodness is particularly problematic for women within a patriarchal culture. As I reflect on the good as a moral category, I turn to *Female Perversions*, Kaplan's brilliant clinical analysis of social and sexual behaviors, for which she uses Flaubert's Emma Bovary as a case study. Perversions, Kaplan argues, ostensibly parody the dominant culture's expectations of what it means to be a good man or a good woman. In the case of women, submission and purity are culturally encoded as prescriptive femininity. Consequently, obedience and virginity are affirmed as normal and, therefore, normative. These expectations, she argues, function to demean and constrain women. Some women become aware that they can never be good enough within the cultural paradigm that obtains. The realization that they do not fit the norm leads some to engage in self-destructive behaviors that include eating disorders and bodily mutilation.[11] Others try to fit themselves into the "natural" order of things, into a "normal" femininity. For Kaplan, such compliance constitutes perversion (*FP* 528). Therefore, regardless of which choice women make, they lose. Although Kaplan's analysis doesn't resolve the dilemma of Bess's desire to be good by transgressing culturally constructed values, it does offer some insight into the cost to women for making choices informed by a deeply held personal belief in goodness. In what follows, I explore the unfolding of Bess's desire and inquire whether she does indeed choose out of her own sense of freedom, whether she is coerced, or both.

The "Good"

Perceptions of the good are ineluctably bound to perceptions of otherness. Von Trier begins *Breaking the Waves* with an elegant short prologue that sets the narrative in motion. The first frame after the title is a close-up of Bess's remarkable face looking directly at the audience. Her image seems to push at the edges of the screen that can barely contain her. Wide-eyed with anticipation and certainty about the rightness of her love for Jan, her expansiveness, generosity and warmth are in stark contrast to the cold and austere faces of the church elders who interrogate her. Bess's simple declaration filled with light and hope: "His name is Jan" is met with the elder's ponderous response: "I do not know him." These two competing images shape the moral landscape upon which battles over competing notions of the good will be fought to the death. In the prologue, Bess and the elders never appear in the same frame during the interrogation that takes place inside the church. The visualization of their apartness is as stunning as it is unbreachable. If the elders value sameness, Bess celebrates difference. Von Trier's visual clues suggest that the twain shall never meet or be reconciled. Insofar as her image is the first and last of the opening sequence, it effectively creates a set of visual bookends that confine the power of the elders to the church. In the last frame before the scene changes to the picture-postcard marking Chapter One, "Bess Gets Married," we see Bess sitting outside the church, bathed in bright sunlight, smiling. The battle lines are drawn: insiders against the outsiders—sameness against difference—the story seems all too familiar.

In the epilogue that begins with the inquest into Bess's death, von Trier returns to the competing, if not contradictory, perspectives on the good that he developed both visually and narratively in the prologue. This time it is not Bess who is interrogated by the church elders, but Dr. Richardson who is being questioned by the coroner about his expert testimony. The coroner states, "You have described the deceased as 'an immature, unstable person. A person, who, due to the trauma of her husband's illness, gave way in obsessive fashion to an exaggerated, perverse form of sexuality'" (*BW* 128). Hesitant and clearly uncomfortable, Dr. Richardson struggles to respond. At first he appears surprised at his own words and then he asks to amend the diagnosis: ". . . [I]f you asked me now, instead of 'neurotic' or 'psychotic,' my diagnosis might quite simply be . . . 'good'"" (*BW* 130). The bewildered coroner responds, "You wish the records . . . to state that from the medical point of view the deceased was suffering from being 'good'? Perhaps this is the psychological defect that led to her death? Is that what we shall write?" (*BW* 130) In the end, in spite of his own belief in Bess's goodness, Dr. Richardson reverts to his original diagnosis. Bess's choice to sacrifice her life for Jan is judged a perversion.

These two scenes are emblematic of the vexing question of the "good" woman. By locating these scenes in spaces defined by patriarchal authority but, nevertheless, allowing for Bess to have the last word, von Trier anticipates the final sequence of the bells to which I will return. The prologue ends with Bess basking in the sun, the scene of the coroner's inquest ends as the camera pans to Jan in a wheelchair accompanied by Dodo and then cuts to Jan on crutches at the cemetery on a beautiful sunny day. From all appearances, Bess did indeed save Jan's life. In between the prologue and the inquest, von Trier creates a compelling argument against a universal or essentialized view of the good as he emphasizes its implicit contingency. Moreover, through the intensity of Bess's struggle to be "a good girl," he forefronts the relativity of moral assumptions and values. Her personal choices are situated within larger communal and cultural contexts. What unfolds, then, is as much a question of whether Bess is good as it is of the dominant perceptions of the good, particularly with regard to women. As I have suggested elsewhere following Zerilli's analysis, in a patriarchal culture women signify as both "culture and chaos, . . . [as] the radical sexual other . . . a cipher, a series of absences to be filled . . . energy to be harnessed . . . [woman is both] the site of sociosymbolic stabilization and destabilization."[12] How this cultural schizophrenia regarding women affects ways in which Bess is judged and how she judges herself are my immediate concern.

Bess's world is inscribed within three overlapping circles: family, religion and marriage. Each encompasses a range of complex and ambivalent attitudes about the nature of the "good" in relation to Bess. Traditional views about women and their role in the community inform and are reaffirmed within the spheres of religion and family—although not without dissent. After all, Bess chooses to marry an outsider, which sets the third sphere apart. Whether her death is seen as a matter of choice or the result of "bondage of some stereotype" (*FP* 528) is the question that von Trier invites viewers to engage. Before turning to this central question, I explore the perceptions of Bess that pertain within her family and religious community. Insofar as both spheres of influence represent a single-minded belief in what Kristeva describes as the law of the Father[13] and Bess's deeply personal faith in love, they are mirror images of one another. Furthermore, by emphasizing competing values within these spheres of patriarchal power, von Trier creates a space for the power of difference, albeit at a very high price.

The cold austere landscape of northern Scotland is symbolic of the rigid and unforgiving moral landscape of the church, its pastor and its elders. The interior of the church is dark, uninviting, and joyless, in contrast to the brightness of its whitewashed exterior. The religious beliefs of this community as expounded by the pastor and the church elders during services, burials, and, finally, in their condemnation and shunning of Bess, are based on their certainty that truth is found in the Word and the Law which are immutable and eternal. Furthermore, they reject all that is considered worldly and sensual. Their Law commands endurance, faith, and obedience. Their god is a god of wrath and justice: rewarding the good and punishing the wicked. The problem, of course, is differentiating one from the other.

Bess's goodness is acknowledged by the pastor at her wedding when he describes how she cleans the church not for worldly praise but for the love of god. However, his praise competes with oblique references to mental and emotional instability made by her mother and others. Although she signifies as the domesticated woman who is necessary to sustain culture; she also signifies as chaos. Where to be good means not to make waves, not to destabilize the "natural" order of things, not to express deeply felt emotions, not to experience pleasure, Bess is undeniably the "other." She is radiant with a love for Jan that seems both unconditional and boundless. Her fearless willingness to trust his love and to believe in its possibilities is counterintuitive to the values of the community. Her otherness is interpreted as a flaw, an emotional deficit.

Both her mother and Dodo describe Bess as simple-minded and excessively emotional. Her mother tells her that she must learn to endure her lot in life without complaint or emotion, as countless women before her have done and will do after her (*BW* 41). When Bess doesn't play by the rules, and when she isn't a good girl because she makes a public display of her grief or anger, she is either threatened with hospitalization or her offending behaviors are controlled by medication. At the airfield where Jan is boarding the helicopter to return to the rig, Bess becomes very agitated and Dodo gives her pills to calm her (*BW* 45). Dr. Richardson at first rejects the idea that Bess ought to be medicated. He acknowledges that her grief and emotional turmoil after Jan's accident are perfectly normal under the circumstances. He makes a point of differentiating himself from Bess's previous doctor, who had hospitalized and medicated her when her brother, Sam, was killed. However, in the end, Dr. Richardson betrays her. When Bess refuses to heed his advice to stop prostituting herself to save Jan's life, Dr. Richardson compels Jan to sign the order to put Bess into a mental hospital for her own good (*BW* 108, 110). His paternalism reflects the attitudes toward women of both the religious and scientific communities.

Von Trier creates a visual and narrative dissonance between the community's expectations and Bess's behaviors. In so doing, he politicizes the discourse, and, I would argue, takes sides. His hand-held camera frequently isolates Bess from others in the scene, particularly in emotionally charged situations. Her joyous, tearful, or anguished face fills the screen before the camera takes in the larger context, whether it be the hospital, her mother's house, Dr. Richardson's office, or the bar where she goes to meet clients. Bess is the heart of the story and von Trier's camera seeks her out as the center around which the other elements revolve. The level of Bess's emotional engagement invariably exceeds that of others. In numerous instances either her mother, Dodo, or the pastor tell her to control her feelings. By focusing so intently on Bess's face, von Trier's camera creates an intimacy between her and the viewer. It also suggests that he is not only empathetic with his character but critical of the emotional withholding that is the cultural norm.

The use of a hand-held camera as well as the film's sepia hue and granular surface give the film a sense of immediacy, inviting the viewer into the film. However, von Trier's insertion of the picture-postcard chapter breaks creates a tension between a sense of being there and having been there. Inasmuch as the viewer is tempted to enter into the world wherein Bess fills the screen with the power of her openness and vulnerability, the postcard images accompanied by sixties and seventies songs nostalgically declare: "Having a wonderful time; wish you were here!" as they dissolve, leaving viewers with a sense of geographic and narrative bleakness. Von Trier describes these interludes as a "God's-eye-view of the landscape in which this story is unfolding, as if he were watching over the characters."[14] Arguably, von Trier's trip back to the psychedelic world of the sixties and seventies, a kind of musical mystery tour, is an ironic reminder that god watching over the characters cannot save them, neither then nor now.

The chapter breaks with musical interludes also function as visual reminders of the multiple worlds in which Bess exists. Effectively, Bess embodies the conflict between two radically different ways of being good in the world. On one hand, she wants to belong by being a good girl, which, under the conditions of patriarchy, requires submission and silence. On the other hand, when she chooses to be good on her own terms, she is cast out by the church elders, her family, and community. The point is made painfully clear when, toward the end of the film, the children of the village stone her as she tries to make her way to the church. As Kaplan argues, there are no safe choices for women. If compliance is a form of self-destruction—a perversion—non-compliance as an indictment of normative values leads to communal recrimination and retribution.

For Bess, marriage signifies living by the rules. Yet the fact that she marries an outsider and, furthermore, that she takes pleasure in their sexual passion for one another puts her at the very the edge of communal acceptability. Jan, after all, does not share their religious worldview, nor does he share their perceptions of Bess. When Dodo tries to tell him that Bess is susceptible, weak, and vulnerable, foreshadowing Bess's choice to save his life, Jan insists that Bess is stronger than both of them. He loves her goodness, openness, sensuality, and strength. When Dodo tells him that Bess "is wrong in the head," he disagrees saying that Bess "just wants it all." To him, Bess is a loving, generous, passionate free spirit whose imagination and faith in the goodness of life is boundless. Like Jan, Dodo loves Bess, but sees her as emotionally unstable and in need of care. At the wedding, when Dodo speaks about Bess, she acknowledges her "good heart," selflessness, and acceptance of outsiders, yet chides her for her lack of good judgment (*BW* 34). She claims that it was Bess's good heart that compelled her to stay even after her husband Sam, Bess's brother, had died. Dodo begins to understand the depths of Bess's love for Jan and recognize her strength and determination to be good on her own terms only after she is cast out by the community.

Bess's understanding of the good reflects the teaching of the church filtered through her deeply personal faith in the power of love. In the traditional view preached by the pastor, the good is synonymous with unconditional love for the Word and the Law. Bess's grief and her unconditional love for Jan exceed this narrow frame of reference. The tension between the literalism and stasis implicit in the traditional interpretation of the good and the dynamic realities of Bess's life is played out in Bess's private conversations with god. Her relationship with god is as conflicted and problematic as her relationship with her religious community and her family. The common denominator is patriarchy. Like her other choices, her choice to speak with god signifies the complex nature of her faith and her desire to be a good girl. For Bess, the good is interpreted as much through the lens of her "otherness" as it is through her need to belong to a community. Therefore, her conversations with god reflect both the traditional values that she internalized and a freedom to desire more than that which her religious community values.

Speaking with god places Bess both inside and outside of the worshipping community, literally and metaphorically. Von Trier situates these deeply personal conversations inside the church as well as in a restaurant, on the boat, and in the hospital where she lies dying. Furthermore, interweaving scenes wherein Bess is speaking with god with those in which she is making love to Jan, trying to cope with the aftermath of his accident, or trying to save his life by prostituting herself, von Trier eroticizes her religious experiences as he sacramentalizes her sexual experiences. He also creates a visual commentary on the different dimensions of power: erotic, religious, familial, climatic, scientific, mechanical, and moral in the guise of the "good." Von Trier

Fig. 4.1 "Bess speaks to god in an empty church—a place where, owing to her gender, she is ordinarily forbidden to speak."
(From the film *Breaking the Waves*. © 1996 Trust Films Svenska AB, Zentropa Productions. All Rights Reserved Still courtesy of October Films.)

underscores the insider/outsider dilemma in which Bess finds herself. The first conversation with god to which viewers are privy takes place immediately after a scene in which Bess and Jan make love on their wedding night. The intimacy of this scene, like that of their lovemaking, is created through von Trier's voyeuristic use of close-ups. As they make love, Jan wonders how Bess managed not to stay away from the boys before she met him: "You must have been lonely. Who did you talk to . . ." (*BW* 37)? Their faces dissolve into an image of Bess kneeling by a church pew thanking god for the gift of Jan's love. The warmth and smallness of the hotel room, their nakedness, and the intensity of their passion are bathed in sepia tones which lose their golden hue as the scene changes to the cold and stark interior of the church. A different kind of emotional intensity characterizes Bess's face and voice as the intimacy of her relationship with god unfolds.

Bess speaks to god in an empty church—a place where, owing to her gender, she is ordinarily forbidden to speak (Fig. 4.1). Furthermore, she not only speaks to god in her own voice but also speaks for god. By attributing to Bess both the voice of the supplicant and the voice of lawgiver, von Trier creates an ironic juxtaposition between Bess and the pastor who also believes that he speaks to god on behalf of the community and for god in proclaiming the Word and the Law. When Bess speaks to god, she raises her face and her voice upward. When she speaks for god (or perhaps as god), she looks down and speaks in an admonishing tone. Arguably, von Trier parodies the traditional moral geography that locates god above his creatures. Her god warns her to be good because, after all, he giveth and taketh away. As she promises to be "good," von Trier cuts to Jan and Bess standing naked and silent in their hotel room. Jan pinches her nipple and Bess's face registers surprise, then pleasure, as the camera cuts to their sexual intercourse. As they climax, Bess simply says thank you, the only spoken words in this scene. This brief interlude ends as von Trier cuts from Jan's snoring to the sound of waves crashing onto the rocks where Jan and Bess brave the elements along the craggy coast. The interweaving of sex, religion, and nature are repeated again. As Jan and Bess make love in an old factory building, the camera cuts to the church where one of the elders is condemning those among them who prefer worldly things. Bess sits distractedly looking away from the pulpit, as her mother looks at her disapprovingly. Her status as an outsider is reinforced when she says to her grandfather, "Stupid that only men can talk at the service." Horrified, he replies, "Hold your tongue, woman."

Bess, of course, doesn't hold her tongue. Reflecting on Calvino's *Invisible Cities*, de Lauretis comments that Calvino's text is "an accurate representation of the paradoxical status of women in Western discourse: while culture originates from women . . . women are all but absent from history and the cultural process."[15] In *Breaking the Waves*, the religious community that passes judgment on Bess begins with the assumption that good girls are meant neither to be seen nor heard. The church law forbids women to speak in church and prohibits them from attending burials. Bess is expected to be "absent from history and the cultural process." In a culture that believes that women are to be silent and absent, Bess is both vocal and present, threatening to transform order into chaos.

In Bess's refusal to be silenced, von Trier situates the paradox of women's lives. To comply, as Kaplan suggests, is to "consign herself forever to the bondage of some stereotype of normal femininity—a perversion, if you will" (*FP* 528). Not to comply is to risk being judged a deviant, a danger to tradition, and, therefore, cast out. The reality of this losing proposition is played out in mixed messages Bess sends when she speaks to god and for god. If being a good girl echoes in her promises and in god's admonitions; so does the impossibility of achieving that status. On one hand, god tells her to endure her loneliness, on the other, he tells her to prove her love for Jan. To prove her love by trying to save Jan's life, she prostitutes herself. Vomiting after her encounter with the man at the back of the bus, she says: "Dear god, I have sinned." In response, god reminds her that Mary Magdalene was one of his dearly beloved (*BW* 87). At times, god is silent. Yet, as she sails for the last time toward the ship to sacrifice her life for Jan's, god tells her that he is always there. When she lies dying, her doubts about her ability to save Jan are not answered. Perhaps her grandfather's admonition is finally heeded: she holds her tongue.

Von Trier's parodic representation of the intractable nature of institutional religion draws on the tension between an external sense of morality in opposition to an internally imagined moral landscape. Von Trier invites viewers to consider who speaks for god—the pastor and the elders or Bess herself. Or, perhaps, no one. For Bess to be good—a good that emerges out of her own desire and love for Jan, she must defy and deny the notion of the good preached by her religious community and affirmed by her family. She breaks out of the "stereotype of normal femininity" (*FP* 528). But what models are there to emulate? Trangressing the cultural norm of the good girl, she finds herself in the role of the "bad" girl, the flip side of the same patriarchal paradigm of how women signify in culture. Whether her decision to prostitute herself is coerced or freely chosen remains be considered. For women, the question of subjectivity or agency is complicated. De Lauretis notes that:

> contemporary work in feminist theory ... (tries) to define the female-gendered subject as one that is outside the ideology of gender: the female subject of feminism is one constructed across a multiplicity of discourses, positions, and meanings, which are often in conflict with one another and inherently (historically) contradictory. A feminist theory of gender, in other words, points to a conception of the subject as multiple, rather than divided or unified, and as excessive or heteronomous vis-à-vis the state ideological apparati and the sociocultural technologies of gender.[16]

In the next section, "Transgressing Goodness," I explore how Bess's obsession with being good is, in and of itself, a transgressive act that reflects multiplicity and excess. Bess is more than the sum of her parts. She is neither the sacrificial good girl who dies for love nor is she the bad girl cast out for sexual misbehavior. In Bess, von Trier creates a character who is as much defined by her culture as she is alienated from it through her own desire. She is everywoman whose life is lived between the cultural expectation that a woman will stand by their man, even if the internal logic of that expectation has fatal consequences, and a sense of her own power to effect change. The value and significance of her life cannot be measured by its outcome, but rather by the process of living her commitment to love another human being unconditionally.

Transgressing Goodness

Critics have puzzled over the meaning of von Trier's title, *Breaking the Waves*.[17] To my mind, it is suggestive of the powerful clash of competing cultural values and the challenge to the "natural" order of things. If, as von Trier claims, *Breaking the Waves* is about the "good," I would argue that it is also about transgressing goodness. Bess's goodness, about which Dodo and Dr. Richardson give public testimony, transcends the moral vision of her community. Her desire to be good exceeds the interpretative capacity of a traditional dualistic either/or, good girl/bad girl framework. The rigidly dualistic normative values of her religious community do not take into account her agency or subjectivity; nor do they affirm the merits of faith lived as the unconditional love for another. Therefore, because their judgment against Bess reflects a narrow moralistic understanding of faith and love, the complex and dynamic aspects of her life are obscured. To inquire whether Bess is a good girl is misleading, if not misguided. It assumes an external reference against which all choices and behaviors can be measured and assessed. In the end, what matters is not whether Bess is a good girl. Rather, her goodness matters, a goodness that allows for vulnerability, that takes risks, that crosses from the familiar to the unknown. If the good is a static moral category that assumes compliance, goodness is dynamic, transgressing, and, therefore, dangerous.

Bess's goodness places her at risk. As Kaplan argues, "For a woman . . . to explore and express the fullness of her sexuality, her ambitions, her emotional and intellectual capacities, her social duties, her tender virtues, would entail who knows what risks and who knows what truly revolutionary alteration to the social conditions that demean and constrain her" (*FP* 528). In Bess, von Trier creates a character who risks goodness as an act of freedom. There is a little evidence that the miracle of "a(n) . . . alteration in the social conditions that demean and constrain" women is imminent. Fittingly, von Trier situates Bess within a traditional religious community, thereby underscoring the limited choices available to women. Furthermore, I believe that von Trier sees Bess's transgressing goodness as both breaking and being broken on the waves of traditional morality. In order to explore Bess's transgressive choices, I turn to three interconnected visual and narrative symbols: music, sex, and the bells. To my mind, they reflect the complex nature of both Bess's faith and von Trier's moral vision. I also consider the "miracle" of the bells which brings the story to its controversial end. Is it von Trier's ironic, or even cynical, response to fate of women? Or, is it an acknowledgment that, in the end, goodness is its own reward?

In the prologue, von Trier introduces music as the signifier of difference and otherness. In response to Bess's petition to marry an outsider, one of the elders asks: "Can you think of anything of real value the outsiders have brought with them" (*BW* 25). Smiling, she responds, "Their music? (25) The irony of this response is startling, particularly when seen in relation to the final moments of the film. Huge bronze bells, that may or may not be Bess transfigured, ring out over the oil rig barely visible in the vast expanse of ocean. In between the prologue and the epilogue, music features as the film's primary leitmotif signaling cultural difference between insiders and outsiders. The fact that von Trier makes music central to the film's moral vision supports the view that he believes religion to be an aesthetic practice rather than a moralizing authority.

Bess's life is permeated with music both inside and outside the church. Traditional hymns are sung during the marriage ceremony; Scottish jigs are played at the wedding reception. Whereas Bess loves all kinds of music, the elders tolerate only their own. The sixties and seventies pop music to which Bess listens signifies freedom, solace, and hope. When she misses Jan, she finds comfort listening to pop songs on the radio late at night. Intolerant of outsiders, the elders are suspicious of their music and its corrupting influence. The difference between their view and that of Jan and his buddies is exemplified in the scene where they listen to pop music as they cavort naked after a shower on the rig. Music as an accompaniment to transgression is also in evidence when Bess tries to seduce Dr. Richardson, another outsider. When Jan asks her to take a lover, she goes to Dr. Richardson's apartment where Elton John's music is playing as she dances on the table—worlds apart from hymn singing in church.

The most striking way in which von Trier uses pop music is as an accompaniment to the postcard images that mark chapter breaks. The images and music are integrally connected—one reinforcing the other and both commenting on the content of the narrative. The images themselves are eerily psychedelic. Filmed in highly saturated colors that distinguish them from the grainy sepia tones of the film itself, the images alter very gradually to a pulsating rhythmic beat. In Chapter One, "Bess Gets Married," an image of a tiny helicopter become visible through thick clouds hanging over the tops of craggy mountain tops as Mott The Hoople sings, "All the Way from Memphis." An incongruous combination at best, but remarkably effective as the camera cuts to Bess who, in full wedding dress, is pacing angrily on the tarmac

awaiting Jan, who is late in arriving from the rig. In another instance, distressed
by Jan's request that she make love with other men and tell him about it, Bess
faints into the arms of Dr. Richardson. The camera cuts to Chapter Five,
"Doubt," where an image of the ruins of a stone building provides the backdrop
to Leonard Cohen singing, "Suzanne takes you down to her place near the river.
You can hear the boats go by. You can spend the night beside her. And you
know that she's half crazy but that's why you want to be there. . . ." The camera
cuts to Bess awakening in Dr. Richardson's office. He advises her to take care
of herself, go dancing—a perplexing suggestion as she struggles to make sense
of ambiguities and doubts.

The surrealism of the idyllic scenes and triteness of the lyrics also
function to relieve some of the tension and horror elicited by the events in the
story. Through the sense of dejà vu that animates them, von Trier seems to
remind viewers that the story is an old one—as are the postcards and music.
Yet, this old story, like other myths of evil, bears repetition. As Jan struggles to
sign the order to have Bess committed to a mental hospital, the camera cuts to
the image of the fjord at evening illuminated by a redskied sunset with a large
tanker in the far distance: Chapter Seven, "Bess's Sacrifice." "If you've been
bad," sings Deep Purple, "Lord, I bet you have, and you've not been good ...
you better close your eyes, you better bow your head. Wait for the ricochet."
Von Trier focuses on a close-up of Bess's face as she is being ferried to the
tanker to buy time for Jan's life. Has she been bad? The question is yet to be
answered. In the final postcard image that marks the Epilogue, a stone bridge
stands over the clear water of a rushing mountain stream as Elton John sings,
"It's a little bit funny, this feeling inside, not one who loves that can easily hide.
. . . I know it's not much, but it's the best I can do, my gift is my song and this
one's for you." The lyrics anticipate the song von Trier offers in the end: a
resounding, if not triumphant, ringing of bells on high. Perhaps this image is
nothing more than another picture postcard with a love song; perhaps not.

Although many critics[18] found the bells in the final scene as excessively
melodramatic, taxing the viewers' ability to suspend disbelief, I see them well
within von Trier's moral vision and filmic imagination. Like the postcards that
mark chapter breaks, the image of the bells offers an alternative perspective on
the immutable law and Word preached in the church. For von Trier, the bells
affirm the possibility of beauty, pleasure, and desire. From the beginning, they
are associated with Bess and her transgressive choices. Three scenes focus on
the absence or presence of bells. The first takes place immediately after the
marriage ceremony. Jan's friend and best man, Terry, who is also an outsider
and non-believer, says to one of the elders standing in front of the church,
"Ring the bells then!" The disapproving elder replies, "Our church has no
bells." Looking up at the steeple, Terry says, "Not too fun, is it." Signifying the
community's refusal to affirm desire, to experience pleasure, the church
steeple—a traditional symbol of male power, is without a bell, impotent by

choice. In the second instance, after a church service, Jan asks the pastor why there are no bells in the belfry. The pastor explains that, "Bells are man's work. We do not need bells in our church to worship God" (*BW* 37). Ever the transgressing voice, Bess whispers to Jan that she had once heard bells, found them beautiful. She wonders whether she and Jan could put them back. Ironically, the only bell actually heard during the film is the clanging bell on the boat that ferries Bess to the big ship where she is assaulted.

Effectively, both Bess and the bells are silenced by the church elders. Neither is welcomed to participate in church services. In Chapter Seven, Bess enters the church dressed like a prostitute as the pastor addresses the congregation with the admonition that to achieve perfection it is necessary to love the Word and the Law unconditionally. Breaking the law with her transgressing voice, she answers from the back of the church: "I don't understand what you are saying. How can you love a word? You cannot love words. You cannot be in love with words. You can love another human being. That's perfection!" Echoing the elder's "Our church has no bells," the minister responds, "No women speak here!"

The symbolic association between Bess and the bells leads logically to the final scene. Silenced in death, the castout Bess is refused a proper burial because her transgressions are judged by elders as reason enough for eternal damnation. However, Jan, who believes in her goodness and in the fact that she saved his life by sacrificing her own, steals her body in order to bury her at sea. Perhaps Bess's final transgression is her escape from the damning law of the Father. Salvation—the reward for her unconditional love—is visualized in the "miracle" of the bells. If women (and bells) are silenced in life, they are given a voice in death—outside the church's sphere of influence. The bells, after all, ring out over the ocean. Does von Trier expect this symbol to be taken literally? I doubt it. Can it be interpreted as an ironic or even cynical interpretation of the status of women in patriarchal religious traditions? I believe that it can. Does he see an imminent "alteration to the social conditions that demean. . . ." women? Probably not.

Arguably, von Trier toys with traditional Christian notions of sacrifice and miracles, but he deliberately subverts them through his implicit criticism of organized or denominational religions that disallow that which he values most: freedom, art, pleasure, desire, and sensuality. In *Breaking the Waves*, he creates a quasi-religious fable for our times which resonates with aspects of literary fantasy as described by Jackson. In *Fantasy, The Literature of Subversion*, she writes that "fantasy characteristically attempts to compensate for a lack resulting from cultural constraints. It is a literature of desire, which seeks that which is experienced as absence or loss."[19] Portraying the religious community as one that silences women, discriminates against outsiders, and has strict rules for separating the saved from the dammed, von Trier offers a critique of these practices by articulating what they lack—empathy and compassion. The fantasy

or "miracle" of the bells makes present the absent church bells and gives voice
to the silenced Bess. The fantastical—the literature of desire is a compensatory
sublime that speaks for the possibilities rejected by the dominant community.

The "miracle" of the bells is ineluctably connected to Bess's sexual
transgressions. Her most serious transgression, the reason she was cast out, I
would argue, is not the fact that she prostituted herself. Rather, it is the pleasure
she took in her sexual intimacy with Jan. This pleasure was so great that they
both believed it to be life-giving. After the accident, Jan is convinced that
having lost his ability to have sexual intercourse, he will die if he can no longer
experience sexual pleasure. The pleasure he describes is not only related to their
physical intimacy but also to the psychic and spiritual intimacy that is essential
to their love. After all, the phone sex they shared when he was on the rig
allowed them great satisfaction. Whether or not Jan asks her to take lovers
because he is heavily medicated or because the injury created a mental
imbalance is not the issue. What matters, it seems to me, is what Bess believes
to be the power of her unconditional love. Jan says, "Love is a mighty power."
He also believes that without the pleasure of sexual love, his life will be
deprived of what is necessary for his very existence.

Just as Bess cannot readily be judged through dualistic categories, their
love also resists the physical/spiritual dualism. Body and spirit are one. To take
pleasure in one is to satisfy the other. In response to Dr. Richardson's anger that
she is prostituting herself to satisfy Jan, "a dirty old man who wants to play the
peeping Tom," Bess tells Dr. Richardson, "Jan and me have a spiritual contact"
(*BW* 103). "I choose for myself. . . . To give Jan his dreams. . . . I don't make
love with them. I make love with Jan. And I save him from dying" (*BW* 103).
Bess's choice to have sex with other men as a way of saving Jan's life puts a
transgressive spin on the traditional understanding of the proper purpose of sex:
procreation. Their sexual intimacy can never again have reproduction as its
goal; yet, ironically, it is a matter of life (or death). If women's bodies and lives
are traditionally valued as commodities or tokens of exchange, in this instance,
von Trier complicates the issue considerably. He recognizes both the traditional
role of women and subverts it by giving it a higher, spiritual calling. But is he
convincing? Does he really expect viewers to see Bess as a woman acting on
her own behalf or is she merely one more woman who loses her self and gives
up her life to satisfy a man's needs? Furthermore, and perhaps even more
perversely, through a curious thea-logical sleight of hand, von Trier expects
viewers to accept the idea that a woman can give up her body for the salvation
of a man. Jan's salvation is inscribed, or perhaps incised, on Bess's body by the
man who rapes and kills her. The cuts she suffers are marks of both punishment
and resistance. For women, agency and freedom come at a price. Bess's choice
to prostitute herself to save Jan is punished by the brethren who cast her out,
and by the rapist/slushier whose needs she doesn't satisfy. If the scars of
rejection and banishment inscribed on her body by the elders are invisible, the

slashes are painfully visible. In both cases, men do what they think Bess deserves, what she "asked for" by not playing by their rules.

Furthermore, von Trier extends the idea of Bess as savior by suggesting a kind of phallic cross-dressing. Believing absolutely in the power of prayer, Bess is convinced that because she prayed for Jan's early return without specifying a safe return, god punished her for her impatience. Therefore, she believes that she is responsible for the accident and, by extension, for his impotence. From the traditional religious and psychoanalytical perspectives that attribute to women the power to castrate men, it seems possible to read von Trier's choice of injury for Jan in relation to the larger religio-cultural issues that he raises in the film. Arguably, Bess takes responsibility not only of saving Jan's life, but also for making amends for his impotence. Within Bess's traditional world, she is permitted neither voice nor desire. Yet, as Adams writes, "Desire is engendered by difference."[20] Furthermore, "desire is the investing of the object with erotic value, this investment is not made in relation to difference as such, but in relation to a gendered difference. The object's erotic value is dependent on the question of whether the man or the woman has the phallus."[21]

Von Trier problematizes the "ownership" of the phallus. In the beginning, Bess transgresses community and family values, marries an outsider, and engages in a highly erotic sexual relationship with her husband. Jan possesses the phallus/penis which Bess regards with awe when she first sees it and which continues to focalize her desire and their sexual intimacy. Furthermore, Jan works on an oil rig whose huge phallic drill bores deeply through the ocean waters into (mother)earth's core. Her mother tells her that she, like all other women, must endure absence—the lack of access to the phallus. Bess, however, balks at the idea of enduring lack; she wants Jan back. The compensatory phone sex in which they indulge in a phone booth virtually at the church door transgresses the communal exhortation to endure absence. Bess's desire is eroticized; she pines for her husband's penis and for her own pleasure. Once Jan is impotent, Bess accepts responsibility for the phallus. Her eroticized desire focuses on keeping Jan alive. As a woman, she is without a penis. But, as a woman who desires for her husband to live, she appropriates his power of creation/procreation: the phallus. She strikes a bargain with god to prove that she loves Jan enough to save his life. She gambles her sex for his life. In the last scene, sex, the phallus, and the bells are reconnected. As she gives Jan his life in return for her own, von Trier imagines Bess's womanly body transfigured into huge bronze womb-like vessels that contain within them the phallic ringer giving voice to her desire. Ironically, the sound of the bells is heard over the ocean and on the oil rig, not in the church that refused her the right to speak.

Conclusion

In the preface to von Trier's film script of *Breaking the Waves*, Stig Björkman notes that the question the writer-director explores is: "Can we believe in miracles?" Furthermore, he writes that von Trier sees this film as a "sensual melodrama . . . a violent passion play about religious dogmatism and erotic obsession where physical love is endowed with life-giving powers of healing."[22] What "miracle" is von Trier asking viewers to believe? Owing to his rejection of religious dogmatism and literal-mindedness, surely he is not suggesting that viewers believe in the literal transfiguration of Bess into the bells. Metaphorically, how does this "miracle" signify? Is Bess to be interpreted as a martyr for misguided male sexual desire? Is her choice, in the end, a perversion, or does it affirm her faith in the possibility that "physical love is indeed endowed with life-giving powers of healing"?

To my mind, Bess is not a martyr. Recounting Reik's writings on masochism and martyrdom, Adams identifies three characteristics of martyrdom: (1) identification with the divine figure; (2) longing for pain in his name; and (3) postponement of pleasure till the next world.[23] Bess herself doesn't identify with a divine martyr. The closest she comes is through god's suggestion that neither her sexual sins, nor those of Mary Magdalene, exclude her from his favorable attention. Her resistance to the pain that enduring Jan's absence, as well as her unwillingness to "sacramentalize" that pain, argues against any notion of longing to suffer "in his name." In the end, Bess is a very ordinary woman. Although she does engage in conversations with god, there is little evidence that she believes in an afterlife where her desires will be gratified. Her desires are far too connected with the materiality of life and sexual intimacy. Furthermore, she accepts being cast out rather than give up her faith in her ability to save his life—a faith in her own powers to heal and sustain life.

Von Trier's eroticization of Bess's religious faith as well as his sacramentalization of her sexual intimacy with Jan affirms the transgressive nature of Bess's goodness as it condemns the self-righteousness dogmatism of the church elders. Arguably, for von Trier, perversion is not Bess's problem. She does not, as Dr. Richardson writes, "give way in an obsessive fashion to a perverse form of sexuality." Rather, perversion is the elders' problem; because they pervert the true nature of religion that von Trier associates with faith, passion and goodness. In *Breaking the Waves*, von Trier makes the case that as long as a "truly revolutionary alteration to the social conditions" is still in the future, women will continue to pay with their lives for the sins of the fathers. Whether Bess is a victim of patriarchy or whether she is heroic in her choice to live and die on her own terms is a question that viewers will invariably need to answer for themselves.

Endnotes

1. Louise J. Kaplan, *Female Perversions: The Temptation of Emma Bovary* (New York: Doubleday, 1991), p. 528. Hereafter cited parenthetically as *FP* with page number.

2. *Breaking the Waves*, written and directed by Lars von Trier, 1996. The screenplay, *Breaking the Waves* (London: Faber and Faber Limited, 1996), will be cited parenthetically as *BW* with page numbers.

3. Critics who point to Christian imagery and symbols include: James M. Wall, *Breaking the Waves*, *The Christian Century*, 114.5 (Feb. 5 1997): pp. 115-7; Mark van De Walle, "Heaven's Weight," in *Artform*, 35.3 (Nov. 1996): pp. 82-88; Brian D. Johnson, "*Breaking the Waves*," *Maclean's*, 109.49 (Dec. 2, 1996): p. 94; Richard Corliss, "*Breaking the Waves*," *Time*, 148.25 (Dec. 2, 1996): p. 81.

4. Critics who suggest mental illness include: Stanley Kaufmann, "*Breaking the Waves*," *The New Republic*, 215.24 (Dec. 9, 1996): pp. 26-8; Harlan Kennedy, "Orbiting Sublimity," *Film Comment*, 32.4 (July-August 1996): pp. 6-8.

5. For a study of women's films of the 1940s see: Mary Ann Doane, *The Desire to Desire: The Woman's Film of the 1940s* (Bloomington and Indianapolis: Indiana University Press, 1987).

6. My reading of film is informed by a number of feminist film theorists. Among the most significant are: Teresa de Lauretis, *Alice Doesn't: Feminism, Semiotics, Film* (Bloomington: Indiana University Press, 1982); Teresa de Lauretis, *Technologies of Gender* (Bloomington: Indiana University Press, 1987); Mary Ann Doane, *The Desire to Desire: The Woman's Film of the 1940s* (Bloomington: Indiana University Press, 1987); Constance Penley, ed., *Feminism and Film Theory* (New York: Routledge, 1988).

7. See: E. C. S., *Breaking the Waves* in *Out* (June 1997), p. 81. I would like to thank Marilyn Reizbaum, my friend and colleague, for the many hours of heated discussion around this very vexing issue.

8. Francine du Plessy Gray, "What women talk about when they talk about Princess Diana," *The New Yorker*, September 15, 1997, pp. 30-1.

9. David Bordwell, *Making Meaning: Inference and Rhetoric in the Interpretation of Cinema* (Cambridge: Harvard University Press, 1989), chap. 4. Symptomatic interpretation is described as follows: Whether sources of meaning are intrapsychic to broadly cultural, they lie outside the conscious control of the individual who produces the utterance. . . . Repressed meaning is what no speaker will own up to" (p. 72).

10. Lars von Trier, "Director's Note - This Film is About 'good,'" in *Breaking the Waves* (London: Faber and Faber Limited, 1996), pp. 20ff.

11. Jennifer Egan, "Cutting," *The New York Times Magazine*, July 27, 1997, pp. 21ff.

12. In an article entitled "Traces of the 'Other' in *Household Saints*" (*Literature and Theology* 12.1 [March, 1998]) I used the categories suggested by Linda M. G. Zerilli, *Signifying Woman* (Ithaca and London: Cornell University Press, 1994), p. 1. She writes that woman signifies as both "culture and chaos" she is "... the radical sexual other...," "... a cipher, a series of absences to be filled ...," "... energy to be harnessed ...," woman is both "the site of sociosymbolic stabilization and destabilization...."

13. Julia Kristeva, "About Chinese Women," in *The Kristeva Reader*, Toril Moi, ed. (New York: Columbia University Press, 1986), p. 154. Kristeva discusses the place of women in the economy of patriarchy.

14. Per Kirkeby, "The Pictures Between the Chapters in *Breaking the Waves*," in op. cit., *Breaking the Waves*, p. 14.

15. de Lauretis, *Alice Doesn't*, p.13.

16. de Lauretis, *Technologies of Gender*, pp. ix-x.

17. For example, Kaufmann, *Breaking the Waves*, p. 26.

18. For example, Johnson, *Breaking the Waves*, p. 94.

19. Rosemary Jackson, *Fantasy: The Literature of Subversion* (London and New York: Methuen, 1981), p. 3. This book was brought to my attention by Meghan Murphy, a student at Bowdoin College, who worked with me in the spring of 1997 on an independent study research project focusing on gender and film.

20. Parveen Adams, "Of Female Bondage," in Teresa Brennan, ed., *Between Feminism and Psychoanalysis* (London and New York: Routledge, 1989), p. 248.

21. Ibid.

22. Stig Björkman, "Preface," in Lars von Trier, *Breaking the Waves* (London: Faber and Faber Limited, 1996), p. 4.

23. Adams, "Of Female Bondage," p. 253.

Part Three: Eating Community

Cinematic Communion? *Babette's Feast*, Transcendental Style, and Interdisciplinarity

Maria Consuelo Maisto

In *Babette's Feast*, two sisters begin to despair that their minister-father's legacy will not survive his anniversary celebration because of the incessant quarreling of the members of their Protestant community. However, the feast of the title, a meal prepared by a Catholic exile in their midst, becomes the occasion not just for reconciliation but also for renewal. Past and present relationships partake in healing and revitalization around a sumptuous feast meant to evoke the eucharistic banquet.

This common interpretation of the 1987 Dutch film directed by Gabriel Axel seems to parallel recent efforts to establish the "field" of Religion and Film after many years of sporadic attempts marked by misunderstanding and even hostility. It may not be an exaggeration to suggest that the most recent conciliatory overtures are due, as in *Babette's Feast*, to the pull of commemorative ritual occasioned by the turn of the millennium and the centennial of the birth of the film medium. Even with reconciliation seemingly in the works, however, there is still an important question that needs to be asked: is this reconciliation really a renewal? To borrow from Julie Klein's and others' research on interdisciplinarity: is the "interdiscipline" of religion and film dependent on "instrumentalism"—each discipline simply borrowing from the other—or can it move toward epistemological "restructuring"?[1]

On another level, this is the very question that *Babette's Feast* is asking of both religion and film through its exploration of the metaphor of communion. What exactly is the nature of the transformation that the film depicts? How, precisely, does the film depict it? And to what degree is reconciliation really renewal in this film? If the film's invitation to interdisciplinarity is to be understood as transformative rather than instrumental, then both religious scholars and students of film must go beyond their initial instincts regarding the film. That is, religious studies scholars must resist the temptation to frame the film's central question according to its theological and ecumenical themes exclusively, while film scholars ought to challenge the tendency to view the film narrowly through the lens of formal or ideological analysis. In the case of each discipline, to take either of these limited approaches is not only to close the door on the possibility of a transformative interdisciplinarity, but also, ironically, to ignore the film *as film*. The religious studies scholar must realize that it is the film's particularly cinematic take on its apparent theme that makes it relevant to students of "Religion and Film" as distinct from, for example, "Religion and Literature." The film scholar must understand that scrutiny of the

83

film's form or ideology begs the question of the formal association between religion and film in existing film theory and practice. Like the feast in the film, then, the developing interdiscipline of Religion and Film is an occasion for reflection on the meaning of (disciplinary) otherness and (academic) community.

My aim in this chapter is to weave together critical and metacritical elements of a discussion of *Babette's Feast* in order to explore otherness and community both in and through the film. I look first at how *Babette's Feast* has traditionally been interpreted by religious studies scholars, especially through the instrumentalist lens of Religion and Literature, and particularly with respect to its presentation of otherness as the beneficent and redemptory agent of communion/community. This interpretation has been strengthened by increasing reliance on film-specific arguments, a result which suggests that religion's encounter with film on the disciplinary level is being re-energized. However, more interaction with film studies is needed. To that end, I examine how filmmaker Paul Schrader's 1972 thesis on "transcendental style" in *Transcendental Style in Film* (hereafter *TSF*)[2]—an example of both formal and ideological analysis—bears up when applied to the film, and consider whether that thesis can serve the kind of transformational interaction which the encounter with otherness, ideally, engenders.

Schrader's work was perhaps the most significant application of formalist, *auteur* criticism to religion and film since Bazin in the 1950s, while *Babette's Feast* has been an important catalyst for some of the resurgent interest in religion and film over the last decade. The two have never, as far as I know, been examined together. Yet *TSF* seems to be a veritable blueprint for a more film-centered, formal understanding of *Babette's Feast* as "religious," while the film reflects on the limitations and contradictions of the transcendental style, challenging and perhaps even changing some of its assumptions about the nature of the transcendental other.

Finally, I explore the implications of each interdisciplinary encounter around *Babette's Feast* and the question of otherness. The film, and religious studies scholars' recent work on it, both illustrates and challenges Schrader's theory of transcendental style, serving as a further example of how instrumentalist interdisciplinarity is always a part of interdisciplinary work. At the same time, Schrader's theory illuminates a different understanding of the film's presentation of otherness and community, and provides a cohesive framework for looking at the film's specifically cinematic qualities. To examine the interaction between these two canonical texts of religion and film with an eye to the question of otherness and interdisciplinarity is to challenge existing disciplinary assumptions ("knowledge") about critical concepts like otherness, transcendence, and film form, and to establish a starting point for a foundational restructuring of the interdiscipline of Religion and Film based on authentic dialogue.

Fig. 5.1 "Even with reconciliation seemingly in the works, however, there is still an important question that needs to be asked: is this reconciliation really a renewal?

(From the film *Babette's Feast*. © 1988 Orion Picture Corporation. Still from the collection of the Museum of Modern Art, New York)

Babette's Feast: The Other as Agent of Renewal

It is understandably difficult for many people to watch Axel's film without having Dinesen's short story in mind; indeed, the film's title sequence all but insists on it by reading "Karen Blixen's *Babette's Feast*." In fact, most analyses of the film use the story as a touchstone against which to understand the film. While this approach is perfectly acceptable, particularly as an exercise in the analysis of adaptation, it poses a familiar challenge to the exercise of Religion and Film. The conflation of story with film, or of techniques of literary interpretation with approaches to film, is typical of many efforts in Religion and Film. This is not to say that all references to the story, or to literary analysis, should be abolished; to do so would be to restrict interdisciplinarity rather than promote it. However, in some cases, treatment of the film and the story combine so seamlessly that it is difficult to tell which is being discussed.[3] This has the effect of denying the particularity of each form, and erroneously equating the two media.

Most discussions of *Babette's Feast* therefore focus on how the film renders and reinforces the story's eucharistic theme and symbols. For example, it is common to note the fish which frame the doorways in the opening sequence of the film; the opening hymn with its reference to the New Jerusalem; and the presence of 12 guests at the feast, with Babette as the Christ-like, salvific figure who initiates the meal. None of these themes or details, however, is usually shown to be cinematic in more than an elementary way. As visual representation or cinematic translation of physical descriptions or themes from the Dinesen story, film is here understood only as a vehicle for the story. At a more complex level, some approaches to the film might include insights into how certain cinematic techniques used in the film have functioned as analogues of literary techniques used by Dinesen. This is a more sophisticated version of the kind of analysis of adaptation mentioned above. It is also harks back to earlier days of film studies' dependence on literary tradition, when comparisons of cinematography to writing (Alexandre Astruc's *le pen-stylo*) and directors to authors (in the French "Tradition of Quality" as well as the *auteur* theory) abounded.

Just as film studies had to move away from, or at least nuance, its association with literature, so must the quest for a transformative type of Religion and Film go beyond dependence on literary techniques. We can see this type of progression in Wendy Wright's essay on the film in the online *Journal of Religion and Film*.[4] Wright mostly ignores the Dinesen story and instead concentrates on how the film is "religious" *as film*.

Wright's argument rests on three progressively more sophisticated arguments. At the most basic level, she points out the film's thematic concerns with religion, acknowledging that they are present primarily in plot, character, and dialogue. In her second argument, she explains how the film explores the foundational myth and symbols of Christianity and contrasts morality and sacramentality as "two modalities of Christian apprehension." Taken together with her first argument, it becomes clear that she is constructing her definition of the genre of religious film by (knowingly or not) employing some elements of a common technique of elementary genre analysis in film studies. This method, which is usually taught in introductory film courses, identifies genre by such elements as plot, theme, iconography, character, and historical time and place. In this effort she strengthens her initial, vague discussion of plot, theme, and character by offering a detailed discussion of iconography—the motifs and symbols that mark the film not simply as religious, but as specifically Christian. Here the familiar elements of fish, hymn, Eucharist, and Christ figure again appear, this time in the context of the film's concern with some of the essential questions confronting Christianity:

> On still another level the film plays with Christian symbols. It seems to ask the question: what does it really mean to live the hope held out by the Christian faith? Does it mean that one is to endure the present world as a place of testing, where the forces of evil are loose, tempting one to turn one's eyes from a truer, not yet realizable fulfillment? Does discipleship consist of moral rectitude, avoiding sin and doing good works? Or is the Christian life perhaps about the realization, at least partially, of that fulfillment here and now? Is discipleship about celebration? About the recognition and embodiment of that final banquet? Is the world a sacrament, a visible means of access to what is yet invisible?

While such a discussion of the film, as mentioned above, can be essentially indistinguishable from a discussion of the Dinesen story, Wright mostly avoids the trap of modified literary analysis. Instead she moves into a discussion of the film's formal structure by invoking John R. May, one of the first scholars to theorize Religion and Film.

> In fact, *Babette's Feast* is structured to recapitulate the central dynamic of the foundational Christian myth. It visually presents a movement from death to resurrection. And it does so by introducing a salvific figure who transfigures the main characters' world through a loving act of self-giving. Film theorist John R. May has suggested that a film's openness to a religious world view may be best be found in those dimensions of the formal structure that represent the visual analogue of religious questions.

Here Wright moves into the most sophisticated of her three arguments. Her exploration of the film's "visual analogy" for the "mythic pattern of ultimacy" effectively begins to shift her discussion away from the categories normally used to study literature. Christian symbolism is still at the heart of this analogy, but this symbolism is explored in its visual, auditory, and temporal incarnations in addition to its plot-centered and thematic ones. More importantly, it is connected to a very specific school of film theory. Wright invokes Andre

Bazin—though not by name—by her reference to the tradition of cinematic realism with which he is associated.

Bazinian realism is grounded in his attention to the potential of a filmic image to be "evaluated not according to what it *adds* to reality [the idea at the heart of formalism, realism's rival school] but what it *reveals* of it"[5] (emphasis mine). The formal techniques at the heart of this realism are the long take: a sustained shot which contains no editing; deep focus: a combination of lens and lighting manipulation that keeps both the foreground and background of a scene in sharp relief; and *mise-en-scene*: all of the material and non-material elements—from costuming, props, lighting, and makeup to figure movement and expression more commonly known as acting—placed in a scene to be filmed by the camera. It is these three cinematic qualities that make it possible for the viewer to apprehend, by means of a contemplative gaze experienced in the physicality of real time, the "reality" revealed by film. Wright defines the "profoundly" religious film as "contemplative" in this tradition. In her analysis of *Babette's Feast*, she compares the pacing of the film (the rhythm effected by the combination of long takes and cuts) to the rhythm of the liturgical rite. The scenes which combine long takes, deep focus and elaborate *mise-en-scene*— most notably the scenes involving the preparation of the feast—she describes as "iconic" and thereby as "enticements to contemplation" as in most religious traditions.

The effect of Wright's progressively more film-centered analysis is to present *Babette's Feast* as a dialectic of form, content, and reception in which "otherness" is symbiotically connected to, even a precondition for, community as an act of grace and redemption. That otherness can be identified as political and religious (Babette as French Catholic); moral (Martine, Philippa, and Lorens engaging duty vs. desire); aesthetic (Babette, Papin, and Philippa as artists); or gendered (Babette, Martine, and Philippa in the context of patriarchal situations). Formally, the first half of the film effects in the viewer a narrative distance through its use of voice-over narration and flashback, underscoring the story's origin as written text[6] rather than as film and preparing the reader for the more visceral connection brought about in the second half of the film. Although Wright does not touch on all of these themes, others have or will; what matters is that from this perspective, the otherness which manifests itself chiefly as alienation or exile is subsumed into and transformed by the feast. On this view, the final two scenes of the film are emblematic of this central truth: Philippa's final words to Babette, "How you will delight the angels!" and the final image of the candle's extinguishing flame, embody a hope of life in death. The film, in Bazinian fashion, invites the viewer into quiet and peaceful contemplation of that reality.

Transcendental Style and the Ideological Other

Unlike the sacramental and salvific character of otherness celebrated in most interpretations of *Babette's Feast*, Paul Schrader sees truly religious otherness as a transcendence which is known *ultimately* through an experience that is at worst alienating, at best distancing. From this perspective, *Babette's Feast* may represent true transcendence only if its aesthetic—its formal style—culminates in this alienation. When Schrader's theory is applied to the film, it becomes clear that this alienation, this "aesthetic of sparseness" as he calls it, is not only identifiable, but indeed defining; the film becomes barely recognizable as the representation of eucharistic salvation that its religious studies interpreters have argued it to be. In fact, it can be said to exalt the secular over the sacred. The disciplinary impasse between religion and film seems here to come again into play, with the difficulty of reconciling interpretations and approaches.

This impasse is illusory, however, because in fact Schrader's approach makes possible an expansion of our understanding of how religion and film can interact and even transform each other. Just as Schrader's theory alters how we can see the film, so does the film alter how we can understand Schrader's theory. To understand how this happens, it is important first to outline Schrader's theory.

In *TSF* Schrader attempts to identify a specific style of filmmaking and film viewing that can be said to be "universally" transcendental, even in particular cultural manifestations. Schrader's theoretical approach is auteurist, structuralist/formalist, and dependent on unstated notions of spectatorship and audience analysis. It is in trying to elaborate the complex relationship between style, reception, and the cultural and religious contexts in which these occur that Schrader runs into trouble. Nevertheless, the insight that he offers into the ability of film to "do" religion *cinematically* is an important addition to Religion and Film, because it provides for a coherent, film-based poetics that can be employed in religious interpretations of film.

Schrader is quite specific that the notion of the transcendent at the center of the concept of transcendental style refers to the actual presence of the holy, a hierophany, as opposed to the representation or analogy of an experience of the holy as is suggested by May's theory. As such, Schrader is also in the tradition of Bazin; it is the viewer who is meant to experience the transcendent through film, not merely to witness a character having that experience. Schrader claims that within the film-viewing experience, this hierophany is best facilitated through a dialectical structure that moves the viewer between experiences of alienation and catharsis. This structure consists in narrative, thematic, and technical manipulations of content and form based on identifiable aesthetics of "sparseness" and "abundance." The aesthetic of sparseness corresponds to the viewer's awareness of "the dull, banal commonplaces of everyday living" represented in and through the film—what Schrader calls "the everyday." The aesthetic of abundance corresponds to the viewer's experience of "disparity"— disorientation and intense emotion effected by the film.

Although each of these aesthetics is expressed through culturally/idiosyncratically informed film direction, according to Schrader filmmakers as far away as France and Japan can produce techniques of transcendental style which are logical in their respective contexts but also universally comprehensible as sparse or abundant. Thus, in Japan, Yasujiro Ozu's subject matter, composition, editing, and acting are ostensibly traceable to traditions of Zen aesthetics such as *mu* (negation and emptiness), and so comprise "sparse" style: static camera placement and deliberate pacing express domestic stories (*shomin-geki*) consisting of non-"dramatic" scenes in which the action is never climactic, oral and visual delivery is expressioness, and intratextual "codas" appear as silent, slow-moving natural scenes. Meanwhile, in the films of Robert Bresson, the sparse style consists in a subversion of western conventions of plot, acting, camerawork, editing, and sound, with as much possible elimination of suspense, emotive expression, camera movement, cutting, and non-essential sound and music. Bresson's affinity for Byzantine art and Jansenist theology are noted approvingly by Schrader to be consistent with the sparse aesthetic of transcendental style. The aesthetics of abundance which affect moments of disparity also operate contextually, jolting the viewer either suddenly or more subtly: in Ozu, a character might suddenly express strong emotion; in Bresson, sound might contradict image.

The point of the experience of disparity is to propel characters, viewers, and film into a "decisive moment," which makes possible the experience of "transcendence." This transcendence consists in what Schrader calls "stasis," a "frozen view of life which does not resolve the disparity but transcends it." Transcendence, for Schrader, effectively consists in the triumph of the aesthetic mode of sparseness. It is not surprising that he sees one of its most effective embodiments in Ozu, because he claims that the transcendental style is in essence an adaptation of (Schrader's understanding of) Zen:

> The desire of Ozu, Bresson, and to lesser degrees, Dreyer and others to express the *aware*, ideal or ecstatic (not synonymous terms, but all transcendent) is formalized in the triad of transcendental style, and it is perhaps not coincidental that these steps correspond to the classic Zen aphorism: "When I began to study Zen, mountains were mountains; when I thought I understood Zen, mountains were not mountains; when I came to full knowledge of Zen, mountains were again mountains." (*TSF* 38)

Schrader sees this aesthetic as having affinity with certain traditions of Protestantism and Eastern orthodoxy, and while it is beyond the scope of this essay to examine Schrader's understanding and use of Zen and other religious traditions which he invokes, it should be sufficient to point out that this attempt to extrapolate a universal from a particular is the central limitation of his theory.

He was later to confirm the critique in an acknowledgement that what he sees as universally transcendental is in fact localized in his own Calvinist background:

> The whole of the *Transcendental Style* hypothesis is that if you reduce your sensual awareness rigorously and for long enough, the inner need will explode and it will be pure because it will not have been siphoned off by easy or exploitative identifications; it will have refined and compressed to its true identity, what Calvin called the *sensus divinatus*, the divine sense. Calvin was a brutal intellectual, an intellectual par excellence, and the goal of all his work was to reduce the window of faith to as small an aperture as possible. We can define and understand the whole world, and all we have to leave is this tiny hole for faith to enter in by. But of course the more you define the world and tinier the aperture, then the more blinding the light of faith becomes in its brilliance. *Transcendental Style* uses the same argument: strip away conventional emotional associations and then you're left with this tiny little pinpoint that hits you at the end and freezes you into stasis.[7]

Schrader's desire to universalize is somewhat mitigated by his attention to the need for explications of transcendental style to be grounded in the particularity of the cinema and cinematic experience. "The spiritual universality of transcendental style may be variously interpreted by theologians, aestheticians, and psychologists; but it can only be demonstrated by critics. At this point one must return to the evidence; one must analyze the films, scenes, and frames, hoping to extract the universal from the particular," he explains (*TSF* 3). If his conclusion about the universal nature of the transcendental other seems questionable, his method is sound, and his analysis of Ozu, Bresson, and others provides an example of how to combine formal analysis with religious concern.

The limitations of existing religious interpretations of *Babette's Feast* can be exposed by now employing Schrader's theory of transcendental style in film. At the same time, however, we can examine how the film addresses, and to some degree redresses, the ideological limitation of Schrader's theory, all the while taking to heart Schrader's insistence that the "evidence" of the film direct its interpretation.

Babette's Feast is certainly structured dialectically, as most critics have observed in discussions of its themes (duty/desire, Catholicism/Protestantism, alienation/reconciliation, etc). Its use of recognizable aesthetics of "sparseness" and "abundance" in the service of those themes is also evident, most obviously in terms of *mise-en-scene*: the cold, bleak settings; stark colors; reserved, pious Norwegian characters; prosaic symbolism; and narrative pace which dominate the first half of the film contrast with the warm, flame-bathed, intimate domestic setting dominated by shrewd and passionate outsiders (Babette and Lorens), rich eucharistic symbolism (12 guests at a feast made possible by the sacrifice and gift of a salvific figure) and luxurious indulgence in sound and color.

Delving a little deeper into the film's dialectical structure, however, we see stronger evidence of its formal complexity. For example, the dialectic of sparseness and abundance is present within each of the three women as well as between them; for all of Babette's worldliness, she is distant and inaccessible to the viewer, for unlike the sisters, we get no detailed look at her past beyond her escape from Paris and loss of husband and son. She is shown mostly in long and medium shots which distance her further while also elevating her to iconic status. Meanwhile, for all of the sisters' austerity, the viewer is invited to empathize with them through detailed narrative flashbacks onto the failed courtships of the past and through lingering closeups of them in both old age and youth. Thus while on the surface of narrative the film seems to associate the sisters with "sparse" style and Babette with "abundant," at the deeper level of form the opposite is true. (This is often how film works formally to undermine its surface appearances, as the *Cahiers* writers Jean-Louis Comolli and Jean Narboni first famously pointed out in their 1969 analysis of the underlying ideology of *Young Mr. Lincoln*.)

The point of the dialectic of sparseness and abundance, of course, is to culminate in a moment of transcendence. In Wright's analysis, that "moment" is identified with the film's invitation to contemplation and, ultimately, Christian hope. However, in Schrader's scheme, the transcendent moment is ultimately the triumph of the aesthetic of sparseness and is in fact *not* clearly redemptive. Furthermore, while Bazinian contemplation is a byproduct of realism, inviting the eye to soak in the detail highlighted by long takes and deep focus, the aesthetic of sparseness rejects realism. "[I]t is more accurately a stylization," Schrader explains.

> Given a selection of inflections, the choice is monotone; a choice of sounds, the choice is silence; a selection of actions, the choice is stillness—there is no question of "reality". . . . The everyday celebrates the bare threshold of existence, those banal occurrences which separate the living from the dead, the physical from the material, those everyday occurrences which so many people equate with life itself. The everyday meticulously sets up the straw man of day-to-day reality (the illusion that the mountain is only a mountain materially), so that it may be knocked down later. . . . The everyday . . . rejects all the biased interpretations of reality, even if they are such conventionally acceptable "realistic" techniques as characterization, multiple point-of-view camerawork, telltale sound effects. In the everyday nothing is expressive, all is coldness. (*TSF* 39)

Seen through Schrader's scheme, the film's realism becomes the element of the "everyday" which ultimately serves the aesthetic of sparseness. How is this realism transformed into the everyday? The expository first half of the film, as many have observed, is a close rendering of the Dinesen story. As such, the film appears to be "realistic" insofar as it is "faithful to the story." However, the film's relationship to the story is transformed by the formal context into which its transcendental style propels it. In *TSF* Schrader exalts Bresson's subversion of western narrative and identificatory conventions as a fundamental example of how the viewer is made to experience the everyday and the disparate. Among the Bressonian techniques most admired by Schrader and present in *Babette's Feast* is the use of "doubling," a term originally coined by Susan Sontag in her analysis of *Diary of a Country Priest*. Doubling refers to Bresson's tendency to present an event twice or even three times, usually by means of interior narration executed via voice-over on the soundtrack. What is seen on the screen is simultaneously told, as when a character is shown leaning against a door while his voice is heard intoning, "I had to lean against the door." Schrader posits that this technique effects disparity by means of an *overemphasis* of the everyday. This is also what happens in Axel's use of the technique. All is presentation, not interpretation (hence the appropriateness of marking the film as Blixen's); the voice-over narration ensures that no point of view is privileged over that of the disembodied authorial voice. Dialogue is minimal; silence overrides the soundtrack. Most of the music is diegetic, and the acting is a stylized miming of the actions, thoughts, and feelings being carefully presented by the narration. Indeed, the entire first half of the film evokes Bresson's technique of narrative doubling, as the images repeat what the narrator recounts, particularly in the sequences which tell the story of Lorens' and Papin's sojourns. Not surprisingly, this is the same distanciation noted in the religious studies analysis, except that its effect is not to propel the film into an aesthetic of abundance but rather into sparseness: the doubling reinforces the "everyday" aesthetic, an important aspect of which, for this film, is the constant reminder that the story is literally "story" and as such is fixed and unchanging. The establishment of this aesthetic culminates in the last bit of voice-over authorial narration, the narrator's statement that the community has descended into querulousness and discord.

Once the aesthetic of the everyday is thus established, the trajectory of transcendental style requires the injection of "disparity." One of the ways in which Schrader defines disparity is as "decisive action [which] breaks the everyday stylization; it is an incredible event within the banal reality which must by and large be taken on faith." In *Babette's Feast* this occurs first in the revelation that Babette has won the lottery. The winning of the lottery is the event that of course leads to the more central disparate event, namely the feast itself. And, as noted above, by this point the voice-over narration has ended, thus showing the rupture of the everyday in form as well as content. The increasing level of disparity experienced by the viewer is then reflected in the sisters' and parishioners' increasing anxiety around the feast, and is expressed in the most overtly "disparate" or "abundant" form used in the film—the nightmare sequence with its surreal/comical images of worldliness and sensuality. The feast is here clearly prefigured to correspond to Schrader's concept of "decisive action":

> . . . [T]he final disparity is an environment which had been becoming more
> and more disparate. It demands commitment. If a viewer accepts that scene, if
> he finds it credible and meaningful—he accepts a good deal more. He accepts
> a philosophical construct which permits total disparity—deep, illogical,
> suprahuman feeling within a cold, unfeeling environment. In effect, he accepts
> a contract such as this: there exists a deep ground of compassion and
> awareness which man and nature can touch intermittently. This, of course, is
> the transcendent. (*TSF* 48)

Significantly, within Schrader's scheme the aesthetic of sparseness still makes possible an experience of grace or hope; thus, an analysis of transcendental style in *Babette's Feast* can reinforce most interpreters' understanding of the film's basic eucharistic theme. In other words, *TSF* transforms the film insofar as its argument can now be made formally and not just thematically. However, *Babette's Feast* also alters Schrader's transcendental style by demonstrating that that style may culminate effectively in abundance *through* sparseness—the Bazinian contemplative moment. This "triumph of abundance" is implicit in Schrader's almost throw-away acknowledgment of the "deep ground of compassion and awareness" that is made manifest by the transcendental style.[8]

It is thus in the interpretation of the final moment of transcendence that the more significant—and mutual—transformations take place, not just between *Babette's Feast* and *TSF* but indeed between a film studies approach to the film and a religious studies approach to the film. By modeling how form and content are layered and interwoven, commenting on each other rather than simply reinforcing each other, the type of film studies analysis represented by *TSF* provides the most logical explanation for the one element of the film that has always seemed to undermine its interpretation as a fairly straightforward representation of Christian redemption through eucharist: Babette at the end of the feast. The film seems to be moving toward the triumph of the aesthetic of abundance. However, the discordant note on which the narration turns from the everyday to the disparate has belied such a smooth formal transition. Furthermore, unlike the other diners, Babette is ultimately untransformed by the experience of the feast. If the film has constructed Babette as a salvific figure, in this instant we are presented with a *Last Temptation of Christ*-like moment of profound ambivalence. Here is neither the triumph of abundance nor sparseness but rather, seemingly, a rejection of grace and redemption altogether.

Alternatively, and in keeping with the coherence of its transcendental style, the final scene can be said to be a moment of stasis in which not just a religious ideology of sparseness, but rather of the *aesthetic* or even the secular (for Babette is never really presented as having or practicing any type of faith, in spite of the cross she wears) is triumphant. Her final words, after all, are that she did what she did only because she is an artist. In this case the final scene in which the candle is extinguished represents not the willing death of a voluntary savior, but rather a deliberate extinguishing, the last grasp of an artist for survival, indeed for immortality. This turns the film into a deliberate negation of the apparent eucharistic theme. The otherness—transcendence—that it celebrates is not in communion but in exile, not in the ethics of self-sacrifice but in the aesthetics of self-expression, not in religion but in film. This is a far different understanding of transcendence than traditional religious studies interpretations have come to see in the film, and so the challenge is to try to understand how this interpretation can still be, in Schrader's words, evocative of "a deep ground of compassion and awareness which man and nature can touch intermittently."

It is important for those who would use film in religious studies to consider whether and how film can undermine what seems otherwise to be apparent. Transcendental style and the ideological formalism of film studies that it can be said to represent challenges and transforms interpretations of *Babette's Feast* that are quick to see the celebration of cinematic communion. At the same time, it is important for those in film studies not to dismiss or discount the interdiscipline of Religion and Film simply because oppositional readings can be made of otherwise overtly religious films like *Babette's Feast*. The fact is that *Babette's Feast* also challenges *TSF* and through it, film studies.

Schrader's insistence on the static moment as the only possible expression of religious transcendence belies a firmly Calvinist ideology masquerading as universal theology. *Babette's Feast* challenges that insistence by granting its dialectic of sparseness and abundance and then challenging Schrader to move back to his original definition of the object of transcendental style: not to resolve disparity but rather to freeze it. Schrader's equation of the notion of stasis with the aesthetic of sparseness is a subtle leap which can be seen as misguided; by his own definition what is frozen is not the sparseness but the *dialectic*. "The decisive action does not resolve disparity, but freezes it into stasis" (*TSF* 49). He refers to stasis as being "locked in conflict," in "frozen motion." The *decisive action*—in the case of *Babette's Feast*, the feast itself—freezes the disparity—the anguish experienced by the community over the sensuousness of the feast, the ambivalence experienced by Babette, the suspense experienced by the viewer. In short, the spiritual effect experienced by the viewer of *Babette's Feast* in the moment of stasis is firmly rooted in a phenomenological reality of religious experience: the constant *tension* and *interaction* between hope and despair, between worship in community or in solitude, between ecumenism and tradition, between the sacred and the secular. As a film, *Babette's Feast* could be said to take no explicit theological or political stances, and its more truly "universal" religious stance both exposes and amends the ideologically biased stance which permeates Schrader's explication of transcendental style.

Interdisciplinary Implications

The above discussion is meant in part to illustrate how two approaches to Religion and Film can yield starkly opposite conclusions in both critical and metacritical terms. Thematically, *Babette's Feast* presents otherness as the agent of the triumph of community; *TSF* presents community ("abundance") as a cog in the progress toward otherness ("sparseness.") I am not suggesting that there is something inherently wrong with the opposition of these conclusions; however, it does seem to support the characterization of Religion and Film as non-interactive. The contexts in which the film and the theory are generally discussed represent religious and film studies' opposing disciplinary approaches to religion and film: in religious studies, the attempt is largely made to see religion in film as a positive (or at least authentic and legitimate) cultural force; in contemporary film studies, the attempt is generally made to expose religion as one of the false universals involved in the interpellation of ideology. This basic antithesis has been a major reason for the disciplinary "othering," rather than interdisciplinary dialogue, that has characterized Religion and Film until so recently.

Another characteristic of Religion and Film suggested by these two responses to *Babette's Feast* and *TSF* is the inescapability of instrumentalism. This is clear from Schrader's use of what is essentially Calvinist theology. And although she moves beyond reliance on literary techniques, Wright's invocation of May still betrays an inherent instrumentalism by its reliance on analogy as a central criterion of analysis. In both cases, film is analyzed according to the degree to which it adheres to a form of accepted/acceptable religious belief or inquiry. My own "use" of Schrader to explicate *Babette's Feast* is also instrumentalist, although it is intended to be so in the service of a transformative interdisciplinarity. As Klein and others have noted, this instrumentalism is one of the early characteristics of interdisciplinarity, analogous to reconciliation but not quite at the level of renewal or restructuring. It is not until each discipline is open to being truly challenged or changed by the other that such restructuring can occur.

The point of any interdisciplinary endeavor should not be to master two or more disciplines so thoroughly that one can address any issue or problem that might arise. The point, rather, should be to open up the possibility of transformation by the other discipline. (Whether this opening is in the service of knowledge as an ultimate, cohesive, and "objective" force or in the conviction that such knowlege is never attainable is a different question.) As scholars of Religion and Film have increasingly sounded the call for more attention to the discourse of Film Studies in order to flesh out its interdisciplinarity, we are confronted with the reality that mere recourse to that discipline is neither simple nor straightforward. If we are interested in a reconciliation between film studies and religious studies leading to a transformative interdisciplinarity, we must first recognize that there is no such singular or "correct" entity as "film studies." Secondly, we must recognize that the trap of instrumentalism does not go away. Using classical or contemporary film theory to support or challenge a religious interpretation (or more accurately, the ideology behind an interpretation) is still "using" film theory. Thirdly, the tendency to demonize the other discipline must not give way to the tendency to canonize it. Just as it is simplistic to view the film *Babette's Feast* only as a Catholic-Protestant polemic, the quest for interdisciplinarity in Religion and Film is ill-served by a demonstration of how the methodologies of one discipline are more "true" to the object of study than the other. The interdiscipline, after all, is to be called Religion *and* Film, not Religion *or* Film or Religion *vs.* Film.

The prospects for interdisciplinary growth in religion and film seem as bright or brighter now than when they were first set forth in the days of Bazin. It seems fitting, then, that his name should again surface here. In the recently rediscovered essay "Cinema and Theology,"[9] Bazin speaks of seeking "greater sophistication in the treatment of religious themes," a sophistication which must "meet simultaneously the requirements of cinematic art and of truly religious experience." He suggests that while the subject matter of traditional religious films "does indeed show specific affinities with the cinema considered as a formidable iconography," *authentic* religious film works *against* the exploitation of these affinities. While he is complaining specifically about the catechisms and hagiographies and biblical epics that comprised the genre of religious film at that time, his words are applicable even to more sophisticated films and their interpretations. Today, authentic religious film might need to work even against the exploitation of *theological* affinities. Bazin's point is that one should not rest easy in the quest to understand the character of "religion and film." Rather than simply searching for or waiting for [exploiting?] "affinities," he is suggesting, it seems to me, the need to be open to otherness—to be open to being challenged and possibly even changed by the other.

Endnotes

1. See Julie Thompson Klein, *Interdisciplinarity: History, Theory, and Practice* (Detroit: Wayne State University, 1990) and *Crossing Boundaries: Knowledge, Disciplinarities, and Interdisciplinarities* (Charlottesville: University Press of Virginia, 1996) as well as William Newell, ed., *Interdisciplinarity: Essays from the Literature* (College Entrance Examination Board, 1998).

2. Schrader, *Transcendental Style in Film* (Berkeley: University of California Press, 1972).

3. In her discussion of the film, for example, Diane Tolomeo Edwards constantly refers to the story's description of events, even when the film bears no cinematic trace of it. She describes Lorens' response to hearing Psalm 85 according to Dinesen's words, not Axel's film. See Edwards, "Babette's Feast, Sacramental Grace, and the Saga of Redemption," *Christianity*

and Literature, 42.3 (Spring, 1993). The fact that the essay, ostensibly about film, appeared in a journal on literature illustrates the problem while somewhat vindicating Edwards' conflation of the two.

4. Wendy Wright, "Babette's Feast: A Religious Film," *The Journal of Religion and Film*, 1.2 (1997): 2 pars. Online. [http://www.unomaha.edu/~wwwjrf/wrightar.htm].

5. Andre Bazin, "The Evolution of the Language of Cinema," in *What is Cinema?* (Berkeley: University of California Press, 1967), p. 28.

6. See Paul Ricoeur's notion of the distanciation of the written word in *Interpretation Theory: Discourse and the Surplus of Meaning* (Baylor: Texas Christian University Press, 1976).

7. Schrader, *Schrader on Schrader*, Kevin Jackson, ed. (London: Faber and Faber, 1990), p. 29.

8. In fact, two of Bresson's films, *Diary of a Country Priest* and *A Man Escaped*, seem to culminate in this "abundance through sparseness"—in the final "all is grace" scene in *Diary* and in the Mozart requiem that ends *A Man Escaped*.

9. In *Bazin at Work: Major Essays and Reviews from the Forties and Fifties*, Bert Cardullo, ed. (New York: Routledge, 1997).

When Your Family is Other, and the Other Your Family: Freedom and Obligation in Frank Capra's *You Can't Take It With You*

Patrick Caruso
S. Brent Plate

> Well Sir, here we are again. We've been getting on pretty good for quite awhile now, and we're much obliged. . . . Remember, all we ask is to go on the way we are, keep our health, as far as anything else is concerned we leave that up to you. Thank you.
> -the dinner prayer of Grandpa Vanderhof

It's a Wonderful Life has become a favorite Christmas-time film, even while few people nowadays know of an earlier Frank Capra film entitled *You Can't Take It With You* that takes up many similar themes. The 1938 *You Can't Take It With You* was actually a much greater financial and critical success during its time than *It's a Wonderful Life*, winning Academy Awards for Best Picture of the year, and Capra winning Best Director.[1] Indeed, the 1946 *It's a Wonderful Life* actually stands as the point of Capra's downfall and is seen by many critics as the last decent film made by Capra, even as it simply rehashed themes of his much better 1930s films, including *It Happened One Night* (1934), *Mr. Deeds Goes to Town* (1936) and *Mr. Smith Goes to Washington* (1939).

In the following we provide an analysis of *You Can't Take It With You*, paying particular attention to the multiple and dynamic relationships portrayed in the film. These relations find their locus in the Vanderhof/Sycamore household, and in particular around the dinner table in the midst of that house, a paradigmatic site of communion/community. Our purpose is not to explore the specific cultural-historical setting of the film as a 1930s United States production, but rather to approach the film formally in order to bring out the tension between *freedom* and *obligation* in the familial relationships of the film. While these contrasting components are inherent in all relationships to varying degrees, we set up the tensions between the two through the filmic-narrative representations of two very different family structures. This tension is of course vital to any understanding of otherness and how the "other" may be treated. Here, the other is in part contextualized by that which is most "not-other"; in other words, the family, the familiar.

On a cursory reading, the two components of freedom and obligation would seem to be antinomies of each other. However, through the contemporary therapeutic school of thought called "contextual therapy" we note that the two terms are bound to each other and depend on each other. Like any mixture of theory and cultural text, this is not a perfect match and we do not imagine the film to be a perfect illustration of this theory of human relationships, yet we are interested in what might happen when we compare and contrast contextual therapy with a cultural text such as a film. We proceed by setting up some background for the film and briefly summarize its narrative, and then turn to describe some of the key issues in contextual therapy. Then the theory and the text are brought together, highlighting the ways the audio-visual nature of the film deals with the two-part relational structure of freedom and obligation, and how these two seemingly opposing structures slide into and build on each other. Our intention is finally to provide a filmic model for how others can and might live together, where the family is estranged and strange people become one's family.

Capra and the film

Capra has often been thought of as a populist, left-leaning film maker who gave voice to the working class in the United States. Himself an immigrant from Italy in 1903 (when he was only six) who had to "pull himself up by his own bootstraps" and all the rest of that North American rhetoric, Capra continually represented the importance of the life of common people who stick to the "traditional" values of hard work, good family, and lots of friends. As such, his films resonate with anti-industrial themes, especially when industry is seen to ignore the common man, and *You Can't Take It With You* was itself called "the most vicious piece of anticapitalist propaganda since Capra made *Mr. Deeds*" by the Columbia Pictures board chairman.[2] And while Capra's liberal-mindedness has been rethought in recent years, his films have remained inspiring for the many who still watch them (many of them have been restored and are readily available in VHS).[3]

Not long before *You Can't Take It With You* was produced, Capra turned forty. By the age of forty he had achieved a lifetime goal, that of, as the title of his autobiography suggests, having his "name above the title" of the film. In the 1930s when this occurred it was the first time in Hollywood's history that a director had become such an *auteur* (and preceded the French *auteur* theories by two decades). So his films would be introduced, for example, as "Frank Capra's *You Can't Take It With You*" and would then include his name again in the title sequence after "Directed by." He was doubly credited in this way, and this fact contributed to his own self-evaluation as a self-made man. Like any so-called self-made man, however, in succeeding decades he would proceed to ostracize many who were close to him, somewhat paralleling the tragic life of "Citizen Kane" epitomized on film only a few years later through the genius of Orson Welles.

While basking in his success Capra recalls, in his preposterous autobiography, that he wanted to remember his own immigrant roots and decided to make films that would remember the "the working stiffs," "the born poor, the afflicted." So he set out looking for film material, he says, "in which 'Love Thy Neighbor' collided head-on with social disorder."[4] He found such material in the play *You Can't Take It With You*, written by Kaufman and Hart, and winner of the Pulitzer Prize. Capra's producer got the play for him for the price of $200,000, a record price for the time. The story allowed him the opportunity "to dramatize Love Thy Neighbor in living drama." Capra claims that "What the world's churches were preaching to apathetic congregations, my universal language of film might say more entertainingly to movie audiences, *if* it could prove, in theatrical conflict, that Christ's spiritual law can be the most powerful sustaining force in anyone's life."[5] Raised Roman Catholic, Capra retained a certain morality of Christianity, merging this with a flirtation with the optimistic Christian Science in the mid-1930s, and finally coming to express in his films the belief in the "Ecumenical Church of Humanism."[6] While the film gives many indications that it could be read through the lens of a certain Christian theology (and even leans toward a liberation theology with its critique of wealth), this is not our focus in this chapter, even as we hope traces of it will remain.

From a biographical point of view there are deep contradictions here. The rugged individualism of Capra's own life meets the generosity (which is also the obligation) of "love thy neighbor." Cynically, we could resolve this contradiction through the idea that the liberal piety represented in his films simply sold well as the nation recovered from the Depression. His recent biographer Joseph McBride notes Capra's irony: "A man whose films attacked the selfish rich, glorified 'the common man' (at least superficially), and preached that 'the only thing you can take with you is the love of your friends' had become a millionaire from those very films."[7] Sympathetically, we could credit Capra as someone who always remembered his roots. Critically and realistically, however, the contradictions remain, for the evidence is quite convincing that Capra was great at rhetoric, he could talk the talk of the poor and downtrodden while enjoying his own lifestyle of the rich and famous. Yet, he did, and his films still continue to, represent a world where love of neighbor is given a sympathetic eye and ear. Even when they verge on the sappy, they are moving and inspiring.

While it is not our intention to come to conclusions on Capra's life here, we do find similar contrasts displayed within the structure of *You Can't Take It With You*, contrasts that move between individuals and communities, freedom and obligation, friends and family.[8] The story within the film centers around a conflict—in general terms, a conflict between two families. One "family" is made up of the loosely-related collection of people who live and work and play in the crumbling Vanderhof/Sycamore mansion; the other that of the (up)tight, well-to-do nuclear family of the Kirbys. In the theatrical version the relationship between Tony Kirby (Tony is played in the film by James Stewart) and Alice Sycamore (Jean Arthur) is the key focus, and while the film version hinges on this relationship, the real point of conflict in the film is brought out between the two patriarchal figures of "Grandpa" Martin Vanderhof (Lionel Barrymore) and Anthony P. Kirby (Edward Arnold). On one hand, *You Can't Take It With You* is the same old story of the rich young man and poor young woman who fall in love and defy the social-symbolic structures that separate them. On the other hand, this plotline is ultimately subsumed by the stronger ideological battles waging between the individualistic-industrialist, represented by Anthony Kirby, and the populist, rich-on-friends common man, represented by Grandpa Vanderhof. Vanderhof used to be a businessman, full of greed and stress, but one day he simply gave all that up and "went down the elevator" (a key visual and verbal metaphor in the film), becoming a "dramatist of the everyday."[9] Kirby *is* the man of wealth, and consequently also of stress (he feeds on bicarbonate soda throughout the film), and is filled with the inevitable mean-spiritedness of such wealth. He is seemingly a man of freedom who does what he wants, but is also bound by a capitalistic code that forces him onward and upward.

The opening scenes of the film introduce us to Wall Street, home of "Kirby and Company," presided over by Anthony P. Kirby himself, who is introduced on screen taking the elevator from street level up to his office.[10] Kirby has just returned from Washington, getting permissions from the U.S. government to build a big munitions plant, thus also giving Kirby the largest monopoly in the world. Kirby claims, "With the world going crazy the next big move is munitions, and Kirby and Company are going to cash in on it." The reply from one of Kirby's cronies is that "a war wouldn't be possible without us." The only thing that stands in the way of this big monopoly is for a single person to sell their house to them so they can level a neighborhood and put up a big munitions factory. That person happens to be Martin Vanderhof, AKA Grandpa.

Once we are shown the world of Kirby, we "go home" with Grandpa Vanderhof and are there introduced to another side of life. A good portion of the film overall is set in the Vanderhof/Sycamore home, particularly the living room, and it is there that the viewer's sympathies are intended to remain. Several of the household interior scenes are filmed as long shots, emphasizing the vast interior space of the living room into which characters come and go. In the middle of the foreground of these long shots is the dining table which is always in process of being set or being utilized for its essential function by the "extended family." The return to this interior long shot throughout the film forces the viewer to step back from time to time and never forget that the relations of this film are set within the narrower context of this wild household. Once we the film viewers are allowed to enter this house, we are introduced to an uncommon, alternative economic structure.

The household is the epitome of what may at first strike the viewer as a type of freedom, of anything goes, of following your dream. As Raymond Carney suggests, the Vanderhof "family" portrayed in the film is a "loose aggregation of more or less independent eccentrics—groups of people who live together in the same household but who sacrifice none of their individualism or independence to the claims of the community they constitute or the responsibilities of mutual interdependency."[11] It is not clear who actually resides in the house on a permanent basis, but the characters seen around the house include Alice's mother and father, Penny and Paul Sycamore (Spring Byington and Samuel S. Hinds); Alice's sister Essie Carmichael and Essie's husband Ed (Ann Miller and Dub Taylor); there is the maid, Rheba (Lillian Yarbo); and then there is an assortment of older men who work in the basement, "inventing things," people like Mr. DePinna, Poppins, and Donald, who is also Rheba's fiancé. Penny Sycamore has become a playwright because someone delivered a typewriter to her home by mistake. Paul makes firecrackers in his basement with the help of Mr. DePinna, an iceman who showed up at the Sycamore doorstep one day and never left. The Sycamores' daughter, Essie, imagines she's a prima ballerina, while Essie's husband Ed, who'd rather play a xylophone than work, spends his free time selling Essie's candy, wrapping each package in paper from a used printing press, providing the candy with hidden messages. Then, of course, there is Alice, and Grandpa himself. Many small things are mentioned in the first half of the film that tell the viewer this is no ordinary household. When Alice asks what time it is, someone mentions that "it was 5:00 about two hours ago," and when the doorbell rings, Grandpa Vanderhof claims that he hasn't heard that sound since Halloween, indicating a certain "open door" policy of the house. And through it all a precariously balanced sign on the wall that reads "Home Sweet Home" is constantly falling and being rehung by one or another of the characters.

In most instances, each member of this odd cast of characters is introduced to the zaniness of the household by way of an invitation to dinner, to join together at the table. Poppins, one of the "basement men," was an accountant who Grandpa Vanderhof met in an office, punching numbers on a calculator. On their meeting Grandpa asks the man if he actually likes what he's doing, and Poppins, timid because he feels the office managers will somehow punish him, whispers that he doesn't really like it. Grandpa asks what he really likes to do, to which Poppins replies, "I like to make things up," and he pulls out a small mechanical rabbit that he has invented from under his desk. Vanderhof is impressed and invites him to dinner. Poppins comes and never leaves. Likewise, we find out that Essie's husband Ed just came to dinner once, fell in love with Essie, and never left. And Essie's dance teacher, the Russian Boris Kolenkhov, seems simply to tolerate Essie's bad dancing so he can be invited to dinner. Even the uptight IRS man who comes to collect from Grandpa—who never pays taxes because he "doesn't believe in them"—was invited to stay for dinner (though he of course does not). Indeed, the very first shot within the house is framed as if the camera were inside the kitchen cupboard where the dishes are stored, and we see Rheba's hands grab some things for dinner as she prepares to set the table. Thus, the table (here the dinner table, but later in the film there are other types of tables) provides the setting for one of the key binding forces of the film, and our analysis continually returns to this prop as it allows us a locus from which to bring together the variety of relationships in the film.

Multiple relationships intersect throughout the household and throughout the film as a whole. Yet, as mentioned above, it is the relationship between Alice and Tony that sets the film in motion. Tony is heir-apparent to his father's vast military-industrial business, and Alice is his secretary. They fall in love even as they are made aware of the difficulties of connecting their drastically different families, particularly as the Kirby family lacks all the endearing zaniness that the film viewer is given to sympathize with through the opening scenes—Mrs. Kirby in particular is depicted as a no-smiles, nasty woman who seems to only care about her social reputation. The tension between the two families is exacerbated by the fact that the tycoon Kirby is trying to buy the beloved Vanderhof/Sycamore house so he can build his new munitions factory there. This fact serves to set a relational context for Tony and Alice, who appear unaware of the plan, that is full of suspense and expectancy from the viewer's point of view. The viewer anxiously awaits the revelation that will let all the parties within the film know the true plot of Kirby and Company to tear down the Vanderhof/Sycamore house.

The ending is a typically sappy Hollywood ending, confirming many critics' suspicions of Capra as an "optimistic Pollyanna."[12] As Charles Maland says of the ending, "Though Capra structures the narrative in such a way as to make Kirby's conversion understandable, though he uses all his knowledge of film language to try to bring the ending off, he doesn't manage to do so. . . . [H]aving the ruthless capitalist converted by the whimsical Grandpa Vanderhof simply strains our imaginations too much."[13] However, given the unidimensional characterizing of Kirby throughout the film, the conversion, we believe, *is* actually managed—though it is a unidimensional conversion and it is not clear how far this conversion goes and what it actually entails. The film ends at the point of possible conversion and the viewers are left to fill out the prospects of what might happen next.

The entire film necessitates that the viewer suspend reality and enter into an imaginative world, a world that, as with the theme of this book as a whole, has high hopes of "imag(in)ing otherness." In the remainder of this essay we will highlight several aspects of the film that have generally been overlooked by previous analyses of the film, particularly as they continue this book's general discussion of "living together with others." To do so means we will first need to take a slight detour and set up several components of a contemporary therapeutic approach called "contextual therapy." Our brief introduction here will pay particular attention to the premises of contextual therapy as they are most relevant to our discussion of *You Can't Take It With You*.

Contextual Therapy

Contextual therapy, both a set of premises and a method, is one of several family therapy approaches with a transgenerational focus.[14] Furthermore, with its emphasis on a relational understanding of life and the dialogical process, contextual therapy is heavily indebted to the thought of Martin Buber.

Contextual therapy claims "that a truly comprehensive grasp of human existence is inevitably composed of both individual and relational realities,"[15] and begins therefore as an integrative approach to understanding human behavior that resists reducing its analysis to an exclusive focus on the individual *or* the family system. Instead, contextual therapy posits that there are four fundamental dimensions to understanding human behavior: (1) objectifiable facts, (2) individual psychology, (3) systems of transactional patterns, and (4) the ethic of due consideration or merited trust.[16] The dimension of objectifiable facts refers to information such as the basic events of a person's development or life-cycle. Internalized motivations for behavior within the individual, or intrapsychic processes, constitute dimension two. The third dimension consists of systemic realities such as rules, roles, boundaries, allegiances, and so on, that highlight processes within the family system as a whole.

The unique contribution of contextual therapy to the broader array of family therapies is its emphasis on the fourth dimension of "relational reality," what is otherwise known as the *ethic of due consideration*. In fact, this emphasis is seen in the very name "contextual therapy": "The term 'context,' then, is used . . . to convey a highly specific meaning: the dynamic and ethical interconnectedness—past, present and future—that exists among people whose very being has significance for each other."[17] In other words, contextual therapy highlights the ethical realm of close relationships. It asks questions such as: Is one person overly burdened in a family? Or, is this person relying on others to carry the load, neglecting their responsibility of active investment in the well-being of the other to whom she or he is in relationship? The contextual approach is concerned with *justice* in human connections and suggests that a balance *between entitlement and obligation*, "between give and take," enhances trust. Two fundamental premises undergird contextual therapy:

> That the *consequences* of one person's decisions and actions can affect the lives of all the people who are significantly related to him, and 2) that *satisfactory relating* for one person is inseparable from the responsible consideration of consequences for all of the people to whom he or she is in significant relationship.[18]

For example, parents' actions yield consequences for their children—positive, negative, and many shades of in-between. These consequences impact parent, child, and reverberate among everyone that either of these two engage in meaningful contact, especially members of future generations.

The ethic of due consideration then asks a person to scan their entire network of relationships and answer questions such as the following:

(1) What do I owe and to whom?

(2) What do I deserve and from whom?

(3) What relationships do I need and want?

(4) What relationships am I bound to retain whether or not I need or want them?[19]

These self-directed questions are asked in the midst of a dialogue with the other, a dialogue that contains essentially two steps, "self-delineation" and "self-validation."[20] Self-delineation is where a person defines her or his own needs and wants, making a claim for what he or she is entitled to in a particular relationship. Self-validation, on the other hand, is the process whereby a person considers the other and offers care. It is through a dialogue that includes self-delineation and self-validation that people can assess the degree of justice that exists between themselves and the other, reworking imbalances that exist and allowing formerly hidden resources to emerge.

Contextual therapy is an understanding of human relationships that emphasizes freedom born of obligation. "Its major goal is to liberate each family member to spontaneously rely on earned entitlement, i.e., on the ethical process of self-validation that is linked to due consideration of significant others."[21] It is through the act of taking stock of one's relationships and then actively investing in them that one gains freedom to creatively enjoy life. "Paradoxically, the individual's goal of *autonomy* is inextricably linked to his capacity for relational accountability."[22] Freedom and obligation do not exist in a kind of dialectic relationship to one another, as much as freedom results from actions that build trust and enable growth in relationships.

Finally, contextual therapy is forward-looking and aims to be preventative. A major locus of concern is the investment of care that parents offer their children, as this is the place where destructive legacies passed down from generation to generation can potentially be reworked. Healing that occurs within the present generation contributes to the well-being of future generations.

Living with...

A household is a place where many dynamics come together. The Greek roots of the word "economy" tells us that economics (what we have come to think of solely as "money") is about households, and about their management. In *You Can't Take It With You* we see two differing economies and two different types of households come into conflict with each other. These two economies bring the relationship between freedom and obligation to the fore. A first glance at the melodramatics of the film shows the Vanderhof/Sycamore household standing for all things free (the audience cheers) while the Kirbys stand for the dreary life of obligation (the audience hisses). However, contextual therapy has a different view of freedom and obligation than we superficially set up here. What we want to spend the remainder of this article discussing is the notion that this seeming antinomy breaks down in a healthy relationship, just as it does through the film; freedom and obligation do not exist in opposition, but as we have just described via contextual therapy, freedom is born of obligation.

While Capra seemed to want to stress an individualistic freedom, a freedom "where everybody does just what he wants," we read the film against these desires and highlight the necessary undergirding of obligation that allows such freedom to occur. If the film is *about* anything, we would argue that it is about relationships. Throughout the film, there is little indication of a private life of any individual; with one key exception, there is no space where a single individual is pictured alone with her or his own thoughts and feelings. In fact, the only scene in the entire film where the camera lingers over only one person is when Anthony Kirby is by himself in his conference room, mentally debating whether to go through with the big merger. (His cronies suspect he is in there "taking a bow to the other Kirbys on the walls.") As the representative of the wealthy individualist, this is significant. Otherwise, a majority of the scenes of the film include vast numbers of people, whether it is the living room of the house, the fancy restaurant where Tony and Alice go to dinner, the crowded prison cells, or the courtroom. Solitude, contemplation, and the inner life of the individual are downplayed throughout. Even Alice, when she leaves town to get away from the problems there, is simply removed from the frame of the film. Her solitude is left off screen.

Likewise, any intimacy between only two people is also downplayed, as intimate conversations are scarce and oftentimes interrupted. However, there are a few crucial scenes where two people are pictured alone, and these are necessary for the plot progression and the structuring of all the key relationships, even as these scenes are typically surrounded by scenes of the teeming masses. The dialogues proceed as follows through the film:

1) Tony and Anthony Sr. in Anthony Sr.'s office

2) Tony and Alice in the office

3) Grandpa and Alice in Alice's bedroom (the bedroom that used to be "Grandma's")

4) Tony and Alice out on a date

5) Tony and Anthony Sr. a second time in the office

6) Grandpa and Anthony Kirby Sr. in the house

The formal structure is quite easily detectable here, with its ABCBA pattern leading to the final transformation and denouement. There are other short dialogues that take place in the film, but these six are the only ones where we have the sense that the two interlocutors are alone. We turn now to note the ways freedom and obligation are emphasized throughout these dialogues, and how they are contextualized within the film.

Within the Kirby family, as we have already mentioned, obligation at first appears to be emphasized. This obligation is however a pseudo-obligation that does not take the other into consideration and thereby actually results in a destructive legacy being passed down from generation to generation. In one of the first scenes of the film, just after Kirby Sr. has come up the elevator and doled out instructions to his "men," Anthony Kirby Sr. is left alone with "Tony" Kirby Jr. As the two men talk in Kirby Sr.'s vast office (conversation #1), the *mise-en-scene* of the shot highlights the ancestry of the Kirby family, the patriarchal lineage which Tony Jr. is expected to assume. At one point, Kirby Sr. strikes a pose leaning on the edge of his desk, precisely imitating one of the forefathers, painted in oil, directly behind him. As the two talk about the big business deal, the ancestral picture is framed between the father and son, emphasizing that heritage is their bond (Fig. 6.1). The importance of heritage is continued when Tony and Alice run into the senior Kirbys with a host of their "friends" around their dinner table in a restaurant where one of the dinner guests, the British Lord Melville, is pictured drawing his family tree on a napkin. The dinner guests are of course impressed. And this emphasis on heritage (and a certain "purity" thereof) becomes especially acute in the tensions brought out through Mrs. Kirby, who disapproves of Alice because she is obviously of the wrong social class. She is concerned that Tony is associating with her and wants to know, "What sort of a family is she from?"

Within the Vanderhof family, as we have also already mentioned, freedom is at first emphasized both superficially and in more meaningful ways. "Everybody at our house does exactly what he wants," is the enticement Grandpa gives to Poppins in an early scene. And this freedom is taken care of (and thereby justified) by "the one who takes care of the lilies of the field" (except that they do have to toil a little). Rather than emphasizing family trees, the response to Lord Melville's "family tree" in the restaurant is that Alice is a "Sycamore," and therefore "already a tree." And rather than strict divisions within the household based on who is related to whom, everyone seems to regard each other with an egalitarian spirit. These aspects are brought together in an early conversation between Alice and Grandpa—inversely mimicking the conversation between father and son Kirby—which denotes that Grandpa is Alice's true father-figure, the one that she asks and receives advice from (conversation #3). (Meanwhile, her biological father is in the basement making fireworks and her biological mother is downstairs writing mystery dramas set in monasteries!) As they talk, it is a mirror that is framed behind them, and when discussion turns to ancestry (i.e., "Grandma") Alice wants to know what Grandma was like, to which Grandpa responds by telling her to look in the mirror (Fig. 6.2). There is a sense of familial history and lineage, but each individual has the freedom to make her or his own life choices. The viewers' sympathies are intended to lie with this relationship rather than that between the Kirbys, for here there is a display of mutual respect and acceptance.

It is therefore not surprising that it is via the courtship of Alice and Tony where the contrasting ethos between the two families is revealed. Compared to the zany endeavors of most members of the Vanderhof/Sycamore house, Alice seems to be the most "normal," working a 9 to 5 job and engaging in a courtship. On the other hand, Tony is the most "abnormal" of the Kirbys, distinguishing himself by wanting to pursue his own occupational and romantic interests rather than those expected of him. Alice and Tony are set apart enough from their own families that they are intially able to begin a relationship with one another, but as their relationship grows the contrasts between their respective families comes clashing together in bold relief. After the office scene that introduces each of them to the film viewer (conversation #2), the first "outing" we are shown between Tony and Alice has them going out to a park to talk, and then to dinner (conversation #4). Their conversation essentially consists of a comparing of their two families—Tony wishes for the freedom of the Vanderhof/Sycamore ethos, but exists in a world in which "the Kirbys have been bankers for about 9,000 years," and that line cannot be broken. When they go out to a fancy dinner, they go to one of the "Kirby's places": i.e., it is filled with snobby rich people. This setting is in vivid contradistinction to the simultaneous dinner taking place in the Vanderhof/Sycamore house where Grandpa delivers the first of his two prayers among the eclectic crowd of the household and their guests. As if the rigidity of the fancy restaurant were too much for them, Tony and Alice create a scene and end up turning the entire restaurant into chaos as they quietly slip out.

The next meeting between Tony and Alice involves the bringing together of both families. We see the Kirby family visiting the Vanderhof/Sycamore house for dinner ("slumming," as they say) and, as expected, all hell breaks lose. Due to a scheduling mix-up, the Vanderhof/Sycamore house is not expecting them, and so is having one of their typical evenings: Essie dances poorly for her teacher Kolenkhov while Ed provides the music on the xylophone, Penny gets out her oil paints and has Mr. DePinna dress up in a Greek Olympic costume imitating a discus thrower, while the other basement workers set off their newly invented firecrackers in the basement. The FBI busts into the house while the Kirbys are visiting, seeking information on the communist-sloganed candy wrappers being sent around (the basement inventors are planning a "Russian Revolution" theme for the 4th of July, simply because it seems to mean more fireworks and they like the color red). Of course the G-men become further suspicious by the presence of the Russian Kolenkhov, and

Fig. 6.1 "As the two talk about the big business deal, the ancestral picture is framed between the father and son, emphasizing that heritage is their bond."

(From the film *You Can't Take It With You*. © Columbia Picture Corporation. Still from the collection of the Museum of Modern Art, New York)

Fig. 6.2 "Alice wants to know what Grandma was like, to which Grandpa responds by telling her to look in the mirror."
(From the film *You Can't Take It With You.* © Columbia Picture Corporation. Still from the collection of the Museum of Modern Art, New York)

by the time all of the fireworks in the basement explode due to Mr. DePinna leaving his lit pipe there, the whole collection of people is in trouble. (A side note: 1938 was also the year that the House Committee on Un-American Activities began to investigate communist influence in Hollywood.) The household is arrested, as are the Kirby family who are seen as accomplices. The chance to bring both families around the table together is foiled.

Tony, for his part, seems more than willing to run from the pseudo-obligations of his family and finds freedom through Alice, and by extension her family. As it turns out, he is the one responsible for the scheduling mix-up that results in the embarrassment of the Kirby's coming to dinner on the wrong night. Alice, for her part, becomes much more concerned about doing things in a proper way and before Tony comes by to pick her up for dinner the first time she directs her household to not do all the crazy things they usually do. Alice and Tony are each in their own way stuck in what contextual therapy calls a "loyalty conflict," defined thus:

> A person's commitments to his [or her] family of origin on the one hand and his [or her] peer commitments on the other hand often collide and conflict in terms of priority [reflecting differing levels of obligation]. Thus, loyalty conflicts seem to be ubiquitous causes of marital and partnership incompatibilities. Of central interest to contextual therapists, loyalty conflicts can be a major deterrent to individual freedom and interpersonal fairness among peers.[23]

Both Alice and Tony feel obligated to their respective families, and yet want to embrace and join with the other. Alice's conflict is that she must behave on the social level of the Kirbys, which also entails a certain felt betrayal of her own family, both of their social status and their valuing the unconditional acceptance of the other. Tony's betrayal involves giving up both the approval of his mother, who wants him to marry a woman of high social status, and his father who expects him to join the lineage of Kirby bankers. Tony feels he deserves freedom from his family to choose as he wishes. The loyalty conflict is an area in which the relationship between freedom and obligation can be seen, and the goal of contextual therapy is to liberate persons from this conflict by gradually shifting one's primary obligation from the family of origin to the *significant other*, thereby reducing the problematic impact of split loyalties.

The crucial turning point of Alice and Tony's "courtship"—and the film as a whole—is indeed in the "court" where they end up after their arrest in the Vanderhof/Sycamore house. Here is the place where decisions about "legislation" and "obligations" (the Latin root *ligare*, meaning "to bind," is at the base of both words) are played out. And it is in the court that Alice and Tony's relationship itself is put on trial. There are two sides to the story and somewhere between is the "bond" (again, the *ligare*) that must connect the two (or, if we want to read this "re-ligiously," it is that which must "re-bind" the two). The table that has brought people together throughout the film has here been replaced by the judge's "bench," a place of judgement that must objectively stand back from the situation to decide what is owed and to whom. The courtroom setting is an explicit representation of the implicit "tribunal" aspect of relationships known in contextual therapy as the "intrinsic relational tribunal."[24]

All the members of both families go before a night court (Kirby has managed to alert his counsel and four well-dressed lawyers show up—"quite an array of talent for a misdemeanor," quips the judge), and it becomes clear to the judge that there is no great conspiracy going on here, that the Kirbys have no part in this, but he must charge the Vanderhof/Sycamores $100 for illegal fireworks. In an image that will be reconfigured in *It's a Wonderful Life*, Grandpa refuses the Kirby's offer to pay the fine ("for this poor, unfortunate family") and instead the whole crowd in the night court, who are the Vanderhofs' friends and have come to support the family, take up a collection and pay the Vanderhofs' fine. The contrast is set up between the man rich-on-money and the man rich-on-friends. As Grandpa has just told Kirby Sr. in the prison cell, making money serves you no good because "you can't take it with you . . . the only thing you can take with you is the love of your friends." Of course the one with the friends is the one with which the viewer is intended to sympathize, and it is clearly the side with which the night-court judge sympathizes, even throwing in a coin of his own into the collection.

More important than the night-court judge's ruling is another judgement that takes place. For in the objectivity of the courtroom Alice is given a different perspective from which to examine her relationship with Tony, and in many ways it is really Tony who is put on trial, for the decision is put into his hands: Will he really forsake the expectations of his family and choose to obligate himself to Alice? The *mise-en-scene* of the night court itself emphasizes Tony's trial. While the entire Vanderhof/Sycamore clan and the Kirby clan are on trial, it is only the Kirbys who stand *facing* the judge. And as the Kirby's multiple lawyers back the Kirbys, Tony is backed by this whole obligation to family—he must stand there alongside them. At the same time, the Vanderhof/Sycamore family stands to the side of the judge, in the position generally given to the jury. Alice stands then as synecdochal juror for the rest of the family and once the final judgement is passed (that they owe $100) Alice likewise makes her judgement by standing on the courtroom table (the table is here a prop not for the gathering and the sharing of a meal, but as a place of judgement) and declaring that she wants nothing to do with Tony and his family. With that she rushes out of the courtroom and off the screen where she will remain until the very end of the film.

Now, once this decision is made, the obvious freedoms of the Vanderhof/Sycamore house and the seeming obligations of the Kirby family that have proceeded straightforwardly throughout the film are crossed. A sense of obligation surfaces in the Vanderhof/Sycamore household as Tony stops by the house trying to find out Alice's whereabouts, but the family refuses to betray her. Further, Grandpa decides that if Alice is going to move away, then so must the entire household—in the end, the household is clearly no democracy—he decides to sell the house to the Kirby-backed real estate agent and move on. At this point the household falls apart, as does the entire neighborhood, for with the selling of the house the entire neighborhood will be torn down to make way for the munitions factory.

Meanwhile, Alice's decision has repercussions on others making decisions. First, it has propelled Tony to make a decision at Kirby and Company and he decides to resign his position. Tony's decision then affects his father. Just as Anthony Kirby Sr. is preparing to finalize a merger that would tear down the Vanderhof/Sycamore's old neighborhood and put up the new Kirby munitions factory, and make him the richest man around, he is struck by something that makes him hesitate. Kirby is about ready to do it, but his experience with Vanderhof has stuck with him (as has a harmonica that Grandpa placed in his pocket while they were in jail together), and here we have the only scene in the entire film with only a single person in frame for a significant period of time. And again, here the prop that dominates the room is the massive conference table, a table designed for a business economy. The solitary contemplation of Kirby Sr. is interrupted twice. First by Kirby's chief competitor who breaks into the conference room and relates how alone in the world "men like them" are. Kirby is then left alone a second time but is now immediately interrupted by Tony Jr. as he walks in to tell his father that he has decided to leave the company (conversation #5). As with their first conversation at the beginning of the film, they are surrounded by ancestral images. Mixed with Vanderhof's accusation of him as a "failure as a man, failure as a human being, even a failure as a father" in the prison cell, Tony's words are one of the key forces that compels Anthony Sr. to finally renege on his "big merger," to go down the elevator (in precisely the same manner that Vanderhof did years ago, and in precisely the opposite manner in which the first scene of the film helps introduce us to Kirby), and to find his way to the Vanderhof/Sycamore household who are in the midst of moving out. Here, in a radical reversal, Kirby Sr. himself acts on his true obligation to family by enacting the ethic of due consideration in his relationship with Tony. He blesses his son's desires for love and work, setting aside the expectations of heritage and family trees, and making a choice for his son's interests. He sets aside a destructive legacy and is himself liberated. His real freedom is born of his enacted obligation to Tony.

The end of the film naturally ends with the "conversion" of Kirby who turns away from his business associates and winds up in the now-empty living room of the Vanderhof/Sycamore house. Kirby goes to Grandpa Vanderhof seeking advice on what he can do now that his son has left him (conversation #6). Grandpa says nothing but replies by taking out his harmonica and prompting Kirby to do so as well. The final scene brings back the zaniness of the household as Kirby and Grandpa play "Polly Wolly Doodle." Tony and Alice meet up, Mrs. Kirby enters, while the others bring their music, dancing, and joyful spirits to the meeting place. The "Home Sweet Home" sign is rehung one last time.

The final scene is set once again at the Vanderhof/Sycamore dinner table as they end up not having to move after all. The table now significantly includes the Kirbys. After Grandpa delivers one of his Americana prayers, the freedom of the table is indulged and all seems right with the world. The estrangements between Anthony Kirby Sr. and Tony, and between Tony and Alice, are re-familiar-ized.

But before we can conclude on this utopian and optimistic note we find it necessary to offer a critique of this ending by mentioning one final element that keeps the film from retaining such a positive vision of living together. For while the Vanderhof/Sycamore household seems to provide an ideal model for community, we find that community is rarely expressed in positive terms without having to simultaneously repress its negative terms. Any community's inclusivity cannot exist without exclusivity. It thus becomes necessary to point out where that exclusion occurs. As we have continued to argue, it is the filmic prop of the table (most importantly the one in the middle of the Vanderhof/Sycamore living room, but also the ones in the restaurant, the courtroom, and Kirby's office) that provides the locus for a bringing together in shared meals and a standing apart in judgement. The table is the place where otherness comes together, where freedom and obligation meet in a relational give and take, and where decisions and judgements are made. In this way, the characters' relationships to the tables throughout the film cue us to the broader dynamics of the film. So, for example, while at first the Vanderhof/Sycamores and the Kirbys do not get the chance to sit together at the table, the final scene includes them all there eating together. A transformation has occurred.

Yet, while telling us something about the characters and the "changes of heart" that bring them together, the table also sets the scene for exclusivity. At the table we see a failure of the inclusivity of the community of the Vanderhof/Sycamore household. While Rheba, the African American maid, and her fiancé Donald take part in much of the social life around the house, they are both excluded from the dinner table. While everyone who walks through the door of the household is invited to dinner, two of those who are ever-present in the house are excluded and carry on their eating in the kitchen. There are egalitarian elements involved in the running of the household economy, and many people actually help to set the dinner table, yet when it comes to the actual sharing of the meal, black people are excluded from the table (Fig. 6.3). This is particularly exacerbated when Elsie's dance teacher, Kolenkhov, stays for dinner and Rheba is asked to set another place for him, which she does before promptly leaving the scene again. Kolenkhov even brings over some of

Fig. 6.3 "At the table we see a failure of the inclusivity of the community."
(From the film *You Can't Take It With You.* © Columbia Picture Corporation. Still from the collection of the Museum of Modern Art, New York)

his own laundry and asks Rheba to do it for him. Of course, Kolenkhov is depicted as an idiot (in some polemic of Capra's against Russia in general), but he still gets to sit at the table. Or again, the exclusivity is highlighted when Donald works with all the men in the basement together, yet when it's time for dinner they all sit at the table while Donald goes to the kitchen with Rheba. (And in one of those all-too-common stereotypes, Donald's first enunciation in the film is to exclaim, "I ain't done nothing but I sure am tired."[25])

While this is in some ways a small piece of the film, it simply cannot be ignored, particularly if the guiding ethos of the household is the rhetoric of freedom to do what one wants. The problem here, as with a vast majority of Hollywood cinema, is as Ed Guerrero puts it in his study on African Americans in film, *Framing Blackness*: "[I]n almost every instance, the representation of black people on the commercial screen has amounted to one grand, multifaceted illusion. For blacks have been subordinated, marginalized, positioned, and devalued in every possible manner to glorify and relentlessly hold in place the white-dominated symbolic order and racial hierarchy of American society."[26] In *You Can't Take It With You*, the freedom of the (white-American) household rests on a hierarchical structure that excludes certain (black-American) others from its table.

And the freedom enjoyed by the many who have seen the film is like any freedom, particularly that evoked by North Americans: an illusion. Such freedom is about as substantial as the filmic images that fade as soon as another light is cast on them. Capra himself represented the epitome of the American Dream, growing up as a poor immigrant, working hard, and making it big in Hollywood. North American freedom allowed such a life. Yet this is only one side of the story (the side that he tells in his autobiography), and the *other* side is told by the others who were ignored and left behind by him in his pursuit of greatness, in his pursuit of having his "name above the title."

Thus, we want to submit that freedom cannot forsake obligation without ceasing to exist in any meaningful way. As free as we want to be, we cannot forget the ties that bind, the obligations to others and of others that prop up our freedom. Freedom from ancestral ties cannot mean ignoring our obligation to those from where we came. Freedom to enjoy a meal around the table is not freedom when it fails to acknowledge its essential indebtedness and obligation to the other. We would like to see representations of how a family might become friends, how friends might become family, and how characters might acknowledge their obligations to others.

Endnotes

1. It was also nominated for best supporting actress (Byington), screenplay, cinematography, editing, and sound recording. Capra also won the New York Film Critics Award for best director for the film.

2. C.V. Whitney to David O. Selznick, 27 December 1938, from the David O. Selznick collection, Humanities Research Center, University of Texas at Austin. Quoted in Thomas Schatz, "Anatomy of a House Director," in *Frank Capra: Authorship and the Studio System*, Robert Sklar and Vito Zagarrio, eds. (Philadelphia: Temple University Press, 1998), p. 31.

3. Joseph McBride's 1992 biography of Capra (*Frank Capra: The Catastrophe of Success*, New York: Simon and Schuster) dispels the myth of Capra's liberal politics and instead argues that Capra simply utilized the rhetoric (visual and verbal) of the left because it seemed to sell better in the 1930s. The biography serves somewhat as a corrective to Capra's own autobiography of 1971, *The Name Above the Title*, by all means a pathetic attempt to continue to put his name in lights when the rest of the world forgot him. Many recent scholarly books on Capra and his films (he is one of those film makers whose films are rarely treated apart from their biography) show a continued interest in his films and life, but most are also quite skeptical toward his self-promotion and shifting sense of identity.

4. Capra, *The Name Above the Title: An Autobiography* (New York: Random House, 1985 [Orig. 1971]), p. 240.

5. Ibid., p. 241.

6. Capra gave this quote at a college presentation in 1978. It is quoted in Charles Maland's *Frank Capra* (New York: Twayne, 1995), p. 92.

7. Joseph McBride, *Frank Capra*, p. 381.

8. Leland Poague argues that "Grandpa is a kind of stand-in for Capra" (*Another Frank Capra* [Cambridge: Cambridge University Press, 1994], pp. 49-63).

9. Leland Poague, *Another Frank Capra*, p. 54.

10. Interestingly enough, we are introduced to Kirby first by a sign outside his Wall Street building which reads "Kirby and Company." This practically mimics the title sequence which immediately precedes the opening scene and which reads, as mentioned above, "Frank Capra's *You Can't Take It With You*." In both, it is the "name above the title" which stands out. This mimicking, of course, heightens the paradox of Capra.

11. Raymond Carney, *American Vision: The Films of Frank Capra* (Cambridge: Cambridge University Press, 1986), p. 400n.

12. We have seen this phrase in so many books referring to this film that we cannot figure out where the original quote is from!

13. Maland, *Frank Capra*, p. 104.

14. *Family Resources: The Hidden Partner in Family Therapy*, Mark A. Karpel, ed. (New York: The Guilford Press, 1986), p. 3.

15. Ivan Boszormenyi-Nagy and Barbara R. Krasner, *Between Give and Take: A Clinical Guide to Contextual Therapy* (New York: Brunner/Mazel Publishers, 1986), p. 7.

16. Ibid., p. 44.

17. Ibid., p. 8.

18. Ibid.

19. Barbara R. Krasner, "Trustworthiness: The Primal Family Resource," in op. cit., *Family Resources*, p. 122.

20. Ibid., p. 130.

21. Boszomenyi-Nagy and Krasner, *Between Give and Take*, pp. 414-415.

22. Ibid., p. 62.

23. *Between Give and Take*, p. 15.

24. Ibid., p. 416.

25. Perhaps interesting to note, the year after *You Can't Take It With You* Hattie McDaniel became the first African-American to win an Academy award, which she received for her portrayal of Vivian Leigh's mammy in *Gone with the Wind*. McDaniel's movie career consisted almost entirely of playing stereotypic maids and other servants.

26. *Framing Blackness: The African American Image in Film* (Philadelphia: Temple University Press, 1993), p. 2.

Part Four: Colonizing Community

"What Happened in the Cave?"
Communities and Outsiders in Films of India

David Jasper

On the blue line of the far distance,
    Flowers a-dazzle, burning,
Fill the air with the fragrance of distilled fire.
The sky is steeped in sunlight, drowning our senses.
The meadow, stored with the yellow-gold mustard flowers,
    Declares the Spring.
In the far distance we see the former times
    And feel the touch of sorrow.
Faded recollections of the bygone Spring well up
They wither and the loss distracts my mind.
Spring attracts me, draws its victims irresistibly,
    Proclaims its mastery in the sway
Of the yellow-gold mustard flowers.

-From *Four Songs of Rabindranath Tagore*[1]

This essay will focus upon two films concerned with what it means to "be Indian" in the first half of the twentieth century—David Lean's *A Passage to India* (1984) and Satyajit Ray's *Aparajito* (1956), the second film of his trilogy about growing up in Bengal which begins with *Pather Panchali* (1955) and concludes with *The World of Apu* (1959). Lean's film is major example of Western commercial cinema. Ray is working within an artistic tradition which is deeply coherent with the great religious epics of Indian literature, and, in the twentieth century, the songs and poetry of the Bengali writer Rabindranath Tagore.

In *A Passage to India*, based on E. M. Forster's 1924 novel, Lean returned to the theme of the British abroad which he had earlier explored in the hugely successful *Bridge on the River Kwai* (1957) and *Lawrence of Arabia* (1962). Though far less epic than these earlier works, *A Passage to India* combines a powerful narrative with a blurring of the central issues and an ultimate refusal to explore the real tensions in Forster's work (and in British India itself), with the result that Lean's post-colonial nostalgia for Empire obscures the novel's hatred of the British presence in India. Oddly, and rather uneasily, the film was made two years after Richard Attenborough's epic film *Gandhi* (1982) which succeeds to some extent in exploring the serious issues which Lean avoids—not only the tensions between the British and India, but the religious politics within India which eventually led to partition in 1948.

English fiction about the British Raj in the twentieth century has been dominated by two works, Forster's *A Passage to India*, and Paul Scott's "Raj Quartet" (1966-1975), the first becoming a major film and the second a hugely successful television series, both starring Peggy Ashcroft. To these may be added, rather palely, a third: Ruth Prawer Jhabvala's *Heat and Dust* (1975), was also made into a film by James Ivory in 1982. All three works explore broadly the same theme—the question of improper or imputed sexual liaisons between young English women and Indians in the last years of the British Raj.

Forster and Scott center their writing around similar fictional events. The incidents of the Marabar Caves and the Bibighar Gardens both involve accusations of rape of English girls by an Indian. The implications are symbolically highly suggestive: that the mighty subcontinent in which the British continue to live their "English" lives is perceived as being inhabited by savages who are capable of any kind of atrocity, and who live, in turn, mysterious lives beyond civilized understanding. A country which is being raped by an uncomprehending colonial power is primitive and, in turn, rapes the innocent English maidens who are overwhelmed by its seduction and mystery. The fiction in each case opens with images of a divided society—on one hand, the city of Chandrapore with its separation of the Indian bazaars from the bland and organized English civil station; and on the other, the English girl running alongside the wall of the Bibighar Gardens, a wall which separates European safety from the wilderness, from the place where "a lane ended and cultivation began."

What Lean fails to reproduce from the novel is Forster's sense of the mysterious romance of the Indian town as opposed to the tedious ordinariness of the English civil station. As Forster described it:

> As for the civil station itself, it provokes no emotion. It charms not, neither does it repel. It is sensibly planned, with a red-brick club on its brow, and further back a grocer's and a cemetery, and the bungalows are disposed along roads that intersect at right angles. It has nothing hideous in it, and only the view is beautiful; it shares nothing with the city except the overarching sky.[2]

Such divisions have translated readily onto the screen in films made for Western audiences, though with a different slant, and suggesting something of the romance of the British Raj itself. They come to confirm different exotic images of India and the nobility (however corrupt) of the British with their impeccable manners and stiff upper lips amidst the tropical heat and the dusty confusion: ancient India—overwhelmingly populated, anarchic, dirty, noisy; the British—rational, organized, Christian, superior.

When we turn, however, to Indian cinema, and in particular the great Bengali director Satyajit Ray in his film *Aparajito*, a very different India emerges, one far more beautiful and ultimately comprehensible. For Ray's themes in this film are universal—themes of growing up, of family life and loves, of the conflict between uneducated older generations and the young who are drawn to the great cities. In

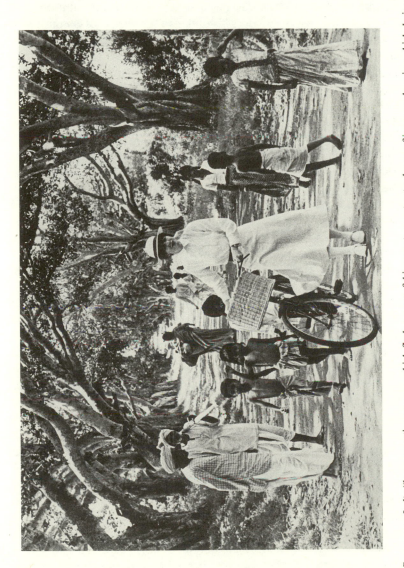

Fig. 7.1 *A Passage to India* "has a narrative urgency which flashes powerful images to construct a drama of incomprehension which derives from the homelessness of the British—without genuine religion, without family, without country."

(From the film *A Passage to India*. © EMI Films. Still from the collection of the Museum of Modern Art, New York)

Ray's films, India remains extraordinary and exotic to Western eyes, but nevertheless believable and inhabited by people whose common experiences we recognize and share. Paradoxically, Ray's profound sense of Bengal is enhanced by the broad cultural influences which have worked upon him, in particular the films of Jean Renoir and the music of Mozart as much as the classics of Indian poetry and the songs of Tagore. Though he describes his films as a "synthesis" of cultures, what emerges is a universality in which Indians are not set against other cultures, but are seen as people struggling with the great common themes of love, parenthood, family dislocation. Ray's fellow filmmaker, the Japanese director Akira Kurosawa, once rather expansively remarked: "Not to have seen the cinema of Ray means existing in the world without seeing the sun or the moon."

In the films of Lean and Ray, India as "place" is crucial. In Lean's vision it is the "other" world—we begin with Miss Quested (Judy Davis) purchasing her ticket in a travel agent with walls decorated with pictures of ocean-going liners and seductive foreign scenes—her first encounter with the mysterious Marabar Caves. When Miss Quested and her prospective mother-in-law, Mrs. Moore (Peggy Ashcroft), arrive in Bombay, the sense of division is accentuated as we follow their progress to the railway station in a rickshaw, between the interior world of the British and the endless, unintelligible world of India. Miss Quested remains tragically trapped within the one, with all its social expectations of the "innocent" young memsahib, while Mrs. Moore is drawn to the other in her crucial meeting with Dr. Aziz (Victor Banerjee) in the Mosque—though this is not the "real" India, but a Moslem world (a division not really acknowledged in the film), Aziz himself the descendent of another race of conquerors who, in their day, had invaded the ancient land, settled and brought their new religion and culture.

Aparajito begins in the sacred city of Benares on the banks of the Ganges, the great river which flows through North India and through Ray's film, from the holy waters which wash the *ghats* (the riverside steps) of the city with their priests and bathers, to the industrial docks of Calcutta with their smoky ships polluting the water and connecting India with the great world to which the young Apu aspires and which he dimly perceives. As in *A Passage to India*, trains are an important motif—railways have been and remain the most important form of transport in India, bequeathed by the Raj and noisily symbolic for Indians of the shift from the rural villages and ancient centers of culture like Benares to the great modern cities of Calcutta, Delhi, or Bombay. In Ray's cinema, trains snake across far horizons, ineluctably drawing their passengers from the country bound by old ties of family, to a new world of industry, dislocation, learning, and ambition. By contrast, however, the sacred waters of the Ganges flow through the Apu trilogy, not dislocating and dividing like the railways, but forming an ancient connection through Indian history and society, from the *ghats* of *Aparajito* to the slow current which carries the poet Apu towards his future bride in *The World of Apu*.

There is no need for the opening scenes of *Aparajito* to tell any story. They rest in a place which is its own story. Lean's work, on the other hand, has a narrative urgency which flashes powerful images to construct a drama of incomprehension which derives from the homelessness of the British—without genuine religion, without family, without country (except the mythic sense of "Empire")—and the unstated sexual awakening of Miss Quested. In one of the more unconvincing, unpleasant, and indeed xenophobic scenes early in the film, she is found alone (always unwise for a white woman in a country which is unprovided with the conventions of Western society), after a rather precarious bicycle ride, in a ruined Hindu temple replete with erotic statuary and inquisitive monkeys. The sexuality of the scene is blatant and crude. Ray's India, on the other hand, simply *is*, not even metaphorically, but literally and wholly present. The people and city of Benares pervade the opening scenes of his film, seen through the eyes of a small boy (the young Apu is played by Pinaki Sengupta), with his beautiful and loving mother Sarbaya (Karuna Bannerjee) and his father Harihar (Kanu Bannerjee), a priest who carries his religion easily and devoutly. From the opening shots, the river and the city pervade the film. The priest feeds the pigeons who fly down and take us to the riverside where sacred observance is mingled with children playing in the water, and people washing and eating. Apu himself is first seen after his mother has complained that he is always out playing in the narrow lanes of the city, and the camera catches his face as it enables the viewer to participate in the game of hide-and-seek Apu plays with his friend. Through the camera lens we enter into Apu's family, which is a universal group like all families, with distant uncles, unpleasant neighbors, typical joys and worries—until it is devastated by the unexpected death of the gentle father. The rhythm of the film is not sustained by the narrative but rather by the visual and spatial contrasts between the provincial city, the village to which Apu and his widowed mother Sarbajaya move, and Calcutta. The powerful mother-son relationship remains constant through these shifts—deep, loving, anguished, and finally severed by the lonely death of Sarbajaya as she pines for the son whose education has carried him away from her physically, intellectually, and spiritually.

As with Forster's novel, there is a schematic quality about Lean's *A Passage to India* as it explores, albeit superficially, the clash of not two but three cultures—British (nominally Christian), Moslem, and Hindu, though this latter distinction is almost lost in the images of "typical" India. The heart of the film, as of the book, ought to be the strange figure of Dr. Godbole, but he becomes almost a joke figure, an Indian pasticed by an English actor, Alec Guinness. Godbole's almost silent and distant commentary on the struggling relationship between Aziz and the British fails to convey the weight of a culture and spirituality which had never absorbed the crass invasions of the British or the imperialist history of the Moslem. What he conveys is, in fact, the British image of almost comic Eastern inscrutability, while the confused and much more accessible character of Mrs. Moore offers the possibility of tragedy seen from the British perspective—India finally kills her as she tries to leave it behind and return to the "real" world of England. Both Mrs. Moore and Miss Quested, in their different ways, represent the impossibility of making the "passage" to India. Ralph Fielding (James Fox), in the film at least, though not the novel, is the educator who alone overcomes cultural divisions, and in the end, to suit the desires of the Western cinema audience, Forster's ambiguous and darkly prophetic ending is eradicated in the film's resolution of the English-Indian relationship in the mutual understanding of Fielding and Aziz—set in the gloriously romantic scenery of the Himalyas—as they settle their differences and accept their different lives cheerfully. Forster, more realistically, recognized that such a friendship between the British schoolmaster and the Indian doctor was a cultural impossibility in the 1920s, at least "not yet. . . . No, not there."[3]

In *A Passage to India*, the British education system, at its best, offers a possible resolution of differences as Godbole is reduced to a ludicrous puppet role. Ray's sense of conflict lies within Indian society itself as the old rural community of family and faith, encapsulated in Apu's patient mother and priestly father, fails before the dangerous onrush of the modern world of "education" and the city. Apu, destined like his father to be a village priest, wins a scholarship to study in Calcutta—three hours by train from his mother's village. In class, in a scene of uneasy comedy, we see him learning the tropes of classical Western rhetoric, being required to define "synecdoche" and "metonymy"—terms utterly alien to his own ancient culture, but symbolizing the passage into the wider world beyond the Bay of Bengal into which the holy river of the Ganges flows. Yet, ironically, Ray is consciously using these rhetorical tropes throughout this most Indian of films to indicate the intrusion of the West and its education system into India. Here, for a moment, India fails to be fully present as the tropes fragment and dislocate its world. The rhetoric class itself becomes awkwardly metonymic of Apu's education and his development away from his mother and her universal values of love and motherhood. At this point, in the pinched character of the college lecturer, the film is at its furthest from the absolutely present world of the opening scenes by the Ganges.

And so, the east/west tensions which so overtly drive the narrative and images of *A Passage to India* also underlie *Aparajito*, but Ray's emotional tone is understated, working by suggestion and fleeting image, so that the interior world of his characters are constantly reflected in the boy Apu in particular as he wanders freely amidst the *ghats*, lanes, and temples of Benares. Ray's characters *see* what is around them mirroring and constituting their own lives. At these moments, the camera alternates between the static, domestic scenes indoors, centered around the tasks of cooking and cleaning, and the movement outside as the viewer becomes one with Apu, catching fleeting glances of shops, characters, pictures of elephants on walls. We see the images which are also impressing themselves on the mind of the young boy. Ultimately, *Aparajito* is a study of growth and survival as one generation moves painfully into another—the title of the film means "The Unvanquished"—and each character, even the dying Sarbajaya, remains powerfully within the poetry of a culture which is changing but at the same time remains whole and one in spite of the traumas of education and movement. Karuna Bannerjee, the actress who plays the mother Sarbajaya, admitted:

> I was absolutely overwhelmed by her personality. It all came so naturally to me. Every word, every look, every small movement, the deep attachment towards the alienated son, they all developed within me, as leaves grow outwards on the branch of a tree. Sounds poetic? But believe me that is exactly how I felt.

The English view of India, on the other hand, allows for no such organic growth of characterization and no such sense of continuity within the tragedies of change. In each part of the trilogy Apu experiences a death—of his sister, his mother, and finally his wife. Each experience is a rite of passage which the boy and young man has to negotiate and absorb into himself. All the Indian characters in Lean's film, however, are seen from the outside, even Aziz, who is played by the fine Bengali actor Victor Banerjee. Nowhere is this externalization more powerfully felt than in the central question of religion—a phenomenon finally as tangential to the Indian life of Chandrapore as it is to the British life of the civil station. For the mysterious and enigmatic Godbole and the echoing caves of Marabar themselves imply little more than we actually see—metaphors for an inaccessible India and a vaguely threatening environment charged with risk and sexual menace when clear boundaries are crossed. Lean's film conveys little sense of the "Holy" since the viewer's reactions are sustained at a superficial, immediate level—the level of a fundamentally simple story propelled by short scenes juxtaposed to maximize the contrasting stereotypes of English and Indians without much attempt to explore character in any further depth. Indeed, to do so would weaken the effect of the film, which could not sustain even Forster's schematic examination in three parts of "Mosque," "Caves," and "Temple" which deliberately excludes the imported religion of the English, Christianity. The film virtually omits the third part of the novel, which is its real heart in Godbole's "Temple," and leaves instead a literal gaping hole in the cave at its center. What happened in the cave—we are left to surmise—is in the deranged and impressionable mind of a young girl in danger of marrying the wrong man.

Ray's film, on the other hand, lingering among the sacred *ghats* of Benares, sees them through the eyes of the boy Apu, with a literal gaze which, precisely because at this innocent stage it is unweighted with symbolic or presumed metaphorical meaning, is extraordinarily illuminative of the ancient, living, sometimes even humorous spirituality of the city and its river (Fig. 7.2). Apu's father, Harihar, carries his priesthood lightly because here there is no need for a Godbole to incarnate a mysterious India—for the life of the city, with its *ghats* and temples, naturally embraces the imagination of a young boy, the domesticity of his mother, and the generous sociability of his father. Here nothing is ever really left behind, as images and environments accumulate not in the progression of a linear

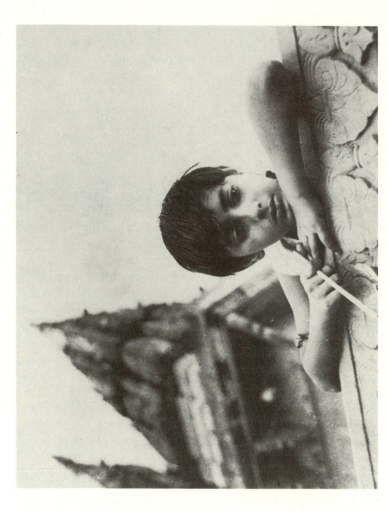

Fig. 7.2 "Ray's film . . . lingering among the sacred *ghats* of Benares, sees them through the eyes of the boy Apu, with a literal gaze which, precisely because at this innocent stage it is unweighted with symbolic or presumed metaphorical meaning, is extraordinarily illuminative of the ancient, living, sometimes even humorous spirituality of the city and its river." (From the film *Aparajito*. © Epic Production. Still from the collection of the Museum of Modern Art, New York)

narrative but with the weight of real lives that must move on beyond death and through generations, yet still retaining and bearing their history. That is why I have chosen to discuss this second film in Ray's trilogy on the life of Apu, because although it is not the most lyrical or even the most moving of the three films, it focuses upon characterization as the others do not—exploring the complexities of a mother-son relationship which is profound and also deeply loving, yet, for precisely that reason must suffer separation as Apu grows into adolescence. When Apu finally walks away at the end of the film, returning to his new life in Calcutta after his mother's death, nothing has been lost as we see here the organic growth of a society—in a sense Apu will always be the village priest, like his father, bearing that vocation as a burden but also a strength through his future life elsewhere. Ray's trilogy is a tribute to India's survival in spite of all the incursions of the West and in spite of Apu's painful education. At the end of *The World of Apu*, we see him walking away again, but this time not from the world of his parents, but, carrying his own son on his shoulders, back into the world which tragedy and disappointment have not been able to defeat or finally subdue.

Painfully and beautifully, *Aparajito* is a film about growth and gain in loss. Ray's camera does not pry into an Indian world constructed by the cinema and seen voyeuristically from the outside. It responds to what it sees—and hears in Ravi Shankar's music. It neither patronizes nor belittles the dirt and squalor in homes which are simply Indian, not European. *A Passage to India*, on the other hand, despite its contrived and manipulative ending, is throughout a film about loss, both for the British and for the Indians, in a way that is not so in Forster's novel, which is more concerned with the division between these two worlds. In Lean's film, Mrs. Moore and Miss Quested, together with Ronnie and the English officials and their wives, are already lost souls from the beginning. Even Mrs. Moore is living out a myth that can never be more than fleetingly real, and withers in the black emptiness of the caves. But the Indians also fail to gather more than two-dimensional status in images of India that move little beyond the tourist brochures of the Taj Mahal or the Himalyan peaks. It is precisely because, perhaps, the English adventure in India was one great story that it is tempting to make films about it, about the passage to India, but the narrative is incapable of touching India itself. That requires a very different kind of cinema—a cinema whose storytelling is not of the adventure kind, not even particularly narrative. Like the great India epics, *The Mahabharata* and *The Ramayana*, it draws its power from its ability to reflect back to what it sees, and a basic attentive stillness and simplicity. As Romesh C. Dutta comments in his translation of *The Mahabharata*, "the poetry of the *Mahabharata* is plain and unpolished, and scarcely stoops to a simile or a figure of speech unless the simile comes naturally to the poet."[4] Satyajit Ray lies wholly within this great tradition of Indian storytelling.

This is not to say, finally, that *A Passage to India* is a particularly bad film. But it is not only about an India which has long ceased to exist in any form, and once existed only as a brief construction of a remarkable group of outsiders who saw it as their mission to try and impose an utterly alien culture upon a whole sub-continent (and even succeeded to a degree—so we see, for example, the continuing importance of their railways for India). It is about an India long pastiched in English literature in such figures as Thackeray's Joseph Sedley in *Vanity Fair*, and even Rudyard Kipling's brilliant Kim. But it is also enmeshed in a tradition of storytelling which Hollywood and Western commercial cinema have taken up and skillfully developed for their own use—a use of narrative, image, and character which barely touches the real life of India, and which Ray utterly avoids, and in *Aparajito* gently brushes against in those two words, "synecdoche" and "metonymy" as they appear disturbingly on the black board of the lecturer in Apu's class in Calcutta. It is a turning point for the young Apu, and, despite his inevitable growth away from his mother, he never succumbs to these tropes, but remains an Indian poet in his soul. Even, for a moment in *The World of Apu*, just before his wedding, he is compared with the god Krishna.

What happened in the cave, in the Marabar Hills, to Miss Quested? Perhaps nothing. Perhaps only the frightened delusions of a community of outsiders who would have been better employed staying at home and, like Jane Austen's Emma, sorting out their lives on a picnic to Boxhill in Surrey. For in the two films we have been considering, the real life of India is happening in Ray's Benares, his Bengali villages and in Calcutta, in a cinema which moves us because it is not sentimental, has no delusions, and faces the future with its past intact.

Endnotes

1. Trans. David Jasper.

2. E. M. Forster, *A Passage to India* (Harmondsworth: Penguin Modern Classics, 1961 [1924]), p. 10.

3. Ibid., p. 317.

4. *The Mahabharata*, trans., Romesh C. Dutta (Bombay: Jaico Publishing House, 1969), p. 184.

Postmodernism and Neo-Orientalism: Peter Brook's *Mahabharata*—Producing India Through a Body of Multicultural Images

Ira Bhaskar

We can reproduce fragmented experiences of different cultures and, since all the media have been doing this for fifteen years, our sensibility has been modified. Thanks to color magazines, travel, and Kodak, Everyman has a well-stocked "musee imaginaire" and is a potential eclectic.
-Charles Jencks[1]

So in postmodern culture, "culture" has become a product in its own right . . . Postmodernism is the consumption of sheer commodification as a process.
-Fredric Jameson[2]

I.

In the latter half of the eighties, Peter Brook's *Mahabharata* played to enthralled audiences all over the world. Brook's nine-hour dramatization of the Indian epic, adapted by Jean-Claude Carriere from the various versions of the text that he and Peter Brook had encountered for a decade before they brought it before an audience, premiered in July 1985 at the Avignon Festival in France.[3] Performed both as an all-night, nine-hour presentation and as three three-hour parts on consecutive nights, the play was received as "the theatrical spectacle of the century."[4] In the fall of 1985 the production toured to festivals in Barcelona, Madrid, Athens, and Lyons. It then opened at Brook's Bouffes du Nord theater in Paris in November. Subsequently, the English language version, a translation of the Carriere text by Brook himself, toured the world in 1987-88 and was performed at different venues in six countries on four continents. Finally, a five-and-a-half hour film version was shot in studios near Paris and released in late 1989. Television channels all over the world screened the film version of this "greatest story of mankind,"[5] and were amazed at the television ratings history that "the epic production" created. In this successful saga of the reception of this "intercultural" marvel[6] it is worth noting that while Brook made several trips to India during his research period, and though he received funding from the Indian government for his production, the play was never performed in India. The film version was first screened in New Delhi in November 1989 under the aegis of the Festival of France in India, and two years later, Doordarshan, the official national television channel, bought the rights, and the film was serialized and telecast from December 1991 onwards.

At over 90,000 stanzas in length, *The Mahabharata* is fifteen times the size of the Bible, and eight times the size of the *Iliad* and the *Odyssey* combined.[7] Successfully converting this phenomenal length of epic poetry into nine hours of gripping narrative and exciting theater could only be the fruition of a labor of love by Brook and Carriere, who devoted a decade of their lives to this project. In the process they not only familiarized the West with "one of the greatest works of humanity,"[8] albeit from India, but were also seen as reuniting *The Mahabharata* "with its land of origin"[9]! A certain section of public opinion in India too, felt a tremendous "debt of gratitude" to Brook for doing a better job "of public relations for Indian culture in the West" than any that even official delegations would have managed.[10] In the process, "national mythology" was not only "extended and enriched," but had "become truly universal."[11]

The universal relevance of this epic from a completely different culture was located by Brook and Carriere, not only in the fundamental human emotions that the text represents and evokes, but also in *The Mahabharata*'s central theme of universal destruction with which the post-nuclear world immediately and pressingly identifies. The reverberating contemporary significance of this ancient text in the context of an all-pervasive anxiety about a post-Cold War world that can accidentally slip into nuclear adventurism continues to be relevant. Even after the defusing of ideological tension with the end of the Cold War, the threat that humanity faces from man's capacity for senseless and destructive action remains palpably real. The "Kali-yuga"[12] that *The Mahabharata* thematizes could not be more vivid than at the present, postmodern moment when the destruction of *Dharma*,[13] exemplified by the Kauravas, seems complete. In embodying the birth and prophesying the end of Kali-yuga, *The Mahabharata* encapsulates a vision of time that would confound Western notions of history as a linear progression of time, human development, and prosperity. Moreover, it is perhaps the capacity of the text to embody universal human emotions while simultaneously destabilizing a response that might smugly distance itself from the narrated events, as either too far back in time or belonging to a different history and culture, that motivated Brook, in his constant search for a direct communion with diverse audiences, to interpret the Indian epic as "the poetical history of mankind."[14]

A laudatory and noble enterprise indeed, but one that certainly raises questions about adaptations, cultural interpretations, and responsibility towards the complex of significances that the original text represents, questions that are not very different essentially from those that Brook might have faced had the text in question been Shakespeare—from the same culture but with the important qualification that it belonged to a different moment in time. In the context of a multicultural interpretation however, these questions begin to reverberate with implications of cultural politics, implications that need to be confronted precisely because the universalizing impulse is only demeaned when set against cultural specificity. That Brook has constantly done this in both his theatrical and film version is obvious not only in the productions, but also repeatedly in the statements with which he has justified and explained his reasons. The implications of Brook's stance, and his enterprise as a whole reveals significances about the postmodern performance culture that might be worth examining as a means of understanding not only some of the characteristic features of postmodernism, with its connections and deviations from both modernism and the avant-garde, but also postmodernism's struggle for a serious self-definition and significance.

That Brook should be seen as a postmodern artist may seem strange, especially since his work can be better understood in the context of avant-garde theater as well as modernism. While his techniques may definitely be identified with the former, it is his multicultural strategy in interpreting *The Mahabharata* that locates him clearly in the postmodern moment. Brook's *Mahabharata* is an interesting postmodern cultural phenomenon in that it demonstrates that with the emergence of a culture of eclecticism that privileges what Bloch called "non-synchronisms,"[15] it is possible to use "randomly chosen images and motifs from pre-modern and non-modern cultures"[16] while "overlaying them with modernist and/or avantgardist strategies."[17] This fascination with other cultures is another form of the primitivism that characterized modernity's dissatisfaction with itself and formed the impetus for the emergence of the avant-garde. The atavistic turn to the "primitive" in the avant-garde may be the embodiment of its relentless critique of the industrial, urban culture of modernity, but the West's erotic and aesthetic fascination with the Orient as well as "other" primitive cultures remains deeply problematic, especially when it is articulated without any sense of the history of colonialism.

It is a well-established critical fact that colonialism, with its contact with different cultures provided the stimulus for much artistic innovation associated with modernism and the avant-garde, and it is ironic when these innovations are used to interpret the culture from which the performance forms have been separated.[18] And when diverse performance traditions are brought to bear upon an alien cultural text, we have a multicultural syncretism that reveals the process by which multiculturalism can be "co-opted" for "commercial or ideological purposes."[19] With the mass-mediated circulation of images of different cultures that feeds the "cultural institution's perpetual need for spectacle and frill"[20] there is a ready-made market in the West for the consumption of the "Other." In this context, is Brook's *Mahabharata* simply a rendering and an interpretation of a "universal" text, or is it an example of the postmodern commodification of culture that sanctions the glossy overlaying of homogenizing images that violates all sense of historical and cultural contextualization in the name of the universal?

The answers to these questions are crucially tied up with a confrontation of the issues involved in the enterprise of interpreting an alien cultural work, along with the issue of confronting the past. That the former has been important in assessing Brook's achievement is obvious from the way in which critical responses and accusations like "cultural piracy,"[21] as the production raising the "problematic specter of . . . Orientalism,"[22] and as exemplifying "one of the most blatant (and accomplished) appropriations of Indian culture in recent years"[23] have punctured the rhapsodic responses that both the play and the film versions elicited from audiences all over the world, including India. While it may seem that the articulation of objections to Brook's treatment of the epic by Indian critics is merely a chauvinistic and proprietorial possessiveness, and hence a form of renegade criticism that needs to be dismissed, it is necessary to address the questions of de-contextualization that these critics have raised. They have a direct bearing not only on Brook's choice of performance techniques, but also on Brook's alleged project of a "dialogue between cultures," an ideal project for the meeting, as Paul Ricoeur put it, of "different civilizations by means other than the shock of conquest and domination."[24] But does "an authentic dialogue" emerge from using the strategy of a multiracial cast and its responses to a simplified narrative of a culturally-specific text, shorn of its cultural, ethical, mythical, and socio-historical nucleus, even if its narrative has the power to elicit universal identification and is wonderfully performed by actors, all of whom have unquestionable dedication to the project?

The larger issue at stake here is whether the quest for a primordial and mythic language of a theatre that communicates instantaneously to a diverse global audience is perhaps really the quest for a share of the cultural market. In that case, the question is not one of a debate of cultures at all, for this would entail a complex narrative and performance strategy through which, in Ricoeur's words, "civilizations confront each other more and more with what is most living and creative in them."[25] In Brook's *Mahabharata* we have neither the Indias that produced *The Mahabharata* nor the various other cultures that are nominally represented through those associated with the production. What we do have is an Orientalist legacy, a perpetuation of the images and concepts of India facilitated first through colonialism and later, in the more recent past through the Indian culture bureaucracy, intent on promoting Indian tourism and culture abroad through its various Festivals of India. Ironically, Brook's grand project of a debate of cultures amounts finally to a validation of postmodernism's conversion of culture into a "product in its own right."[26]

Does this imply, however, that Brook's attempt at bringing different cultural perspectives to bear on *The Mahabharata* was doomed to failure from the very beginning because texts are locked in their cultural contexts and are not really accessible to those outside? Is the "universal" an ultimately elusive experience? The point is certainly not to advocate the position of the "ethnic insider"[27] as the privileged locus of the interpretative act, but rather to suggest that there are different ways of responding to the alien cultural text without compromising either the universal human experience that all art aspires for and embodies, or a specific cultural matrix that an epic implies, given the fact, of course, that one chooses to interpret it with the scope and significance of an epic.

Abstraction into a stylized mode is one way of dealing with an alien cultural text, especially when the references are unknown to the audience, necessitating a focus on shared human experiences. A completely different strategy of response could be the attempt to be authentic, to be faithful to the text, the context, and Brook and Carriere did spend several years thinking about and researching for the project. The task before them was no mean one—to condense the longest narrative poem into a nine-hour dramatic performance or a six-hour film would be daunting to say the least, especially since Brook took it upon himself to interpret a distinctive culture to a world alien to it. The choices of interpretative and performance strategies before Brook and Carriere involved several thorny issues: questions of language, representations, and signification; accessibility of the material in terms of ideas, attitudes, and even emotions. The resolution of these questions would reflect their positioning vis-a-vis the culture they had chosen to "interpret." These questions become important because they contain the larger one of allegiance.

While Brook was obviously committed to the idea of a shared body of human experience that could be tapped through performance, he was equally committed to giving it shape and form through the images and spirit of India, even while using a multiracial cast to embody his former conviction. These two impulses are not necessarily in conflict with each other, unless seen as such. For Brook, however, this was certainly a problem:

> To tell this story we had to avoid evoking India too strongly *so as to not lead us away from human identification,* but also we had to nevertheless tell it as a story rooted in Indian earth.[28]

One can only surmise that Brook did not want to alienate his non-Indian audience, and would therefore tell his "Indian story" in terms that would be as acceptable and accessible to them as possible, while ironically describing this intention as one that was the most "human" option available. That Brook remained the alienated outsider throughout his association with the project is obvious in that he chooses to describe it in these terms. For Brook, the question of universality seems to be linked up with universal accessibility and acceptability, and the strategies of interpretation would naturally be colored by the latter. The issue here is simply that as a mode of response to an alien text and culture, Brook was not really interested in attempting, however difficult it might have been, to interpret from within. The point is not that he should have, but that he need not convey that this is what he was doing.[29]

These contradictions of his position would not have arisen had Brook chosen to respond differently to his project of claiming *The Mahabharata* for the world. An adaptation would surely have distilled the essentially universal dimension of the narrative, without having to confront its particular cultural embodiment, since it would have meant adapting the story to his own cultural context. Kurosawa's *Throne of Blood,* an adaptation of Shakespeare's *Macbeth,* demonstrates that essential human responses and emotions are universal precisely because they find an echo in completely different cultures. To have taken *The Mahabharata* and made it Shakespearean would have wonderfully served the "universal" objective, especially since Brook believes that "the work is Shakespearean in the true sense of the word. Its form is essentially Indian but it's based on universal conflicts and ideals."[30] This anachronistic evaluation of *The Mahabharata,* with its positing of Shakespeare as *the* yardstick of the universal, reveals significantly that the Eurocentric response to culture is very much a reality, despite the claims of multicultural conviction and practice.

Though Brook does not adapt *The Mahabharata* entirely to a Shakespearean or to any other Western model, it is undeniable that Shakespeare is an important presence in his version. In his conception of character, in some of the performance modes that he uses, even in the language of ultimate doom and destruction, the production has more Shakespearean elements than Indian. The point is not that it should be Indian, but rather, why did Brook not go the whole way and adapt the epic to a Western context? Why did he feel the need to cling to some form of cultural authenticity, communicated especially through an attempt to convey "the flavor" of India,[31] as if it were a curry powder one could buy in a supermarket? That Brook does not understand the Sanskrit term *rasa,*[32] most inadequately translated as "flavor," is obvious from the way in which the production relies so heavily on the evocation of this flavor through a reliance on the easily identifiable exotic images and sounds of India and the East generally. The interplay of the "essential" and the "contextual" to produce an appropriate response, integral to the idea of rasa, is completely missing in Brook's understanding of ancient Indian performance traditions or its aesthetics. All he can do is to extract these traditions from their social and ritualistic contexts, converting them into abstract stylizations that reflect postmodernism's cannibalizing of alien traditions, a residual feature of modernism. Though modernity's fascination with the "other" is definitely problematic, one cannot at the same time overlook the fact that often alien traditions and elements were used as a form of self-critique, where the sources of rejuvenation were seen to lie outside the deadening matrix of Western, industrialized, urban experience. Markedly, the borrowing from Oriental traditions in Brook's case hardly seems to perform any such critical role. Meant to convey the feel of "Indian-ness," it does not seem to matter to Brook that by dehistoricizing the expressive modes that he is using, and by combining them in random ways, he achieves not so much the effect of universality, but rather that of a melange that trivializes and, at best, can only exoticize the culture in question.

It should be thus obvious that Brook uses several strategies to turn *The Mahabharata* into a performance text without committing himself to any one finally. He uses an abstract, stylized, symbolic mode while simultaneously attempting to evoke a specifically Indian cultural context. He attempts an adaptation of a kind in the way in which several features of the performance are reminiscent of a Shakespearean text, but finally this does not reverberate with the kind of associations that an adaptation should evoke, of the culture that it is being adapted to—in the way in which Kurosawa's *Throne of Blood,* for instance, evokes not Shakespearean England through Scottish history, but Japanese Samurai culture. The reason, of course, is that Brook intended that several different cultural traditions be invoked and brought to bear on *The Mahabharata*, so that through the multicultural interaction, *The Mahabharata* could be claimed as a universal text, and he would simultaneously prove that "geography and history cease to exist."[33] Brook also believes that we are all a "part of a limited culture" and that therefore a "dialogue between cultures" would ensure one's full potential.[34] But if multiculturalism is invoked as a humanizing and universalizing gesture, it should not be at the cost of the historical and cultural reality in which the performance text is rooted, but rather, if one may quote Shohat and Stam, should be "a gesture toward historical lucidity, a matter not of charity but of justice," and therefore function as "part of an indispensable re-envisioning of the global politics of culture."[35] To accept this version of multiculturalism would be to accept not only that diverse peoples from diverse parts of the world can identify with and perform *The Mahabharata,* which of course should be so obvious that it need not be stated, but also as Rustom Bharucha, countering Brook's view of *The Mahabharata* as a text that is "Indian but it is universal," puts it, "*The Mahabharata* is universal because it is Indian."[36] To fear that, by evoking India too strongly, "human" (should one read Western?) identification would be compromised reveals such an extreme form of Eurocentrism that its multicultural face is only a form of pretension, but one whose currency ensures success.

At the end of the film version of *The Mahabharata,* everybody accepts that it is a great story, that anyone can and may perform in it, that India has beautiful textiles and artifacts, but some strange beliefs, traditions, and even rituals. But what do people get to know about the history, the culture, the structure of beliefs of the societies that produced *The Mahabharata?* What do we know of the performance traditions of the societies that performed it? And what do we know of those alien societies whose performance traditions are also used by Brook in a multicultural effort to universalize the text? And if Brook's version does not even address these questions, let alone attempt to answer them, then his multiculturalism is not the political and humane vision implied in the project of "the dialogue between cultures,"[37] but rather "an empty signifier," an ethnic "pluralism" that promotes "commercial or ideological purposes."[38]

II.

Brook's film version of *The Mahabharata* is beset with certain conceptual contradictions from the very beginning, mainly because he neither wants to adapt the text to a different culture, nor does he really want to explain India to the world. And yet, he cannot let go of a desire to retain some images of India, for they actually ensure the exotic interest of the East for his viewers, but at the same time will not go with a "wholly Indian production" because otherwise "the barrier would have remained."[39] Did Brook fear that an "Indian production" would have committed him to a faithful rendering of "the deepest and most thought-out notions of Indian culture"[40] embodied in *The Mahabharata* which he could evade the responsibility of by using the multicultural strategy? And if Brook was not willing to bring about a "reaffiliation," which a meaningful and committed multiculturalism implies,[41] then he is certainly open to the charges of appropriation with which various critics have responded.

To be sure, Brook faced no mean task when he decided to bring *The Mahabharata* on to the world stage. The text is not only an ancient Indian text that still pervades modern India's sociocultural life, but one that has taken root in several performance traditions with their own sociocultural, ritualistic, and aesthetic functions. Obviously, Brook's performance context was different, and therefore one would not expect him to have *The Mahabharata* performed in an Indian mode. However, it is his attitude to these traditions that is revealing. Brook wanted "to eliminate classical Indian art at all levels: in acting, in dance, in song, in music" in favor of "a popular form," which he believes is "exactly our own" and which would therefore justify using a popular idiom that is not necessarily Indian.[42] This privileging of the "popular" as a performance mode— a typically postmodern response—especially when it is divorced from a political intent, has two fundamental problems. By eliminating cultural distinctions in the belief that popular forms encode elemental human responses as opposed to the classical which is culturally specific, Brook demonstrates a lack of a historical consciousness, in that he refuses to recognize that "the popular" has a completely different significance in the present moment of commodified cultural circulation. If he is referring to "folk" forms when he uses the term "popular," then a recognition of their ritualistic connotations and functions, which are specific to each culture, is unavoidable. Moreover, in India there is a continuity between the classical and the folk forms of performance, a relationship that Brook would rather obscure to serve his postmodern, multicultural strategy.

That Brook is aligned with the "popular" as opposed to the "classical" in Indian art is, however, itself a debatable point. While it is certainly true that Classical Indian dance, music, and art are more or less absent from his enactment of *The Mahabharata*, it is not entirely so.[43] There are certain gestures and movements that evoke Classical iconography and dance techniques, and are in fact very effectively used by Brook. On the other hand, folk elements, rather than a popular Indian performance tradition, are also present in the form of either dramatic props or the *mise-en-scene*, and even certain gestures from the martial arts, which again are not specifically Indian, but could be vaguely identified with the East generally. Other aspects of the performance (for example the costumes and the acting styles) cannot be exclusively identified with any kind of a folk tradition, either Eastern or Western. The acting combines psychological realism in the Stanislavskian mode with often a Shakespearean touch, while the costumes evoke some aspects of folk India, but also a Classicism that belongs to different historical periods. Does this repertoire of mixed modes and styles make the performance resonate with implications that connect the classical with the folk, the high with the low, the East with the West, the specific with the universal, or does it in fact present a melange that is hardly a multicultural understanding of either human performance or narrative traditions but rather feeds the obsessive need for spectacle that has increasingly pervaded mass culture from the beginning of modernity?

Spectacle is not, however, in itself a derogatory category. Its sensuous, visual, evocative quality definitely has the potential to convey pleasure of an aesthetic, emotional, and even mental-intellectual kind. In its cinematic form and combined with a rigorous, historical, social, and cultural insight, spectacle can communicate the truth of human experience in vivid, perceptual, and cognitive terms which in its appeal to all the human faculties can be a holistically satisfying experience. But when the spectacular dimension of a representation is divorced from an analytical vision or becomes the vehicle of a retrograde politics or feeds curiosity without sympathy and understanding, it can become exploitative in its titillation of the emotions or the exoticizing of the Other.

Brook has constantly claimed that he was not interested in India for its exotic quality. And yet the opening sequence of the film version establishes the Orientalist gaze that more or less colors the entire perspective of the film. Brook's camera fluidly follows a young boy who, having emerged from a rustic doorway wonderingly walks into a room that is beautifully lit with *diyas* (brass lamps) that are positioned along the room and some suspended from the ceiling. It is a breathtaking scene that establishes one of the major performance spaces for the film: the Kaurava court/palace interior that is constructed with some well-known icons associated with Indian culture. Apart from the lamps, the seating area with the white furnishings on the floor, the image of a deity with a garland of marigolds around it, and all the paraphernalia of worship before it convey the feel of an "authentic" Indian setting. The boy walks through this space, pauses before the deity, bends to touch a mound of *kumkum*,[44] jerks back to dust off his hands, goes through another doorway to discover a *charpai*[45] and a mask of Ganesha[46] hanging from the wall, moves through yet another doorway into a primordial cave-like room where he comes across an ancient sage in meditation, Vyasa.[47] Vyasa welcomes him and informs him that he is about to narrate to him the story of his race, which is "the poetical history of mankind."[48] Ganesha, the divine scribe arrives to record the narration and the scene is set for the performance of the story that Vyasa is narrating to the young boy. It is an interesting scene that overlays modernist Pirandellian techniques of performance over an attempted folk quality of the experience, and a scene that raises some very interesting questions. Who is the boy whom Brook and Carriere have introduced into the performance, and who is he supposed to represent? Is he generic, universal man; Modern man; Indian; or a representative of the West looking at the East?

Brook did not intend to literally realize an element of the original text wherein the story of his ancestors is narrated to a young prince so that he "prepares himself for life."[49] But the figure of a young boy, at the very beginning, he felt, would bring an extremely simple, human atmosphere to this rather solemn and grandiose story. As the child listens and asks questions he would embody the responses of the audience, and at the end as he walks away bearing *The Mahabharata*, he is literally the viewers who when they leave carry *The Mahabharata* within them. The external framework of the performance is provided by the narration of the story of the conflict between the Kauravas and the Pandavas, one of the central foci of *The Mahabharata*, to a young boy by the sage Vyasa, the composer of the epic poem. The identity of the former is not clearly identified, presumably because there is a symbolic function that he performs. The fiction of narration that Brook provides for the enactment of the epic takes the audience back to the moment of the creation and inscription of the epic, for Ganesha, the divine scribe, completes the trio who represent the creation, the inscription, and the reception of the epic. In a Pirandellian gesture, they witness the embodiment of the narrated text, often weaving in and out, mingling with the characters that Vyasa has created. Despite these ruptures of dramatic illusion, the performance takes place within the fictional construct of the narration that provides the framework of Brook's text. The movement of the opening sequence clearly suggests that the audience is being transported, through this performance, back to a prehistoric, mythic age when men were close to the gods, magically potent and creative. The evocation of primitive space—the cave of Vyasa—and prehistoric time universalizes the context of the text while simultaneously keeping the suggestion of India in place with the cultural icons with which the *mise-en-scene* is replete. Neither the evocation of primordial time, nor the specific images of the culture, however, capture the Indian notion of time, the framework of yugas within which the text has a role to play.

On the other hand, this sequence does foster the sense of a primordial narrative situation that attempts through the boy to connect with the contemporary moment, especially that of the performance. There is, however, ambivalence in the conception of the figure of the boy. He has a double function, for he is a character in Brook's fiction while simultaneously representing the doubts and responses of a modern audience to this ancient tale. His wondering stance as he walks through the opening sequence would seem strange if one were to take him as a representative of his race, the fictional role that he is to play. For, if he is the descendant of the Bharatas, and dressed in Indian clothes as he is, he ought not to be so completely alienated from the surroundings in which he finds himself. His responses to the space through which he wanders, his gesture of discomfort as he dusts off the *kumkum* that he has bent to feel, his inappropriate response to the place of worship with its elaborate paraphernalia, his wonder at the mask of Ganesha that he comes across all come from the wondering surprise of a foreigner confronting interesting images for the first time, rather than the pleasure of recognition of one who discovers his own past history.

This reading of him as a representative, modern Indian is full of problems, for he is obviously alienated from his traditions, a reading that could be easily contested on sociological grounds. How alienated is the modern Indian? And who is this Indian that Brook is pointing to: the expatriate or the native? The representative Indian is not an easy configuration either, given the religious and cultural diversity of the country. And if Brook is pointing to the modern Hindu, and perhaps he is, for the boy certainly knows the names of both Ganesha and Krishna, his responses in this sequence are inappropriate. Given all this, the boy certainly seems to represent a modern audience (especially a Western one) and literalizes their encounter with a strange culture—the West looking at the East as it were. This seems to be the basic structural principle of this sequence, if not Brook's entire production. In that case, why bother to dress him up as Indian or call him a descendant of the Bharatas, unless Brook is attempting to claim the text for the world very literally, in which case the boy is just generic modern man confronting the hoary past of mankind. If this abstract, universal gesture is a correct reading, then the cultural icons are meaningless. But since they have an important evocative role to play in the performance, it seems more appropriate to read Brook's enterprise as an attempt to represent the culture of the chosen text; an attempt, however, that should acknowledge the foreignness of its perspective. In which case, Brook needs to be much more honest about his intentions if such they are, for otherwise the claim that the boy is a representative of the Bharatas and *The Mahabharata* "the poetical history of mankind," cannot but be read as the West's appropriation of an Oriental text in the name of universality.

The Orientalist gaze, responsible for some of the basic contradictions of the opening sequence, colors the entire narrative despite some sporadic attempts at actually capturing the essence of the culture that Brook attempts to represent. To this gaze, India appears in its rich, exotic colors, customs, and rituals as

either a primitive, tribal culture or else a mystical, spiritual entity that is forever
out of reach. What is accessible are its artifacts, its textiles, clothes, especially
when they have a designer finish to them, and perhaps only that in the vision of
The Mahabharata that is a warning of the imminence of global destruction. To
foreground this universal message, Brook obfuscates the historical and political
specificities of even the central conflict that he chooses to depict. Hence, the
princesses Gandhari and Kunti, as well as the three sisters, Amba, Ambika and
Ambalika, daughters of the King of Kashi, all make an appearance out of
nowhere to marry into the Kuru clan, their significance restricted to their role as
mothers of the children they bear.[50] The political alliances that these marriages
symbolized and the allegiances that they brought into effect (which were of a
crucial significance during the great battle) are elided by Brook for a fairy tale
rendering in which princes and princesses have an imaginary or, at best, a
mythical existence. Were Brook to merely even suggest that Gandhari came
from Khandahar, in Central Asia, that Kunti was Krishna's paternal aunt, while
the sisters from Kashi are from the eastern kingdom of Benaras, his rendering
would militate with a significance of political alliances and their impact on
governance that is an important aspect of the *The Mahabharata* and of
understanding any historical situation. The point, however, is precisely that
Brook is not interested in history. Ironically, it is the Indians who are
supposedly ahistorical in their attitude. While the mythic is an important
component of any construction of ancient history, especially in India, Brook's
response to this issue is an extremely impoverished one. In an enterprise of this
nature, it is not enough to say that his intentions were not to attempt "a
reconstruction of Dravidian and Aryan India of three thousand years ago" or
that he would not presume to "present the symbolism of Hindu philosophy,"[51]
for without a conscious reconstruction of some kind, without an attempt at
understanding and representing the philosophy of the culture that creates a text,
any attempt at representation can only be a facile one.

That Brook's production suffers on this count, apart from the more
serious count of cultural appropriation, would be obvious if one were to
question the premises of the representational choices that have been made in his
interpretation. It is obvious to anyone who knows India that there is an attempt
at creating a homogeneous image of the country that is not even necessarily
identified with Hindu identity. That a recognizable and accessible image of the
culture is important to Brook would be clear if one were to examine the *mise-
en-scene* and the costumes that designer Chloe Obolensky has worked on with
him. She has emphasized that documentation has been the most important
consideration while conceptualizing the realization of the text.[52] But one
wonders what exactly she is referring to. For the costumes have been designed
and tailored to her specifications of those designs that would be most appealing
to a foreign audience, and have nothing to do with historical and regional-cultural
authenticity (Fig. 8.1). Though based upon "authentic" Indian styles, they manifest a

Fig. 8.1 "[T]he costumes have been designed and tailored to her specifications of those designs that would be most appealing to a foreign audience, and have nothing to do with historical and regional-cultural authenticity." (From the film *The Mahabharata*. Production Still.)

complete disregard of the geographical and historical context. The costumes of both the men and the women are a melange of elements from different parts of the country, from different historical periods and from different class and caste backgrounds. Which logic would justify a combination of Mughal kurtas with South Indian upper class *angavastrams* (a kind of shawl) for the men on the one hand, and tribal jewelry, folk embroidery, gypsy skirts, and expensive silk weaves worn by upper class women for the costumes of the women, on the other? The only logic that seems operative here is that of the market, for the images that are thus created are easily exportable images of the exotic East. This is not to dispute Obolensky's claim that the textiles, the fabrics, even the designs are Indian, but to suggest that authenticity has to do with history, geography, and sociology; that documentation does not mean picking randomly those images that are most appealing, no matter where they come from so long as they are within the confines of a recognizable Indian boundary and from some point in time in Indian history that can stretch over five to six thousand years. Indian adaptations of *The Mahabharata* work within the regional and cultural context in which the text and the performance tradition have a significance. These details are therefore worked out in accordance with those traditions, and do not claim historical authenticity, but only the contemporary relevance of the text in that specific context. In Brook's case, however, there is no such context; only a free-floating narrative that, abstracted from its cultural matrix, can more easily bear its universal message. What role do the cultural signifiers perform in his version of the text then, for they hardly seem to carry the burden of cultural signification? The attempted authenticity when deprived of cultural and philosophical value can only function at the level of a surface image that does not resonate with a significant understanding.

Brook's rendering of the religious and ritualistic beliefs of Hindu society that are reflected in *The Mahabharata* is indicative of just such a reduction of the culture to the level of a superficial image. Almost every important performance space is evoked with an image of a deity enshrined in one area, with garlands and objects of worship before it. We also see the characters at some stage or other involved in some ritual associated with the act of worship, whether it be Draupadi setting lit *diyas* (earthen oil lamps) on a pond during the Pandavas' exile, or Duryodhana and Dussasana in an obscure ritual that enables them to visualize the absent Arjuna's encounter with Shiva, or Karna's encounter with Parshurama, or the evocation of Shiva and Kali in mantras by Salya, Karna's charioteer, during the final stages of the war. None of these scenes, however, resonate with the beliefs and ideas that structure a culture. In fact, the mere inclusion of certain Sanskrit terms is not enough to evoke an entire worldview. Thus, while words like *kshatriya* and *Dharma* recur throughout the performance, the code of values that they embody remain elusive. The attempt at implying those through aesthetic images of a culture can only be reductive and extremely demeaning and dangerous when they disguise an ideological purpose. The strange gestures of Duryodhana before the shrine;

the serpentine ring of fire that he brings into being; the portrayal of Parshurama; the ascetic, as a half-savage uttering the strange words "vala, vala, vala" all perpetuate a spirituality that in these examples doesn't seem very different from a kind of black magic. The Orientalist mystique of India is well ensconced in Brook's text, furthered by the occasional inclusion of Sanskrit mantras, words that are not subtitled or explained, commented upon, or refracted through the text in any gesture of illumination. Thus, the evocation to Shiva and Kali[53] by Salya in the middle of the war—"Om Namaha Shivaya, Om Bhadra Kali"— comes completely out of the blue and does not carry any textual or cultural resonance. Without such signification, the authenticity of the mantra or the objects used as props can only be seen as exploitative, for the only aims it serves are those of marketing an exotic product and in terms that would be completely accessible to those alien to it.

Accessibility is not in itself a mark of an exploitative attitude to an alien text, but only becomes such if the complexity, the cultural vision it encodes, the beliefs that it embodies are all sacrificed for a structure that in its comprehensibility is also extremely impoverished. Extracting a teleological narrative of a family feud from *The Mahabharata,* Brook and Carriere have created a story that has no political, economic, social, cultural, or philosophical implications. And to imagine *The Mahabharata,* that along with *The Ramayana,* still forms the basis of the ethical life of Hindu culture, that provides the literary matrix for the music, dance, and performance traditions— both folk and classical—of the country, that embodies the most complex and thought-out philosophical ideas of the culture, as just a martial tale of warring families is to impose a reading that reductively denies the Other any identity apart from the one imposed upon it.

The predominance of the martial arts as performance technique in Brook's rendering is extremely revealing. Divorced from the respective contexts in which the martial arts were ways of life, homogenized into an image of the ancient East in general, the use of the martial arts presents not just India, but in one stroke the entire East as primitive, tribal societies that spent all their time fighting each other (Fig. 8.2). That the martial arts have established traditions all over the East is a well-known fact. But that these traditions have developed differently and have different functions in Eastern societies would not be evident from Brook's text. There are folk performance traditions in India that have emerged from the martial arts that often use episodes from *The Mahabharata* as performance text. But there are other folk traditions that also perform sections of *The Mahabharata* but are not derived from the martial arts.[54] That Brook prefers the former as his dominant mode of depicting the conflict of the Kauravas and the Pandavas is indicative of the interpretative choices that he has made. While extremely appropriate and evocative as a technique to depict conflict on the stage, to use a theatrical device derived from the martial arts to portray the Great War on film is extremely impoverishing.

Fig. 8.2 "[T]he use of the martial arts presents not just India, but in one stroke the entire East as primitive, tribal societies that spent all their time fighting each other." (From the film *The Mahabharata*. Production still)

One is not trying to suggest that Brook ought to have given us a spectacular display of an armed conflict in true Hollywood style, but rather that cinema is an audio-visual medium that works very differently from the stage. Having chosen to literally depict the War, Brook can hardly avoid confronting the elaborate and very real descriptions that he would have found in any version of *The Mahabharata* that he may have used for that section. This is not only to say that the horses, the elephants, the chariots, the arms of war are all missing from Brook's version; but that the kind of sparse theatrical mode that he chooses to use in the third section of the film creates an image of an extremely primitive, tribal society. This is, of course, in keeping with the rest of the narrative as we have it from Brook. So that while on the one hand, the images evoke an opulent culture, on the other the imagery of the war scenes derived from the martial arts evokes a tribal society that has not developed into the political kingdoms that *The Mahabharata* records. Brook's attitude embodies the contradictions of an Orientalist response that sees the Orient as an exotic land of riches while simultaneously constructing it as primitive, in order to deny it any historical or political agency. The subsequent result is a universalized narrative, extracted from a specific, cultural, and historical context, which is not sufficiently abstract to function as a stylized account of the human condition. Since cultural signifiers do exist in the text one would expect that the culture they signify is taken seriously and not reduced to words and images that remain empty signifiers since they do not come to grips with the concepts that they are meant to signify.

One such signifier is the mask of Ganesha that the boy comes across, hanging from the wall in the opening sequence. Together with the rustic *charpai*, the mask is clearly meant to reference a folk theater tradition where masks are often used to intensify and elevate the emotional effect of a scene. A little later, an actor appears wearing the mask, impersonating Ganesha, the divine scribe who is also evoked on every auspicious occasion by Hindus. After a short account of the origin of the elephant-head, given by Ganesha to the boy to satisfy the curiosity of a foreign audience, the enactment of Vyasa's poem begins. A little later, the same actor (Bruce Myers) takes off the mask to become Krishna. While the eclectic use of traditions—Indian folk and Western modernist—is definitely postmodern, it is hardly politically or historically allusive in this context. In fact, while the conflation of the Ganesha/Krishna figure may seem a very interesting theatrical device from a Western point of view, it is extremely problematic from an Indian one. Krishna is an avatar of Vishnu while Ganesha is the son of Shiva and Parvati and is therefore certainly not interchangeable with the former. Folk theatrical traditions in India have ritualistic functions and can hardly be apprehended outside the context of the cultural and religious beliefs of the community. The Ganesha mask may point to those traditions, but its actual use in Brook's text is to serve the modernist alienation technique that Brook uses to frame his narrative. The device does not facilitate an apprehension of a theatrical tradition of performing *The Mahabharata*, for instance, or lead the audience to discover the religious or ritualistic beliefs of the community. Divorced from its context, the mask is an empty signifier whose sole purpose is to decorate Brook's narrative as an "authentic" symbol of an alien culture, just as the martial arts tradition that he uses functions at best as an exercise in performance technique and not as revelatory about the culture at all.

That Brook is perhaps not interested in the latter seems the only conclusion one can come to when one examines his treatment of the key philosophical concepts of *The Mahabharata*. Brook's text constantly refers to Dharma, and he takes some pains to indicate how central this concept is to his narrative. Vyasa is composing his poem "to engrave Dharma in the hearts of men" for they have forgotten "the essentials."[55] But the complex associations of the term, even as defined by Carriere in his introduction to the play, as the "law on which rests the order of the world" or "the personal and secret order each human being recognizes as his own"[56] do not provide a framework or "a Hindu perspective of action in the larger, cosmic context."[57] Dharma cannot be understood without an understanding of *karma*,[58] *svadharma*,[59] and *sanskara*,[60] and certainly not without any reference to the cycle of rebirth and past lives within which each human life has meaning and which finally only ends with *moksha*, or deliverance. While the metaphysical and philosophical implications of these concepts are worked out and expounded in *The Bhagavad Gita*, which Gautam Dasgupta calls "the epicenter of the poem, the fulcrum on which rests the entire thrust of this monumental drama of humanity,"[61] these ideas imbue the entire narrative and form the determinants of human and social action in *The Mahabharata*. The *Gita* is thus integral to the epic, and therefore the ideas that it explores do not seem unfamiliar. In Brook's version, however, this is not so. The *Gita* is nominally present, but the infinitely reduced version with a quick summary of the main ideas can hardly make them reverberate through the text as they do in the original. In fact, the concept of *karma yoga*, the path of action as one of the means to deliverance, or *moksha* (the other two being knowledge and faith), the lesson given to Arjuna on the field of battle by Krishna, seems to emerge from out of the blue with no prior referencing in the text. It is not surprising that a Western audience would laugh at Krishna's advice to Arjuna to act but not reflect on the fruits of action, for, as Rustom Bharucha has pointed out, not only does it go against their ideology of capitalism and self-interest, but it has not been supported through the action of the epic at all.[62] It is therefore also possible for Christopher Innes to say that while what Brook rejects in modern society is sufficiently clear, "the spiritual alternative to be affirmed turns out to be indefinable. The myth is hollow at the centre."[63] To an Indian, steeped in the tradition of *The Upanishads*[64] and *The Bhagavad Gita* within which tradition *The Mahabharata* also belongs, this response may seem absolutely incomprehensible, but not so for Brook and Carriere, to whom *"The Mahabharata gives no answer. It simply gives immense nourishment."*[65]

This is not to suggest that Brook ought to have treated his version of *The Mahabharata* as revelatory injunction, but rather that he certainly needed to confront the notion of narrative as cultural signification, especially when cultural signifiers are retained in a performative adaptation. The responsibility of the former can easily be evaded by using the strategy of a universalizing discourse, whereby cultural specificity is condemned as narrow provincialism. In contrast, multicultural syncretism can embody a global vision of culture wherein no cultural formation occupies a privileged standing. While this perspective is completely appropriate for the politics of cultural relations and also possesses normative value, when it comes to the question of a creative adaptation of a text for an intercultural performance, a multicultural syncretic performance mode can come into serious conflict with the values and ideas that the chosen text embodies. Brook envisioned a multiracial cast, the members of which would bring their individual cultural traditions to bear upon an alien cultural text as the prime example of a "debate of cultures" that could take place within the space of the performance arena and affirm the universality of human experience. While his actors have certainly proved his faith in their ability to embody the monumental drama of *The Mahabharata*, and that a text is performatively accessible to anyone—whether we understand more about their respective cultures through their performance or enough about the culture whose experiences they are concretizing—is another question.

The latter project is a much more difficult one and one for which syncretism may not be the answer. As Paul Ricoeur has pointed out, syncretisms are "residual phenomena" and "do not involve anything creative." Moreover, they

> must be opposed by communication, that is, a dramatic relation in which I affirm myself in my origins and give myself to another's imagination *in accordance with his different civilization.* Human truth lies only in this process in which civilizations confront each other more and more with what *is most living and creative in them.*[66]

The emphases in the above quotation can be used to recognize the need to respect and value difference through an attempt at a sympathetic understanding that does not fuse differences for a homogeneous vision or image. Syncretism "as a perennial resource for the arts"[67] is only effective when it builds upon a syncretism in the culture that is being interpreted. Otherwise, instead of being mutually illuminative of the cultures in question, a syncretic image or technique can misinterpret, misinform and even more dangerously, appropriate an image of these cultures for an ideological purpose, like the Orientalist construction of the Orient that can only be reprehensible. That Brook's *Mahabharata* is guilty of this along with his reviewers, like Richard Schechener who celebrate the "syncretism" of the work, is illustrative of the deep-seated Eurocentrism that is residual in professed affiliations to multicultural syncretism.

A few examples from Brook's *Mahabharata* might prove the point. Brook's delineation of the character of Bhima as performed by Mamadou Dioume, an otherwise powerful Senegalese actor, especially from the second part onwards often degenerates into a caricature of primitive, tribal earthiness. The tomfoolery in the Bhima-Hidimbi-Ghatotkacha episode is certainly not from the original text and, as a syncretic interpretation, one wonders what it reveals either of Senegalese or Indian society. While Brook and reviewers like David Williams have dismissed accusations of a racist bias in the casting of the characters,[68] the naturalism of certain sequences is certainly questionable, as Sadanand Menon has pointed out.[69] Bhima's response to Ghatotkacha's birth, born fully grown as he is, "already so big, so black,"[70] draws attention to the kind of racial stereotyping that a multicultural response should definitely avoid. The demonic power of Ghatotkacha, a primitive savage, who has to be tricked by Krishna into deploying black magic to rout the Kaurava army, to be killed by Karna in the process, is another example of an attempted inter-cultural interpretation that is offensive to both the cultures involved. That Krishna is needed to intervene and evokes Ghatotkacha in a strange ritual, manipulating him to an angry, destructive rage through clever suggestions about the danger to his father is an instance of the perpetuation of the stereotype of the passionate but anti-intellectual nature of the primitive.

Brook's portrayal of Krishna's intervention in this episode is in keeping with his conception of Krishna's role in the epic. He is depicted as one who takes on the burden of all those actions that frustrate a moral justification precisely because he is a god who seems to serve a higher principle beyond human comprehension. The responsibility for the deaths of Abhimanyu, Ghatotkacha, Karna, Bhishma, and Duryodhana is assumed by Krishna, for otherwise the incidents are horribly inexplicable. By attempting to shift the culpability for these deaths from the Pandavas into the realm of divine retribution, Brook completely reduces the significances of the Indian notion of destiny and karma that is worked out in the original text. By explicating the moral enigma that Krishna represents as the opaqueness of divine intention, Brook not only mystifies Indian philosophical ideas, but also deprives his characters of *karmic*[71] motivations for their actions, since they then come across as motivated either by their passions/feelings or manipulated by Krishna. That all the characters act in accordance with their *swadharma*, evolved through the *sanskara* of their past lives is completely elided by Brook's text, for this is a realm of signification that would be too alien to a foreign audience. In order to make the text more accessible, Brook translates the struggle against *adharma*[72] into the battle of good against evil, with Krishna, the enigmatic man-god, on the side of the former. While such transformations make sense in complete adaptations to a different culture, in the event of an attempt to explicate an alien text, they can only be seen as either an inability to come to terms with the culture in question, or a deliberate repression of meaning in order that certain codified responses to strange cultures surface. That Ghatotkacha is seen by Krishna as "the demon of eclipses and illusions,"[73] is evoked in a strange ritual, is the nephew of a cannibal *rakshasa* (demon) and functions as an amoral, destructive force contributes to a perception of both African and Indian culture (for Krishna is past master of the power that Ghatotkacha embodies, so Brook would have us believe) as primitive and spiritually suspect, for the impression of their spirituality as essentially black magic is consistently evoked, be it in the context of Ghatotkacha, or Parshurama, or Duryodhana, or even, finally, Krishna. The syncretic, cultural act—the creative interaction of different cultures—is here ironically nothing but a subservience to a vision of the director's that remains Eurocentric and exploitative.

Both Mallika Sarabhai and Yoshi Oida, who play Draupadi and Drona, respectively, have affirmed in different ways the power that Brook exerted over the production. While encouraging individual, cultural inputs into the interpretative responses of the actors, Brook nevertheless had a clear idea of which cultural input would conform to his vision and which did not. Sarabhai, the only Indian in the production, was often put aside in her objections to implications that she felt would go against the grain of the text, with the alibi that their audience was primarily Western. One wonders how much of herself and her culture Sarabhai actually put into her role. There is nothing in her performance that would suggest her training as a classical dancer, neither movement nor expression. As one of the worst and most wooden performances of the production, Sarabhai's does not suggest the creative dynamism of interculturalism, but rather the stifling of indigenous potential in favor of towing a multicultural vision that must remain consistent and cannot accommodate a performance tradition that may initially seem incomprehensible to Brook's audience. That Sarabhai herself does not feel any resentment at being controlled is a testimony to the subtle, suggestive power of Brook's final control, despite his assumed attitude of a director who gives complete freedom to his actors, allowing them to discover their own potentials for their roles and their own interpretations.[74]

Oida's acceptance of Brook's suggestion of an image evocative of Japanese culture to signify Drona's death in the production is another example of Brook's control and his deployment of a syncretic image in service of the multicultural philosophy of his enterprise. When Drona learns of his son's death and the will to fight leaves him, he decides to give up his life. He removes his armor, and in a gesture evocative of a violent samurai death, lifts a pot of blood and pours it over his head before sitting down in a yogic posture of meditation, waiting for life to leave his body (Fig. 8.3). Dhrishtadyumya, Dhrupad's son, comes forward to slay him. The fusion of the samurai tradition with the yogic one, with the blood dripping down his face and body as Drona sits in

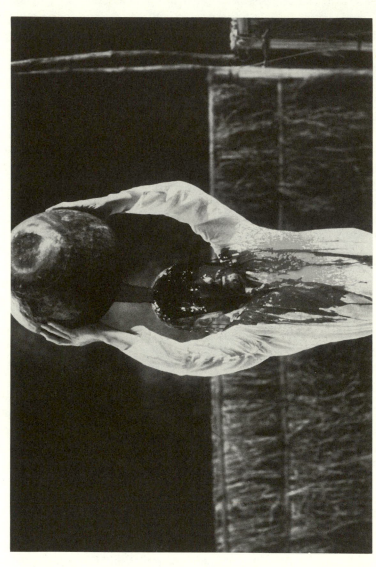

Fig. 8.3 "When Drona learns of his son's death and the will to fight leaves him, he decides to give up his life. He removes his armor, and in a gesture evocative of a violent samurai death, lifts a pot of blood and pours it over his head before sitting down in a yogic posture of meditation, waiting for life to leave his body (From the film *The Mahabharata*. Production still)

meditation, is a syncretic image, but one whose significance militates against the imagery. Drona's death is certainly a violent one, and the image of the blood being poured over his head will bring to the fore the violence of samurai culture. But the implications of the yogic posture are entirely contradictory. Brook may have intended the contrast between Drona's philosophical acceptance of his death and the violent treachery with which he was killed. But the image of Drona pouring the pot of blood over his head suggests a strange ritual of death that only mystifies both the traditions being signified—the samurai and the yogic. Ultimately, what is affirmed once again is the mystique of the Orient, a gesture that does not open up the possibilities of a committed understanding, but rather serves the Orientalist curiosity with expected images.

Where Brook succeeds is precisely in those aspects of the production where he is most at home, namely the stark, simplified, yet psychologized acting technique, the evocation of tragic waste at the end of the battle as Vyasa, Gandhari, and Dhritarashtra—literally and metaphorically the blind king, responsible for this desolation—walk over the battlefield strewn with bodies; or in the extremely Shakespearean moment when Yudhishthira prophesizes in Virata's court, the birth of the Kalyug that they have heralded. In fact, the dramatization is so effectively Shakespearean, tragic flaws and all, that it is a real pity that Brook didn't opt completely for a cultural adaptation, but insisted on retaining images of Indian culture without taking the trouble to illumine adequately enough the context and the matrix of those images. For, in fact, when he does, as in the Ekalavya episode, he is able to convey insights about the cultural context that are otherwise almost negligible in the production. Eklavya, is a minor character, dispensable as far as the story goes. But by focusing upon this episode, Brook, almost contrary to his dramatization principle which eliminates everything except that which is necessary for the furthering of the central narrative, is able to suggest, as Bharucha points out, "the interplay of authority and obedience in the tradition of the teacher-student relationship."[75] At this point Brook is not just telling the story, but rather highlighting an important aspect of the *guru-shishya parampara* (teacher-student tradition), central to the culture of the age of *The Mahabharata,* a significance that gets refracted into the text as a commentary on the Pandavas' and the Kauravas' relationship with their elders, especially Drona and Bhishma.

Similarly, during the dice game and Draupadi's humiliation in the Kaurava court, her appeal to Krishna to protect her honor is poignantly effected. While there are possibilities for improving this scene, the pace, development and tension are extremely dramatic. Draupadi's helpless situation, but powerful invocation to Madhava (Krishna), her only recourse amidst her horrifying humiliation, is effective precisely because Brook chooses to incorporate the actual Sanskrit *sloka* (verse) from the original text, sung in Sanskrit in the incantatory mode for sloka enunciation. Without subtitles, Brook's Western audiences would have definitely missed the literal meaning of the words.

However, the dramatization definitely communicates the power of faith that is the core of the Bhakti tradition in Indian philosophy, and later of a similar tradition in poetry.[76] Needless to say, the effects of this sequence are derived from the much-maligned Classical or high tradition as opposed to Brook's declared privileging of the low or folk tradition as the inspiration for his interpretation of *The Mahabharata.* With a powerful narrative like *The Mahabharata,* which has a symbolic significance that seems to transcend time and culture and would elicit a powerful response from the audience anyway, Brook need not have worried about accessibility and should have devoted his energies to coming to grips with the culture that his text embodies. His project of universal signification would not have been derailed by cultural contextualization. However, an opposed impulse in Brook's project was also that of exporting the exotic images of Indian culture while simultaneously claiming affiliation with a multicultural syncretism. The realization of this motive has entangled Brook in a whole host of political, ideological, and cultural contradictions that he, swept away in the postmodern culture of "commodity aesthetics"[77] has hardly confronted.

III.

> The point is not to eliminate the productive tension between the political and the aesthetic, between history and the text, between engagement and the mission of art. The point is to heighten that tension, even to rediscover it and to bring it back into focus in the arts as well as in criticism.[78]

On the face of it, Brook's *The Mahabharata* can be seen as a typical example of a postmodern style as James Collins defines it: "a radical eclecticism built on juxtapositions of conflicting discourses (high art, popular culture, contemporary and historical, etc.) where the text becomes a 'site' of intersecting modes of representation."[79] While eclecticism has more or less come to be recognized as the hallmark of the postmodern, the key word in Collins' version of what Andreas Huyssens would define as the "postmodernism of resistance"[80] is "radical." A measure of Brook's radicality would enable us to determine whether his text is merely a reflection of the postmodern cultural context in its fascination with other cultures, its primitivist nostalgia, its randomly chosen images and motifs reflective of a culture of eclecticism and commodity aesthetics, embodying therefore an "easy postmodernism of the 'anything goes' variety," or an example of the "postmodernism of resistance."

The answer to this problem can come from examining another aspect of Collins' discussion of the postmodern—the emphasis placed on cultural context by so many postmodern artists who have taken up a situational position in their desire to speak "in the language of a particular culture" renewing an interest in "the historical traditions that constitute it."[81] The potential for constructing "polylogic rather than dialogic relationships with the 'already said'" can transform postmodern eclecticism's appropriative tendencies into historically dynamic, analytical insights about the relationships "among the layers of accumulated representations" and "the morphological continuity of specific culture(s)."[82] But to do that it would be absolutely essential to confront the issue of a specific historical context and not obfuscate it as Brook has done. While interesting as an idea, Brook's entire project of interpreting *The Mahabharata* for modern audiences has been marred by the contradictions of vision and purpose that Brook, reacting to the pressures of the postmodern cultural market, has got himself entangled in. Unable to confront the deep-seated Eurocentrism of earlier attempts at interpreting Oriental texts, almost unwittingly perhaps falling in line with this tradition, Brook has managed to exoticize the culture that he and Carriere dedicated a decade of their life to. He may have been able to avoid it if he had actually realized, as Shohat and Stam point out, that "a radical multiculturalism . . . has to do less with artifacts, canons, and representations than with the communities 'behind' the artifacts."[83] The result would have been not an exoticizing of other cultures, but a "normalizing"[84] of them. In the process, Brook would not have eliminated "the productive tension between the political and the aesthetic, between history and the text, between engagement and the mission of art," and would have been able to actually demonstrate a "postmodernism of resistance."[85]

Endnotes

1. Charles Jencks, *The Language of Postmodern Architecture* (New York: Rizzoli, 1984), p. 95. Cited by James Collins, "Postmodernism and Cultural Practice: Redefining the Parameters," *Screen*, 28.2 (Spring 1987), p. 25.

2. Fredric Jameson, *Postmodernism, or, The Cultural Logic of Late Capitalism* (Durham: Duke University Press, 1993), p. x.

3. The genesis and the history of their interest in and involvement with the epic has been recounted by both Brook and Carriere in various interviews. Apparently Brook first encountered an image from *The Mahabharata* in 1966 while doing a play about Vietnam. A young Indian, Asif Currimbhoy, came up to him with a six-page play on the *Bhagavad Gita* which excited Brook's interest. He toyed with the idea of beginning his Vietnam play with the central image from the *Bhagavad Gita*—that of a warrior on the verge of battle stopping dead in his tracks to ask the fundamental question about why he should fight and destroy those who, while his enemies, are actually his kith and kin. Arjuna's (one of the Pandavas) question is answered by Krishna (believed to be an incarnation of the Lord Vishnu of the Hindu Trinity, born as a human to rid the world of evil), and what follows is the renowned *Bhagavad Gita*, which even today forms the core of Hindu philosophical and ethical thought. Though Brook did not use the image for the play *US*, his interest had been piqued, and in 1975 over several months, he and Carriere received *The Mahabharata,* in the Indian tradition, orally from Philippe Lavastine, a Sanskrit professor. Following their commitment to make it their next project, Brook and Carriere, and later the actors, made several visits to

India, and witnessed several performances of parts of *The Mahabharata* in several different performative traditions of India—Theyyem, Mudiattu, Yakshagana, Chaau, and Jatra, to name a few. From the myriad impressions generated by these visits they drew the images for their version of *The Mahabharata.* See the interviews of Peter Brook; Jean-Claude Carriere; the musician, Toshi Tsuchitori; the designer, Chloe Obolensky; and three of the actors by Richard Schechner, Mathilde La Bordonnie, Joel Jouanneau, and Georges Banu in *The Drama Review,* 30 (Spring 1986), hereafter cited as the *TDR* interviews. Also see the Foreword and Introduction to the script of the play, Jean-Claude Carriere's *The Mahabharata: A Play based upon the Indian Classic Epic,* trans. from the French by Peter Brook (New York: Harper & Row, 1987).

4. Vijay Mishra, "The Great Indian Epic and Peter Brook," David Williams, ed. *Peter Brook and The Mahabharata: Critical Perspectives* (London & New York: Routledge, 1991), p. 201.

5. From the SBS Television's (Australia) advertisement for the "Special Encore" screening of *The Mahabharata* within two weeks of the very successful first telecast of the film on October 7, 1989. From the material circulated as part of the press handout for the New Delhi screening on November 1, 1989.

6. The production with its multiracial cast was seen as a wonderful example of the interculturalism of Brook's work. Richard Schechner thinks that of "all the intentionally intercultural productions" he had ever seen the *Mahabharata* was "the finest example of something genuinely syncretic," the *TDR* interviews, op. cit., p. 57.

7. *The Mahabharata,* and the other Indian epic, the *Ramayana,* are foundational texts of Hindu culture. Believed traditionally to have been composed by sage Vyasa, *The Mahabharata* is a poem that has over the centuries had additions by successive generations of brahmin priests who interpolated sections on morality, philosophy, theology and statecraft into the central narrative of conflict and strife between two related families. The Kauravas cheat their cousins, the Pandavas, of their legitimate share of the kingdom after defeating them in an unfair game of dice. After a thirteen-year exile, the Pandavas return as agreed to claim their share only to be repulsed. A massive war—the battle of Kurukshetra—is fought that aligns all the major and minor kingdoms of the region on one side or the other. The Kauravas are defeated, but not before an almost apocalytic end is enacted. Not quite, however; for one of the descendants of the Pandavas survives to rebuild the edifice of righteousness that the Kauravas had completely destroyed. *The Mahabharata* has been considered traditionally to be *itihasa* or history, and while the mythic and poetic qualities of the epic are undisputed, scholars do accept that there is a historical basis to the poem and have dated the battle of Kurukshetra at approximately 3200 BC. There is no agreement between scholars about the date of composition, and they have placed the poem somewhere between 400 BC and 200 AD. The discrepancy between the dates of the battle and those of the poem's composition are glaringly evident. In this context, it is worth remembering that Sanskrit literature and treatises were orally passed on from generation to generation. It is possible then that no written evidence of the text may be available before the dates mentioned, but that the core of the poem had been composed much earlier and handed down to successive generations. Even today *The Mahabharata,* with its central theological and philosophical composition, the *Bhagavad Gita,* is central to the social, cultural, ritualistic, and aesthetic life of Hindu India.

8. Peter Brook, Foreword to Carriere's play, p. xiv.

9. Georges Banu, the *TDR* interviews, p. 68. In the context of a culture in which *The Mahabharata* is not only a living performance text in more ways than one, but also one that is still seen as the foundation of its ethical and philosophical tenets, Banu's comment is absurd, to say the least.

10. Amita Malik, "Peter Brook's epic experiment," *The Statesman*, November 5, 1989.

11. Divya Raina, "Epic Effort," *The Sunday Observer*, November 5, 1989, p. 14.

12. The "age of Kali"—the dark age of destruction, and moral and social degradation. In Hindu mythology, each world cycle is divided into four ages, or *yugas*. These are: 1. *Krta* or *Satya,* 2. *Treta,* 3. *Dvapar,* and 4. *Kali*—the present period. The first three have already elapsed and we are living through the fourth. See Heinrich Zimmer, *Myths and Symbols in Indian Art and Civilization*, Joseph Campbell, ed. (Princeton: Princeton University Press, 1974 [1946]), pp. 11-19 for a definition and discussion of the concept of the *yugas*. Carriere and Brook use the sense of kali-yuga as "the age of destruction" throughout their rendering of the epic. Yudhishthira, the eldest of the Pandavas, prophesies the beginning of "the age of Kali, the black time," just before the battle of Kurukshetra.

13. The cosmic order of the universe, upon which is based the moral order of the world. Its multiple significances include religion, duty, law, morality, and custom. See Zimmer, *Myths and Symbols* for a discussion of *dharma*, pp. 13-16. Also see Margaret and James Stutley's *A Dictionary of Hinduism: Its Mythology, Folklore and Development—1500 BC-AD 1500* (New Delhi: Heritage Publishers, 1986), p. 76. Carriere describes *dharma* thus, saying that "truth," "justice," or "duty" fall short of the mark: "Dharma is the law on which rests the order of the world. Dharma is also the personal and secret order each human being recognises as his own, the law he must obey. And the dharma of the individual, if it is respected, is the warrant of its faithful reflection of a cosmic order" (Carriere's introduction to the text of the play, p. xii).

14. The text of the play, op. cit., p. 3. Carriere explains his use of the title of the epic: *Maha* in Sanskrit means "great" or "complete." *Bharata* is the name of the legendary ancestor of the Pandavas and Kauravas, and therefore the name implies a family or clan. "The title can therefore be understood as 'The Great History of the Bharatas.' But in an extended meaning, bharata means Hindu, and even more generally, man. So it can also be interpreted as 'The Great History of Mankind'" (Introduction to the text of the play, p. viii). Bharata, even today is the Hindi name for India. That is why the epic in India has always been regarded as its ancient "history."

15. Cited by Andreas Huyssen, "Mapping the Postmodern," *After the Great Divide* (Bloomington: Indiana, 1986), p. 187.

16. Ibid., p. 196.

17. Ibid., p. 197.

18. Ella Shohat and Robert Stam, in their discussion of the meaning of Eurocentrism, cite Barbara Kirshenblatt-Gimblett who says that the West "separates forms from their performers, converts those forms into influences, brings those influences into the center, leaves the living sources on the margin, and pats itself on the back for being so cosmopolitan." See their *Unthinking Eurocentrism: Multiculturalism and the Media* (London & New York: Routledge, 1994), p. 3.

19. Ibid., p. 47.

20. Andreas Huyssen, "Mapping the Postmodern," p. 185.

21. Sadanand Menon, "Peter Brook's *Mahabharata*: Demise of 'Interculturalism,'" *The Economic Times*, Dec 18, 1991. This article was reprinted from *The Hindu*, Dec 29, 1989 where it had appeared as a review of the Delhi premiere of the film, to coincide with the beginning of the television screenings.

22. Gautam Dasgupta, *"The Mahabharata*: Peter Brook's 'Orientalism,'" *Performing Arts Journal 30,* vol. X no. 3 (1987), p. 10.

23. Rustom Bharucha, "Peter Brook's *'Mahabharata'*: A View from India," *Framework* 35, (1988), p. 35.

24. Paul Ricoeur, "Universal Civilization and National Cultures," in *History and Truth*, trans. Chas. A. Kelby (Evanston: Northwestern University Press, 1965), p. 283.

25. Ibid.

26. Fredric Jameson, *Postmodernism*, p. x.

27. From Paul Gilroy's phrase "ethnic insiderism." Cited by Shohat and Stam, *Unthinking Eurocentrism*, p. 343. They speak of the need to avoid the twin traps of "ethnic insiderism" and facile appropriation.

28. Brook, the *TDR* interviews, p. 68.

29. In Brook's claim, for instance that they wanted to tell the story as one "rooted in Indian earth," or Carriere's claim that he did not translate some of the Sanskrit words like *kshatrya* or *dharma* into French because they represented "the deepest and most thought-out notions of Indian culture" (the *TDR* interviews, pp. 68, 73).

30. Ibid., p.64.

31. "In the music, in the costumes, in the movements, we have tried to suggest the flavor of India without pretending to be what we are not" (Brook in his foreword to his English translation of Carriere's play, p. xvi). Rustom Bharucha has pointed out that had Brook been aware of "the numerous metaphors of cooking that had beeen used in Bharata's *Natyashastra* and other aesthetic commentaries on the *rasa* (literally "taste") of a performance, he might have used the the word with more caution." Flavor is the "outcome of a process wherein specific ingredients have been seasoned and blended with spices in particular combinations," and therefore the "flavor" of Indian culture has a "definite context" that cannot be ignored or suggested through a melange of images that have not been contextualised (Cf. Bharucha, "Peter Brook's *'Mahabharata'*: A View from India," p. 37).

32. The term implies essence and therefore can signify sap, juice, water, mercury etc. as the essence of life. In performance theory, Bharata's *Natyashastra* outlines the rasa theory of aesthetics. The theory posits that a performance must endeavour to represent and evoke the essential human emotions enabling the spectator to experience and savor them. The aesthetic experience restores the equanimity of mind and in its heightened emotional state is comparable to a spiritual experience.

33. Brook, the *TDR* interviews, p. 55.

34. Brook to Melvyn Bragg in the program "A Portrait of Brook" presented by Bragg on CBS.

35. Ella Shohat and Robert Stam, *Unthinking Eurocentrism*, p. 359.

36. Rustom Bharucha, "Peter Brook's *'Mahabharata,'*" p. 34.

37. Peter Brook to Melvyn Bragg on CBS.

38. Shohat and Stam, *Unthinking Eurocentrism*, p. 47.

39. Carriere in conversation with Richard Schechner and Peter Brook, the *TDR* interviews, p. 63.

40. As expressed by Carriere, the *TDR* interviews, p. 73.

41. Shohat and Stam, *Unthinking Eurocentrism*, p. 345.

42. Brook, the *TDR* interviews, p. 70. There is some confusion here in Brook's statements, especially as to the implication of the term "popular," and the popular performance style that

he identifies as similar to a Western one. For popular performance in India can only be identified with the style of popular Indian cinema that in its dominant melodramatic mode is extremely different from that of the psychological realism of Western popular forms. But perhaps he means "folk" forms of performance for he does state that they "mustn't speak from above but from below," implying a connection with the audience that works at a primordial level. But folk traditions of performance are fast disappearing or are being transformed radically under the pressure of mass mediated and commodified cultures of the contemporary globalized environment. Where folk forms still have a significance, they cannot be divorced from their specific ritualistic and cultural functions.

43. Mallika Sarabhai, the only Indian in Brook's team of actors, is a well-known Classical dancer of the "Bharatanatyam" form. However, she has hardly used her dance training in the performance. As an actress, she is perhaps the least effective of Brook's troupe.

44. A maroon-colored powder used by Hindus, especially women, on their forehead as a mark of identity. The symbol has multiple significances. Its use symbolizes a mark of obeisance and respect for the Universal Spirit that is the center of Consciousness and resides in the middle of the forehead, as does Shiva's third eye. Its use also signifies a mark of respect for the feminine, creative principle of the universe. Apart from these abstract, philosophical significances, the use of kumkum is also a sign of femininity, of marriage, and of course of religious identity. Kumkum is a must in all ritual worship.

45. A rustic cot made of bamboo poles and woven with jute rope.

46. The elephant-headed son of Shiva, the Destroyer of the Hindu Trinity of Brahma, the Creator, and Vishnu, the Preserver. According to myth, Ganesha was created by his mother Parvati while Shiva was away. One day asked by her to keep guard while she bathed, Ganesha refused his father Shiva entry into his mother's chamber. Annoyed, Shiva kills him only to face an uncontrollably angry Parvati. In order to pacify her he agrees to bring him back to life, but only after he acquires the head of the first living being that Shiva comes across. That very moment, an elephant passes by, and Ganesha is brought to life, but now has an elephant head. Ganesha was blessed with a boon from his mother that he would be one of the most important of the Gods. He is invoked before every major ceremony. No ritual worship can begin before an invocation to Ganesha. According to tradition, he is also the scribe of *The Mahabharata,* and writes as Vyasa composes the epic. As a patron of the performing arts, he is invoked before every performance. The mask of Ganesha is a common prop in several folk theater traditions.

47. Considered the author of *The Mahabharata.*

48. See note 14.

49. Brook explained the role of the child to Georges Banu as one who is "there to receive and give us that which is in *The Mahabharata*." Even in the original text the story was told to a young king so that he could prepare himself for life. Brook did not want to begin with a king because then there would be a distance for the audience. On the other hand, he felt that they would be able to identify directly with and sympathize with a child. (Cf. the *TDR* interviews, p. 71.)

50. Amba, Ambika and Ambalika are the daughters of the King of Benaras or Kashi. The three princesses are won in a tournament by Bhishma, the grandfather of the Kauravas and the Pandavas. While Ambika and Ambalika are married to Bhishma's two brothers Vichitravirya and Chitrangada, Amba asks Bhishma to marry her. Bound by a vow of celibacy, Bhishma declines and asks Amba to return home. Amba had been in love with King Salya. When she goes to him and offers herself in marriage, he declines to accept her since she was another man's prize. Amba burns with the desire to avenge herself against Bhishma, and retires to the forest to gain power by extreme asceticism. Pleased by her devotion, Shiva

grants her her wish on the condition that she can realize it only in her next life. Amba burns herself, and is then reborn as Prince Shikhandi, who kills Bhishma in the great battle of Kurukshetra. In the battle, Shikhandi fights on the side of the Pandavas, and his killing of Bhishma marks an important setback for the Kauravas. Gandhari and Kunti are the wives of Dhritarashtra and Pandu and the mothers of the Kauravas and the Pandavas respectively. Gandhari is from Khandahar in Central Asia while Kunti is the daughter of Sura, a Yadava King from northern India, and also the aunt of Krishna. In the battle Gandhari's family fought for the Kauravas while that of Kunti were on the side of the Pandavas.

51. Brook in his foreword to the text of Carriere's play, p. xvi.

52. "My base is always in documentation" (Chloe Obolensky to Georges Banu, the *TDR* interviews, p. 79).

53. Kali is the Goddess of Destruction venerated all over India, but especially in Bengal. As the consort and wife of Shiva, she also has benign forms and in that manifestation is known as Uma or Parvati. Kali also symbolizes eternal time and hence, she both gives life and destroys it. For a detailed discussion of the implications of Kali, see Stutley, *A Dictionary of Hinduism*, pp. 137-38.

54. Kalaraipayattu is a martial art form from Kerala that has influenced folk as well as classical theater like Kathakali. Other forms like Kutiyattam do not use techniques from the martial arts. This pattern is evident in folk theater in different parts of the country. The Chau theatrical form from the eastern part of India (the states of Bengal, Bihar and Orissa) has also been influenced by the martial art of the region, while the repertoire includes themes from both the epics and other texts of legends like the *Puranas*.

55. Vyasa to the Boy, in Carriere's text of the play, p. 107.

56. Carriere's text of the play, p. xii.

57. Rustom Bharucha, "Peter Brook's '*Mahabharata*,'" p. 39.

58. Like *dharma*, *karma* too is a concept that cannot be translated into a single-word equivalent. It literally means action, but is identified with *dharma* as duty. The *Bhagavad Gita* contains the most well-known exposition on the doctrine of *karma-yoga*, or the path of action, as one mode of liberation from the cycles of birth. Krishna advocates performing one's duty without thought of the consequences as the path of the true *karma-yogi*, the one who fulfils his duty as action.

59. That which every individual recognizes as the law that s/he must obey. As Carriere puts it, "the dharma of the individual, if it is respected, is the warrant of its faithful reflection of a cosmic order" (Introduction to the text of the play, p. xii). Rustom Bharucha points out that any discussion/delineation of the concept of "swadharma" would have to take into account the culture in which a person is born (desa), the period of historic time in which s/he lives (kala), the efforts required at different stages of the individual's life (srama), and the innate psychobiological traits which are the heritage of an individual's previous lives (gunas) ("Peter Brook's '*Mahabharata*,'" p. 39).

60. The actions and experiences that an individual accumulates through previous lives, and which therefore effect the "innate psychobiological traits" (Bharucha) and the destiny of the individual in the present.

61. Gautam Dasgupta, "*The Mahabharata*: Peter Brook's 'Orientalism,'" p. 12.

62. Bharucha, "Peter Brook's '*Mahabharata*,'" p. 38.

63. Christopher Innes, *Avant-Garde Theatre: 1892-1992* (London & New York: Routledge, 1993), p. 147.

64. *Upanishads* are Hindu philosophical texts that explore the question of the reality and meaning of the universe and of mankind within it. The form of these texts is generally that of scholastic and philosophical discourse between either a teacher and his disciples, or between scholars debating a theoretical and philosophical point. They are said to have been composed between 700 and 300 BC.

65. Brook, the *TDR* interviews, p. 71.

66. Paul Ricoeur, "Universal Civilization and National Cultures," p. 283. The emphasis in this quotation is mine.

67. Shohat and Stam, *Unthinking Eurocentrism*, p. 313.

68. In an interview with Banu, Brook responded to the question about whether he had cast actors to incarnate certain aspects of humanity by saying that he does not work by beginning with schematic ideas and does not do casting "a la UNESCO," (the *TDR* interviews, p. 68). David Williams while taking into account the criticisms against Brook from the post-colonialist perspectives of critics like Gautam Dasgupta, Rustom Bharucha, and Sadanand Menon feels that Brook is always going to be the "villain" in such post-colonialist readings simply because he represents the "economic, and *ipso facto* cultural, power and hierarchy of the west throughout the history of its relationship with Asia." However, throughout the history of Brook's Center, "cultural difference and individuality have been cherished and celebrated within the work as sources of creative friction," and that there is no question of the "kind of patronizing tokenism implicit in suggestions of a UNESCO-style company casting policy." In countering Sadanand Menon's charge of a racist bias in the casting and roles of black actors like Mamadou Dioume who are either cast in the racist stereotypes of the ignoble savage, the natural cannibal, or as demonic forces, Williams is at pains to point out that a number of white actors were tried for the role and found inadequate. He concedes that Brook should have been more aware of the possibility and probability of such critical responses. However, he insists that the only principle followed by Brook in his working with a multiracial cast has always been to open himself and his productions to the "creative input of culturally diverse individuals within the company." See David Williams, "Theatre of Innocence and of Experience: Peter Brook's International Centre—An Introduction," in his edited volume, *Peter Brook and The Mahabharata: Critical Perspectives*, op. cit., pp. 24-28.

69. Sadanand Menon is strongly critical of Brook's "naturalism" in a script that claims to resist it throughout. The black Bhima while in exile in the forest meets a force of the forest, a *rakshasi*, naturally a black woman. They mate and "naturally" have a black son, Ghatotkacha. Moreover, when Bhima fulfils his vow to avenge Draupadi's humiliation at the hands of Dushasana by killing him and drinking his blood, what is reinforced "is a viewpoint that subconsciously pervades the narrative—the White West's conviction of the 'primitivism' of the African and the Asian, the racist stereotype of the 'ignoble savage,' of the black man's natural cannibalism." Menon finds this "filling in of our imagination and fantasy . . . revoltingly negative and . . . outrageously crude." He feels that it is obvious that "Brook lacked the guts to show a white man drinking human blood" ("Peter Brook's *Mahabharata*").

70. See the text of the play, p. 90.

71. Here the word "karmic" is related to the idea of *dharma* as governed by one's past *sanskara*. See notes 58, 59, and 60.

72. That which is not *dharma*. While Brook claims in an interview that the concepts of "good and evil are replaced by understanding and ignorance" and that in *The Mahabharata* there is a battle between the two since "our planet . . . is covered with the darkness, not of the devil, but the darkness of stupidity, the darkness of ignorance," his production does not reflect these ideas. See Brook's interview with David Britton, "Theatre, Popular and Special, and the

Perils of Cultural Piracy," in David Williams, ed. *Peter Brook and The Mahabharata: Critical Perspectives,* op. cit., p. 55.

73. The text of the play, p. 189.

74. Mallika Sarabhai, though strongly supportive of Brook's encouragement and support of his actors, also points out that during the course of the rehearsals she would often "quibble, or defend some detail ferociously." But Carriere would explain that a "European audience deprived of any frames of reference" for the epic would understand Brook's and his version more clearly. That Brook had complete control over the actors and the interpretation is obvious from the fact that, despite her objections to details and to certain responses to characters, Sarabhai still states "unequivocally" that she feels that Brook's representation is right and that there is nothing there that she would be ashamed of, or for which she "would have to apologize to Indians" (In David Williams, ed. *Peter Brook and The Mahabharata: Critical Perspectives,* op. cit., pp. 101, 103.

75. Rustom Bharucha, "Peter Brook's '*Mahabharata*,'" p. 41. Eklavaya is a minor character in the epic. Nevertheless, he is extremely important in terms of the function he performs in the narrative, both in terms of the plot and the theme. Eklavaya is devoted to Drona, the guru of the Kauravas and Pandavas. Ekalavaya approaches Drona and requests Drona to accept him as a pupil. After testing him Drona refuses saying that he is of low birth and he cannot accept him. Ekalavaya withdraws into the forest and remains devoted to Drona, worshipping a mud idol of his guru for inspiration while he continues training himself. One day Drona discovers his skill as Ekalavaya has pierced seven arrows in the jaws of a dog in the span of a single bark. Drona is not pleased, and demands Ekalavaya's right thumb as his "guru dakshina" or the teacher's reward. Ekalavaya obliges, and Drona thus ensures that Arjuna, the Pandava, remains his most accomplished pupil.

76. The word *bhakti* literally means "devotion," and signifies the cult of personal devotion as a means of realizing God. In his discourse to Arjuna that forms the "Bhagavada Gita" in the *Mahabharata*, Krishna explains the three paths to self-realization and liberation from the cycles of birth—Bhakti or devotion, Karma or selfless action, and Gyana or Knowledge. Beginning in the medieval period, from the twelfth century onwards in India, the Bhakti cult brought about a virtual cultural renaissance in the country—a movement that saw the birth of several vernacular literatures. At the center of this moment were saint poets from the lower classes. During the nineteenth-century era of social reform and later during the national movement, the lives and examples of the Bhakti saints were used to communicate the message of social and religious equality, and make a bid for reform within indigenous traditions since the radical nature of the Bhakti movement centered in its rejection of the ritualistic structure of Brahmanical, Hindu religion. Its widespread popularity came from the simple and egalitarian message of faith and devotion to a personal God that the saints preached.

77. Andreas Huyssen, "Mapping the Postmodern," p. 210.

78. Ibid., p. 221.

79. James Collins, "Postmodernism and Cultural Practice: Redefining the Parameters," *Screen*, 28.2 (Spring 1987): p. 12.

80. Huyssen distinguishes the "postmodernism of resistance" from the "easy postmodernism of the 'anything goes' variety," ("Mapping the Postmodern, p. 220).

81. James Collins, "Postmodernism and Cultural Practice," p. 21.

82. Ibid., p. 22.

83. Shohat and Stam, *Unthinking Eurocentrism*, p. 47.

84. From Shohat and Stam's "the media can normalize as well as exoticize other cultures," Ibid., p. 347.

85. I would like to thank Brent Plate, David Jasper and Richard Allen for their invaluable comments on earlier drafts of this paper.

Part Five: Ending Community

Imagining Nothing and
Imaging Otherness in Buddhist Film

Francisca Cho

The category of "otherness" is by now a well-established construct in academic discourse and it engages the substantive realms of social and cultural studies as well as the methodological concerns of hermeneutics and epistemology. It is also a category that is saturated with the political and intellectual history of the West, and which speaks in the idiom of Western European and American encounters with alien communities. The East Asian context of the following essay might very well demand an alternative narrative of otherness, informed by that regions' own representations of outsiders and barbarians. Although this task is too large and peripheral to my current purpose, a more limited focus on the Buddhist manifestations of otherness is highly instructive. What the examination reveals, in sum, is the semiotic reversibility of "otherness," both socially and spiritually, which in turn questions the stability of the concept itself.

Because Buddhism is most distinct and identifiable in its monastic incarnation, the community of Buddhist monks and nuns (known as the *sangha*) comprises an "other" set apart by its desire to abandon secular life in exchange for higher spiritual goods. The self-segregation of the monastic institution, which divides a community against itself, has been particularly troubling in the East Asian context, and it also conforms to contemporary Western perceptions of the marginal status of many religious communities. In response, Buddhist discourse has countered the social problem of otherness through a metaphysical strategy that both inverts and enriches the otherness of spiritual transcendence. One might even say that it has been a specialty of Chan Buddhism, in particular, to deconstruct the otherness of enlightenment, which in turn has consequences for the social location of religious practice. This Chan response will be the keystone of the film analysis to come, but it also offers interesting perspectives for relating religion and art generally, as we shall see. Concomitantly, the Buddhist irony towards the construct of otherness will hopefully encourage the Western intellect to treat this concept more playfully, as an illusory instrument capable of drawing and redrawing false boundaries solely for the purpose of the real insights that such sport can reveal.

Within this broader framework, the other contribution of this paper is to argue for what I call a non-ideological, cultic way of viewing film. The growing interest in the relationship between religion and film provides us with an opportunity to articulate fully the way in which visual images signify meaning. As scholars of religion who are immersed in logocentric forms of communication, it is tempting to treat film as yet another text that discloses itself in the same way. It is interesting, I propose, to try to articulate and appreciate film as a "cultic" experience that participates in a broader and distinctly non-logocentric tradition of religious signification. The cultic mode of signification can be elaborated through a theory of religious meaning that dovetails with Chan Buddhist "antidiscourses" about the experience of otherness, or religious breakthrough. Hence, the theoretical portion of this essay is inextricably bound up with the religious and cultural milieu in which the analysis is situated.

The Buddhist film

Why Has Bodhi-Dharma Left for the East? is a Buddhist film. The title is derived from a Chan (Zen) Buddhist koan, which is a public record of dialogues between medieval Chinese masters and their disciples.[1] The figure Bodhidharma (460-534) that is evoked in this koan riddle is the Indian monk who journeyed to China and whom Chan Buddhism recognizes as the first patriarch of its lineage. The film tells the story of three contemporary Buddhist monks living in a dilapidated hermitage on a remote mountaintop above the main temple complex, and high above a bustling city. Haejin is the orphan child who was discovered and adopted by Hyegok, the Chan master of the temple. Kibong is the young disciple who abandoned his impoverished mother and sister in order to seek self-transcendence through religion. Hyegok, the mature master, guides both disciples as he himself moves towards death. The Korean director, Bae Yong-kyun, was drawn to Asian philosophy as a troubled adolescent and spent some time in Buddhist study and practice. In college, Bae focused on painting and art history, eventually earned a doctorate and joined the Faculty of Fine Arts as a teacher of painting. In fulfilling a lifelong dream of making a film, Bae completely circumvented the mainstream film industry and single-handedly wrote, directed, filmed, and edited *Bodhi*. It was released in 1989, after ten years in the making, and garnered recognition at the Cannes Film Festival and Korea's first ever director's prize at the Locarno Film Festival.

The label of "Buddhism" or "Buddhist" can be somewhat of a burden, as Bae admits. He states, "I'm afraid to call myself a Buddhist because belief cannot be attained easily nor can it be measured."[2] *Bodhi* would probably disappoint the viewer in search of discursive explanations of Buddhist dogma. If this betrays the point of calling *Bodhi* a Buddhist film, then Bae's own self-accounting, at least, follows Buddhist tradition. "The ten years I committed to the making of *Bodhi* were a kind of practice for me," he states. "Even though I didn't practice conventionally, the process of creating that movie was like holding a koan in one's mind."[3] To harness one's art as one's spiritual practice

Fig. 9.1 "Following Hyegok's careful instructions, Kibong cremates the body of his teacher in an old chest, pounds the bones and sprinkles the ash and dust on the mountain."

(From the film *Why has the Bodhi-Dharma Left for the East?*. Still courtesy of Milestone Film & Video, New York) invokes centuries of Chan tradition, which was perhaps most broadly—and certainly most famously—realized in Japanese Zen.[4] The *zenga*, or Zen arts of Japan, is comprised mostly of the paintings and calligraphy of Zen masters, but has also been associated with all manner of cultural practices (e.g., tea ceremony, flower arrangement, Nō drama), making for a broad aesthetic association. If some object to such a broad usage of the term Zen art, its very existence nevertheless exemplifies the Chan wisdom that enlightenment is "nothing special," that it inheres in the mundane things of this world and that it can be expressed through worldly activity—a wisdom that is traditionally and paradoxically contemplated in isolated hermitages.

The tension presupposed by the dichotomy of spiritual and worldly disciplines has long dogged East Asian Buddhism's embrace of the arts, and self-reflexively forms a central motif in the telling of *Bodhi*. Kibong is the most conflicted figure in the movie—a young man who has abandoned his responsibilities to his family for the higher goal of spiritual release. His flight to the mountaintop and his search for freedom, however, succeeds only in exchanging the burdens of ordinary life for the burden of spiritual desire. Chan Buddhism recognizes this irony of religion, leading the ninth century Master Linji (J. Rinzai) to famously prompt his disciples to "kill the Buddha." The otherness and distance of what spiritual discipline seeks are illusions that must ultimately be violated. The perceived absence of the Buddha in the ordinary world breeds an anguish that Kibong attempts to master through his protracted austerities. Kibong finally attains his release from both worldly and spiritual burdens through the methodical task of attending to the death of his master. Following Hyegok's careful instructions, Kibong cremates the body of his teacher in an old chest (Fig. 9.1), pounds the bones and sprinkles the ash and dust on the mountain. Hyegok's passage from distinct human form to an indistinguishable extension of nature enacts the endless passage between form and emptiness that is at the heart of Chan doctrine. What this polarizing language obstructs, however, is an understanding of their ultimate interchangeability. As the master intones to a lumbering frog in the opening lines of the film, "There is no beginning and no end. Nothing is immutable; everything changes. That thing which does not come into being, does not die." The master's reversion to emptiness is indistinguishable from any form-governed presence.

In its visual mode, the film's mountain setting and its intense and ravishing contemplation of earth, water, and fire asserts a presence that is vivid and perhaps sufficient to stand in for the absent Buddha that Kibong seeks (Fig. 9.2). Bae's painterly attentiveness to imagery—for indeed, *Bodhi* is primarily a visual rather than a narrative film—draws self-consciously from traditional Chan icons and landscapes. The enforced contemplative pace of these images, especially brilliant when screened in the film's original 35 millimeter stock, challenges the viewer in much the same way as the enforced stillness of meditation. When these visual elements are applied to the quest of Kibong, the effect is highly evocative of the Chinese poetic trope of "Seeking the Recluse" that emerged during the Six Dynasties era (from the third century). The consistent conceit of this poetic theme is the absence of the recluse. The eight century poet Qiu Wei writes:

> On the precipitous peak, a bracken hut,
> A climb straight up of thirty *li*.
> I knock at the gate—no servant boy;
> I peak in the room—only a table and bench.
> If (or since) he's not abroad in his covered cart,
> He must be fishing in the autumn waters.
> This way and that, we do not meet
> After all that effort, in vain I gaze, awed.
> The color of grass in new rain,
> The sound of pines in an evening window.
> Arriving here at the summit of solitude,
> Perfect contentment washes over my heart.
> While there's been no understanding of guest and host,
> There is something of the sense of limpid purity.
> When my desire abated, then did I descend the mountain,
> What need is there to see the master?[5]

The recluse's absence is an incarnation of silence that renders the recluse and his presence superfluous because the poet's encounter with this absence is still beneficial. The absence is not literally a "nothing," of course, for the poet arrives "at the summit of solitude." The mountaintop that is the ubiquitous symbol of world renunciation is a space that allows the poet to stand in for the recluse and obtain a reverse enlightenment of aesthetic experience. For Kibong, the absent Buddha is configured in the passing of his master, which enables him to act upon his own realization—filmically narrated as a debate between two silhouetted figures that represent his splintered self—that it is impossible to be free of the world without embracing everything that is in it, particularly the suffering. Kibong enacts the mutual interpenetration of form and emptiness by leaving the mountain and reintegrating himself into the world below.

The construct of "otherness" is best understood in *Bodhi*, as well as in Chan Buddhism generally, both as a real and an illusory spiritual condition. Kibong's dilemma and resolution exemplifies a conflict between Chan ideology and Chan epistemological skepticism. The former asserts "original purity," or the doctrine that all beings, and, indeed even the insentient elements of nature itself, are possessed of "Buddha nature." Buddhism's telltale critical impulse, however, manifests itself in Chan's rejection of all truth claims as themselves the source of spiritual delusion. Bernard Faure refers to these conflicting impulses as Chan's "metaphysics of presence" and its subversion, respectively.[6] The metaphysics of presence is ultimately privileged, however, by Chan's spiritual orientation, which deploys its critical epistemological arsenal only as a means to a higher form of breakthrough.

The language of "sudden enlightenment" in Chan speaks of a bona fide irruption that disrupts the flow of ordinary experience; in Faure's words, an "irruption of the 'other'—the *totaliter aliter*" which is a positive catastrophe attested to by advanced practitioners.[7] The genuineness of this radical intuition is nevertheless endangered and alienated by the rationalizing effects of religious dogma and practice. Chan's images and narratives of violence conveys a tradition's attempt to combat linguistic rigidity in the context of institutional and historical practices.

Kibong's flight into spiritual isolation is indicative of a faulty concept of otherness that fails to grasp Buddhism's metaphysics of presence. This theme is present in other Buddhist-themed films from Korea, such as Im Kwon-taek's *Mandala* (1981) and *Come, Come, Come Upward* (1989), and Chung Ji-young's *Beyond the Mountain* (1991). Similar to the tale of Kibong in *Bodhi,* the protagonists of Im's films struggle with the polarized demands of religious retreat and community responsibility. David James argues that the primary point of Im's films is a humanistic concern with Korea's modern social condition. The drama and syntax of Im's work are provided by two opposing cultural and historical forces— the religious and the social, and the characters who struggle to resolve them.[8] For James, Im is more socially than religiously conscientious, and the director tests the responsiveness of Buddhist constructs in their ability to pose larger possibilities for Korean cultural discourse. One can also discern a strong social consciousness in Bae Yong-kyun's depiction of Kibong. During a trip to the city, Kibong pays a visit to his old, blind mother. His presence unannounced, he silently aids her pathetic figure as she fumbles about for her medication. Her helplessness is cruelly highlighted by the original purpose of Kibong's trip into the city—to beg alms in order to buy Chinese medicine for his ailing spiritual master. If the poverty and social deprivation that is Kibong's original milieu relentlessly tugs at his religious commitments, his final act of leaving the Chan hermitage overcomes the construct of otherness in exemplary Chan form.

The metaphysics of presence is perhaps the best rubric for interpreting the Buddhist ideological significations of the film. The otherness that is imagined to be distant and absent is repeatedly resolved through a metaphysics of presence. This mechanism is also apparent in the tale of the orphan novice Haejin. Unlike Kibong, the child Haejin has little experience of the world below the mountain. Haejin's innocence to the suffering of the world is significantly cued by the fact that he has no memories of his mother. When asked by Kibong if he is sad about the mother he has never known, Haejin responds, "How can I be sad, since I don't remember?" The film proceeds to destroy this presumption of Haejin's immunity to the world as it depicts his experience of killing a bird and being consequently haunted by the cries of its mate. One might discern a karmic circularity in these events as the death of the bird propels the death of Haejin's innocence of the world, narratively rendered as his plunge from a cliff to the waters below, startled by the maggot-ridden corpse of the bird and the fluttering of its mate. His initial struggles to swim give way to an inanimate and redemptive stillness, which allows his body to float to safety. The closure provided by this episode comes on the heels of the retributive scene of Haejin's karmic drama, when Haejin encounters a group of boys on an outing in the mountain. The scene cuts in on the idyllic play of the boys in a river. Eventually, Haejin is clearly distinguishable by his shaven head. The scene evolves deftly from children's guileless amusements to a spontaneous and ominous resolution—aided by slow motion photography—when the kids make repeated attempts to push Haejin under the water. The absent suffering and the absent mother are made present in Haejin's encounter with the birds, who, as a species, are perhaps perceptibly human in their tendency to bond for life. The indistinguishable capacity for attachment in human and animal alike underscores the Buddhist cosmological view that all things are created by the capacity of desire. Human and animal are juxtaposed in a different way a little further into Haejin's story. After surviving the river and wandering confusedly through the woods, Haejin sleeps and dreams of his mother. She opens her mouth and her image meshes with the bellow of an ox—a pervasive Buddhist icon—that had earlier escaped into the forest. The appearance of the ox comprises Bae Yong-kyun's most overt use of Chan art. The "oxherding pictures" go back to eleventh century China, when allegorical poems about Chan enlightenment were put together with illustrations that liken the journey to enlightenment to the oxherder who sights, chases, and finally rides an ox home through the forest. The allegorical association of the ox is clearly indicated in *Bodhi*. Two close-up shots of Kibong in solid and imposing meditation bracket the scene in which the ox—located in some narratively disjunctive space—breaks open from its confinement. Kibong's act of meditative concentration initiates a symbolic process of spiritual attainment that ties into Haejin's story. Before the slumber that brings his dream of his mother, Haejin encounters and chases the ox through the forest. The dream suggests another affirmation of the metaphysics of presence in which the formerly absent mother merges with the bovine cipher of Haejin's spiritual evolution. Absence and presence are interchangeable signs. Upon awakening, the ox leads Haejin back to the hermitage.

The metaphysics of presence has been used thus far to detail the Buddhist significations of *Bodhi*'s narrative structure. What does it offer for deciphering the film's attempts to *image* otherness; to portray the film's resolutions in visual form? Bae Yong-kyun's self-conscious use of traditional Chan imagery offers a visible clue. The director's use of landscape, setting, and specific icons such as birds, ox, frogs, and circles, all have the effect of animating classic Chan paintings on the screen. But we must resist the temptation to reduce the Buddhist significations of the film to a catalogue of visual Chan signs. A larger clue is offered, perhaps, in the director's description of his filmic art as Buddhist practice. The film moves beyond corresponding specific images to overt ideological meanings and offers the vestiges of an artist's own experience of insight—an experience that can be recreated by the viewer. The habit of viewing that this statement presumes, however, is worth explaining in some detail. Although the film image can be direct in its mimicking of reality, the act of *reading* images is intrinsically theory laden. I will take a detour

Fig. 9.2 "In its visual mode, the film's mountain setting and its intense and ravishing contemplation of earth, water, and fire asserts a presence that is vivid and perhaps sufficient to stand in for the absent Buddha that Kibong seeks." (From the film *Why has the Bodhi-Dharma Left for the East?*. Still courtesy of Milestone Film & Video, New York)

from the film, then, in order to sketch out the specific theory of reading that informs my treatment of *Bodhi*. This theory of reading ultimately will bring us back to the Buddhist metaphysics of presence.

Reading films: the ideological versus the cultic

The growing body of scholarly literature on the use of film in the study of religions attests to the charge that the vast majority of publications within religion and film treat film as if it is narratively and structurally no different than a novel or theological text.[9] In *Screening the Sacred: Religion, Myth, and Ideology in Popular American Film*, editors Joel W. Martin and Conrad E. Oswalt identify three primary modes of analyzing, as well as classifying, films with religious content. The *theological* mode deals with explicitly Christian and Jewish symbols and applies to them traditional methods of theological analysis. The *mythological* mode defines religion more broadly by seeking out psychological and cross-cultural archetypes of thought and action, particularly in "secular" films. The *ideological* mode evinces a postmodern concern with religion in its political and social dimensions, and often seeks to unmask the symbiosis between religious traditions and class, race, and gender structures.[10] All three modes of approach to classifying and interpreting film are extensions of methods applied to literary and theological texts.

These are recognizable ways of constituting the religious "meaning" of film that can be set apart from other forms of religious signification. For the purpose of putting two of these forms into contrastive relief, I designate the familiar, text-derived form of religious significance described above as examples of "ideological reading." I choose the phrase "ideological reading" (which subsumes the politically concerned, critical ideological mode of analysis) for etymological reasons. The root word "*ideo*" or "*ide(a)*" refers to a mental act or cognitive form of signification, giving to "ideology" its substantive meaning of a body of belief, doctrine, or myth. As a cognitive act, ideological meaning is primarily logocentric, and conforms to the significations and logic of speech. Hence, the primary quality of ideological readings is that it focuses on discursive claims. Whether or not the content is explicitly denominational, an ideological reading encompasses the strategy of reading novels and films as reasoned forms of religious expression. It also includes, alternatively, the strategy of critical ideological analysis because its task of unpacking the images and processes of representation also presumes logocentric structures of meaning.[11]

The theological, mythological, and ideological modes of film analysis can all be equally contrasted to what I call the cultic mode of signification. I interpret *Bodhi* as cultic art in which ideological content is subservient to its significance as ritual function. Although rituals usually have ideological content, their "meaning" is defined more relevantly as an event. The religious significance of these events, since we must attempt to verbalize it in some way, is that they create or manifest a momentous form of "presence." In our discourse, of course, we want to know how this "presence" may be understood, both by the practitioners and by us, the theorists. Very extensive definitions of this presence demonstrate how easily the ideological reading can overtake the cultic form of appreciation. One example is offered by Mircea Eliade's understanding of the sacrality of all art, by which he means that art functions as hierophany.[12] Eliade uses a theophantic model that imitates the Christian mystery of the Incarnation. Art is sacred because it reveals the divine by means of "something other" than itself. Crucial to this model is the doctrine that the divine is formless and limitless—completely "Other" (God), which through art can paradoxically take on limited material form (the Incarnation). Although Eliade's approach to art participates in a cultic reading, it is overshadowed by the ideological interpretation supplied by his use of explicitly Christian categories. A critical question that is raised by this example is whether or not, in our limited academic discourse, it is ever possible to avoid the hegemony of ideological readings. Before attending to this issue, I will first account for my own version of cultic reading.

The model that I employ borrows from David Freedberg's theory of response based on his art historical study of images.[13] According to Freedberg's cross-cultural theory, the power of images is that they make real what is represented, and hence present what is otherwise absent. The absent/present object can be understood as historical or spiritual, depending on the image and the viewer's culturally conditioned response to it. There is an inherent religious signification in this process, however, in that the painter's status as magician or seer in pre-modern cultures puts the artist on a par with divine creators. In Buddhist East Asia, this status is attested to by the numerous miracle tales of images that come alive, often in response to the behests and needs of the pious. The tales invest Buddhist icons with the power of movement and speech, and their lifelike quality is emphasized by details such as their ability to grow hair. These tales arise from an active cult of icons in which images are enlivened by the worshipper. Thus if artists have the ability to breathe life into icons, then this power is also dependent on a cultic imagination and a context of cultic practice.[14] Such a cultural environment mandates the perspicacity of the image maker, sometimes even in spite of himself, as the following tale recounts. An old book from the Silla dynasty (seventh to tenth century Korea) tells of how a court artist was ordered to paint a portrait of the Chinese Emperor's favorite beauty. While completing the finishing touches, the artist is so moved by his lifelike creation that he trembles and his brush slips, marking a mole below the portrait's navel. The Emperor is infuriated by this evidence of the painter's intimacy with the lady, but the artist is liberated from a death sentence after he successfully paints the lovely woman that the Emperor dreamt of the previous night. This lady turns out to be an image of the Bodhisattva Guanyin.[15]

The appearance of the Bodhisattva in the Emperor's dream proves to be the artist's saving grace, but as a vehicle, it also reiterates the painter's status as an almost unwitting conduit of reality. Eliade invokes this status for modern secular artists as well—although most have little use for overt religious symbols, their creative activity nevertheless "camouflages" a cosmic religiosity.[16] One might accuse Eliade of having it backwards—it is not the ideological symbols that are so interesting but rather the power behind them that elicits our response. The slide from artistic representation to cultic presence that is at the center of Freedberg's theory of response, in any case, is a psychological and behavioral construct that is separate from the many and varied ideological interpretations that can be put upon it. To be sure, the constructs of psychology are no less declamatory than the dogmas of Christianity, but in Freedberg's hands, they have a broad application that makes for much theoretical usefulness. The cultic power of art is the universal ability of art to provoke responses by virtue of the human tendency to move from the gaze, to arousal, to the enlivening of the image. Quite importantly, Freedberg's theory of response does not require ideological self-awareness in order to be activated and appreciated. Indeed, Freedberg emphatically proposes that cognitive understanding and rationalization—he is concerned primarily with the discourse of art criticism—functions to mask and repress cultic responses to art.[17] The broad applicability of Freedberg's theory of response is also evident in its indifference to distinctions between "high" and "low" art, and ultimately to the distinction between religious and secular art. In refusing to be bound by these ideology-based distinctions, Freedberg's insights into the power of images offer a clarity and simplicity that avoid the awkwardness of premises such as the "camouflaging of the sacred."

A cultic reading of the religious, or more specifically, the Buddhist significance of *Bodhi* is consistent with how most Buddhists have read and responded to Buddhist icons in the popular ritual context. This is, to some degree, an observation about cultural differences. The ideological bias in how religion is defined and studied—that is, the privileging of belief systems over ritual praxis—is often traced to the doorstep of Protestant Christianity. It has been charged that the study of religion as a discipline has been overly infected by this denominational bias. Buddhist studies has been informed by the Protestant ethic since its beginnings, with its emphasis on doctrine and canonical texts, and only of late has followed its colleagues in "primitive" religions in employing alternative definitions of religion.[18] David Freedberg's own study of art history also posits the exceptional nature of the Protestant attitude and urges the fruitfulness of a cultic understanding of Christian images and practices. The ideological-cultic polarity, then, is indicative of an academic cleavage in the understanding of religion.

There is a particular difficulty, however, in advocating a cultic understanding of religious significance. If I am serious about this notion of meaning, then I can do no better than to halt my own discourse and simply commend the reader to a viewing of the film. But this too presents a problem. Westerners who survive the pace and subverted narrative conventions of *Bodhi* will invariably want to know what it "means." The obstacle lies in the broader cultural prevalence of the ideological notion of meaning. My task, then, is to *describe* the nature of cultic response rather than to provoke one. My rational discourse cannot metamorphose into the cultic experience that it describes, but it can hopefully aid the reader to recognize it. This descriptive task is historical in that it appeals to the evidence of specific cultures, and normative in that it advocates the reality and importance of the cultic mode of religious signification. Both the historical and normative endeavors are nevertheless themselves ideological in how they signify. Just as a theory of the novel must always speak in an idiom that is separate from that of fiction itself, I cannot avoid discursive language in arguing for the theoretical construct of cultic power.

The Buddhist metaphysics of presence that I utilized in the narrative interpretation of *Bodhi* also provides an intellectual basis for the reading/viewing of film as a form of cultic power. With this new application of Buddhist thought, I turn to Buddhism as the *source* of my theory making rather than as the *object* of ideological clarification. In other words, Buddhism is the instrument of my analysis rather than its target.[19] My use of Buddhist theory to ground an understanding of cultic power is related to the historical dimension of my descriptive task. To reiterate, Buddhist icons and the Buddhist practices surrounding them have traditionally been experienced as cultic rather than as ideological forms of meaning.[20] This Buddhist experience instantiates a more pervasive phenomenon in East Asia, where even pre-Buddhist icons—the ghost money and funerary tablets used in the native practice of ancestor worship, for example—serve as signs that trap within themselves the power of ultimate reality.[21] What I add to these observations is the claim that Buddhist ideological discourse provides the most effective framework for appreciating this phenomenon—within Buddhism and potentially beyond. Thus my use of Buddhist sources is more than an effort to interpret Buddhist practices through the lens of its own theories. It is a claim about the efficacy of the Buddhist theory *qua* theory, whatever the context of practice. Conversely, because the purpose of the Buddhist theory is to clarify the nature and operations of cultic power *generally*, its effect is to slight Buddhism's denominational distinctness. Against the strategy of using film in the service of religious ideological disclosure, one can reduce the Buddhism of *Bodhi* to nothing more than the cultic power of art itself.

What Is Chan Art?

There is a historical precedent for the cultic interpretation of Buddhism in pre-modern literati reflections on the relationship between Chan practice and art. Pre-modern China has steadily produced critical reflections on literature and art. Of particular interest, however, is the theoretical discussions of poetry and painting that make explicit analogies to Chan Buddhism. These critical discussions originate not with Buddhist monk-scholastics but with literati-artists more associated with neo-Confucian circles. Yan Yu's *Canglang Shihua* (Poetry Talk from the Ocean Wave) from the thirteenth century, and Dong Qichang's *Huazhi* (Purport of Painting) from the seventeenth century are two of the most influential. In these discourses, painting and poetry are understood as acts of self-cultivation that lead to enlightenment (*wu*). The problem for modern interpreters is how to understand this claim. Is it metaphorical, in that artistic achievement *is like* the breakthrough of spiritual enlightenment, or is it substantive, in that the art is synonymous with Buddhist practice? While this forms the overt question, analysis is often informed by more implicit assumptions about how to define religion generally.

A catalogue of the Boston Museum of Fine Arts' centennial exhibition of Chan painting and calligraphy states, "The most obvious criterion for establishing what Ch'an art is lies in its subject matter, and the evolution of Ch'an art can best be followed through the gradual development of this repertoire of typical Ch'an themes."[22] The criterion invokes common sense, perhaps against the broad aesthetic definitions that can lead to the conclusion that most Japanese art, for example, is Chan/Zen in spirit. The focus on overt subject matter and content, however, favors an ideological interpretation and obscures the concern with cultic experience that lies at the heart of these literati discourses. The Tang era (618-906) was traditionally viewed as the golden age of both Chan Buddhism and Chinese poetry, and beginning in the Song (960-1279), literati speculations display a keen interest in the mechanics of both.[23] The general characterization is that poetry, like enlightenment, leaps upon the poet after he gives himself over to the cultivation of emptiness and quietude of the mind, which enables him to tap into the depth of reality and have perfect intuitive control over the poetic medium. It cannot be taught verbally, and yet requires, according to some, disciplined study of the Tang masters. The concern is overtly with methodology—of how to practice poetry—and the criticism replicates Chan concerns with how to use and understand words properly in order to spark an enlightenment experience. The Chan concern with language not only lends itself to reflections on the process of poetry, but, conversely, one can readily read the utterances of Chan masters—so fondly collected and utilized as meditative devices during this era—as inspired poetry.

James Cahill speculates upon the shared characteristics of art and religion very broadly and suggests: ". . . although both can be discussed in rational terms, truly significant choices in both must be made on non-rational grounds; and on these choices may hang one's spiritual fulfillment, one's very 'salvation.'"[24] Cahill insists that the religious language of enlightenment as applied to the breakthroughs of art is only partly metaphorical. And yet Cahill ultimately obscures this insight when he decides that Dong Qichang's theory of painting uses Chan purely as an analogy; that there is, in fact, no real Buddhist aesthetic basis or content in Dong's landscape paintings. The criterion of "Chan content" is purely ideological. Thus accordingly, Chan paintings must "present, through analyzable artistic means, a vision of nature and of natural phenomena that is consistent with the Chan mode of experience."[25] In other words, the paintings must—through both subject and technique—offer a discursive representation of Buddhist doctrine, particularly the ideals of spontaneity and immediacy associated with the Chan concept of "sudden enlightenment."

Richard Lynn similarly warns in his study of Chinese poetic criticism that we should not confuse the use of Chan terminology by poets with the practice of Chan itself.[26] Lynn has a valid point. Yan Yu uses the Chan language of stages of enlightenment to classify the evolution and lineage of poetic traditions. This penchant for classification is pervasive in Chinese thought and highly realized in Chinese Buddhism itself. Beginning with the strategy of *panjiao*, or "dividing the teachings" of Indian texts into a hierarchy of Buddhist revelations, and culminating in the lineage wars of Chan that established the dichotomies of "Northern" and "Southern," and "gradual" and "sudden" schools, Buddhist terminology provides a rich resource for sectarian categorization schemes. It is interesting that the recurrent dichotomies in Buddhist classifications reflect a larger tension repeated in many discursive Chinese traditions. As Peter Gregory points out, the conflict between Confucianism and Daoism is one historical expression of this tension, which may be most broadly described as the conflict between affirmation of tradition and the desire for freedom. The division is also replicated *within* discrete traditions, such as Confucianism's breakdown into competing schools.[27] The polarity is clearly represented again in Chinese aesthetic-literary theory, and perhaps here, the Chan language is, in fact, merely expressive of broad cultural binary classifications.

The caveat notwithstanding, I do not believe it is Lynn's or Cahill's intention to reduce Chan language to a mere functionary of a broader cultural polarity. Lynn's distinction between Chan language and Chan *itself*, after all, presumes the substantiality of something called "real" Chan. It is only by clarifying what we take this Chan to be that we will be able to resolve the issue of the affinity between Buddhism and art. As we have already seen, Lynn and Cahill reflect a pervasive Western prejudice in the study of religion by defining Chan ideologically. It is only through the presence of Chan "content" that we can speak of a Buddhist aesthetic. This same doctrinal content is used by Lynn to disprove the affinity between poetic and spiritual enlightenment: Inasmuch as poetic enlightenment is described as the perfect fusion of artist and reality through the medium of words, Lynn avers, it is by definition inimical to Chan because Buddhists "deny the value and very existence of objective reality."[28]

Lynn's representation of Buddhist thought is conveniently selective, but this is not the focus of my objection. It is, rather, the strategy of ideological representation itself. Both Lynn and Cahill conclude that the ideology that drives the artistic practices of their respective subjects is more Confucian than Buddhist, perpetuating the mandarin obsession of most sinologists to claim Chinese culture as the legacy of Confucian tradition.[29] This conceit willfully overlooks the active exchanges and mutual influence between the literati and Chan monks beginning in the Northern Song period (960-1126), which is reflected in the output of such literati as the renowned writer, poet, and calligrapher Su Shi, as well as in the deep philosophical impact of Buddhism on Neo-Confucian thought and practice. Exclusivity is a demand of the construct of ideology, however. When scholars attempt to determine whether an individual is more truly a Buddhist or Confucian at heart, they not only make staggering assumptions about the nature of identity, they act as functionaries of their own intellectual categories. But is determining whether Dong Qichang was more authentically himself in his Confucian voice than his Buddhist voice really possible, or even helpful?

We must reconfigure our strategy of signification. I believe that the critical reflections on art and poetry by the Chinese literati are more constructively read as indigenous insights into the similarity of art and religion in their cultic manifestations. This awareness is evident beginning in the Song dynasty, when critics began to make the distinction between painting as a mere craft striving for technical likeness, and as an art expressive of an individual's superior mental and spiritual capacities. Backing this latter emphasis is the unanimous concern with process, or the act of painting, rather than with specific artistic styles.[30] As Lynn more helpfully points out, Yan Yu's notion of "entering the spirit" (*rushen*) through poetry has nothing to do with placid landscape imagery—the kind that might readily come to mind as "Chan content." Yan signifies instead the highest achievement of any and all poetry, "the fusion of a spontaneous and effortless poetic *act* with a poetic medium that can perfectly articulate immediate 'pure experience.'"[31] This emphasis on the poetic *act* or event is no different from the Chan understanding of the enlightenment irruption into otherness.

Cultic Presence and the Metaphysics of Presence

In the first part of this essay, the metaphysics of presence has helped us to articulate the Buddhist ideological significations of *Why Has Bodhi-Dharma Left for the East?* It can now help us to formulate an understanding of cultic power, and therefore a Buddhist basis for appropriating Freedberg's theory of response. What is gained by this is not only a manner of interpreting the Buddhist film, but an explicit ontological grounding for Freedberg's theory.

   Bodhi's visual rootedness in the mountain top and hermitage is a spatial evocation of the primary ideological understanding of Mahāyana Buddhism that the Buddha—and the otherness that he signifies—are realities that are simultaneously absent and present. As the supreme and perfect enlightened one, the Buddha embodies the absence of all conceptuality and illusion. This absent quality of Buddhahood is often "presented" in the form of silence, or, at the very least, in the tradition's consistent denigration of speech. This suspicion of semiotic attempts to represent truth is itself expressed in a rich variety of representations. Some famous narrative depictions include the tale of the Buddha's own initial refusal to teach the dharma, the Buddha's nonverbal transmission of the dharma to his disciple Mahākāśyapa by holding up a flower (which is the charter myth for the Chan conceit of a direct "mind to mind" lineage transmission), and the Bodhisattva Vimalakīrti's silent response that bests all his rivals in doctrinal debate. The absence of speech is also configured as the absence of images, as in the supposed aniconism of the early Buddhist tradition. But here too, images are utilized to signify this absence. They may be semantically direct, such as Liang Kai's thirteenth century painting of the sixth Chan Patriarch Huineng tearing up Buddhist texts, or highly figurative, such as the ubiquitous Chan empty circle (Zen ensō) which simultaneously configures the signs of completeness and emptiness.

   As Buddhism's literary and artistic heritages convey, absence must be signified in order to be soteriologically effective, and therefore this absence can be located somewhere—in the Buddha's biography and very body, and, subsequently, in his relics, reliquary mounds, and pilgrimage sites; in the signifying silences of the tradition, and the icons of absence. In being located, and therefore taking *place*, this absence is both "presented" and "present."[32] The ubiquitous popularity of relic worship in Buddhism is one manifestation of faith in the presence of the Buddha even after his historical departure. As a monastic tradition, Chan has also been partial to landscape settings—the isolated mountains that signify as well as afford actual retreat from the world and the opportunity for contemplative insight, which ultimately, as in Zibong's case, confounds the duality of worldliness and spirituality; of absence and presence.

   The metaphysics of presence is a powerful tool for understanding a range of Buddhist practices—often deceptively broken down into the opposition between monastic and popular. What is consistent about these practices— pilgrimage, the cult of relics and icons, world-renouncing retreat and meditative contemplation—is that they are different ways of evoking and instantiating the phenomenon of religious presence. Furthermore, this description can extend beyond Buddhist practices to religious practice generally. The significant point is this: the phenomenon of presence is not a function of the ideological sign, but rather an extension of cultic practice. The sign is entirely arbitrary, not just in relation to what it signifies (which is the standard semiotic wisdom), but in terms of its efficacy for bringing about the experience of otherness. Meditation upon the Bodhidharma, a mountain, a circle, are all acceptable. What Chan wisdom specifically adds is that if the sign is semantically valorized and clung to, then its cultic power is often destroyed. In that case, the sign itself must be destroyed, just as the master Gutei cut off the finger of the boy servant who imitated the master's one finger Zen.[33]

Given the essential yet ultimately arbitrary nature of the sign, it is even more important to articulate a theory of what makes it "work." Freedberg's psychological framework for understanding the power of images is immensely augmented by the Buddhist ontological insight that one can access absolute reality in *nothing else* but the conventional and arbitrary sign. This ensures that the sign will change according to history, cultural context, and even personal preference. The sign's efficacy, again, is a matter of its context of practice rather than its semantic meaning. Yan Yu's ideal of "entering the spirit" through poetry exemplifies this point. Artistic expression, to the degree that we define it as a numinous fusion of discipline and freedom (irrespective of whatever ideological content may be imposed upon it), encircles the Chan habit of using words in a performative rather than descriptive capacity. It is the sign used as a perlocutionary device—that is, to produce an effect or response that engages the experience of emptiness/otherness as an emerging, present reality.[34]

We perhaps have the makings of an historical and theoretical justification for reading and viewing *Bodhi* as an example of cultic religious significance. It is, of course, quite feasible and undoubtedly useful to read it ideologically. But in attending to the question of how this film images otherness, one must speak of culture specific strategies of experiencing images. My interpretation of *Bodhi* as a "Buddhist film" begins by taking its cue from the work's ideological markings, but parlays this resource into an argument for a different way of signifying religious meaning. This form of signification is given a Buddhist ontological basis in recognition of the fact that it is a theoretical construct that I must discursively defend. It is nevertheless descriptive of a real form of experience of meaning that is vital to recognize in our own intellectual considerations of the religious power of film. Unfortunately, as Freedberg points out, this kind of power assumes a habit of sustained and contemplative viewing that is lost to contemporary culture.[35] The observation is particularly apt when applied to the culturally strange experience of viewing *Bodhi*, assuming that Hollywood is taken as the comparative norm. Indeed, because of the pervasive popularity of Hollywood cinema with audiences all around the world, and conversely, the role of Western audience expectations in the making of successful Asian arthouse films, the dominant mode of Asian film criticism is ideological.[36] Here I mean ideological in the narrow sense of critiquing and unmasking the economic and cultural forms of hegemony that inform the making of internationally successful Asian films. If our current global economic and cultural infrastructures necessitate privileging ideological modes of reading—both for offensive and defensive purposes—then it is even more incumbent upon us to retrieve and imagine other ways of imagining reality. *Bodhi* may actually conform to Western expectations of Asian spiritual inscrutability, but this form of "recognition" glosses over the once pervasive experience of cultic signification.

Let us return to another look at *Bodhi*, then, and describe a portion of it in specifically cultic rather than ideological perspective. I will do so by concentrating on one aspect of the film *qua* film—specifically, its quality of montage, or sequence and juxtapositioning of scenes. One of the challenging aspects of watching *Bodhi* is its tendency to violate the convention of narrative continuity. It jumps back and forth, for example, between the present identity of Kibong as a Buddhist monk and his past life as a householder without any warning or any indication that the two are even the same person. Pointing to other crosscut scenes, one reviewer of the film remarks, "Temporal and spatial leaps like these cause us to wonder which part of the film is reality, which part dream."[37] Bae's nonlinear deployment of montage is evident from the very beginning of the film, and underscored by the fact that the first fifteen minutes is devoid of any story establishing dialogue or narration. I will focus on this portion of the film and explore how its montage shapes the viewing experience.

The opening shot dwells on a young man at a railroad crossing, his figure dominated by the flashing red light that looms in the foreground. The next scene jumps to a closely cropped shot of a window, beautifully dilapidated and traditional in its paper and wood construction. The soundtrack switches from clanging city noises to the sound of idyllic insects, impinged by the gentle voice of an old man calling the name "Haejin." The window opens to reveal a serene courtyard. The scene cuts to a cluster of ripe berries hanging from a tree, which is picked and eaten by a young child whose face is mostly obscured by the tight camera frame. Back in the hermitage courtyard, an old monk picks up a piece of a fallen window frame and fits it back in place. At this point the viewer has been "introduced" to the three characters of the film—Kibong, Hyegok, and Haejin, but these opening scenes hardly do the work of conventional establishing shots. Instead of story, the emphasis is on images, as made evident in the subsequent sequence of tightly framed shapes and textures: Water is scooped from a pear-shaped gourd into a round cup. The roundness of the cup is echoed in a shot of Haejin's bald head reflected in rippling pond water. Boiling water is poured into the cup, and the scene cuts to a back shot of Hyegok seated on a veranda drinking tea. Another cut to a looming shot of a golden Buddha statue, centered on its imperturbable face.

Bodhi has been observed to "[teach] not through its narrative but through its overpowering visual offerings."[38] That these visual scrutinies are meant to "teach" anything at all is perhaps conveyed by the next shot. The old master Hyegok reads from a sutra, offering the only spoken lines in the film's opening, and appears to preach to a retreating and indifferent frog (in a cut-away shot) about the interchangeability of beginnings and endings, and of life and death. The didactic Buddhist content of this verbal intrusion binds the montage of opening shots into a visual koan that signifies meaning through the very process of upsetting the expectations of narrative and logical coherence. If koans are accounts of the non sequitur verbal and physical exchanges between Chan masters and their disciples, then the visual entry into *Bodhi*—as well as much of its unfolding—is similar in its non-narrative aspects. *Bodhi*'s montage does not convey an obvious storyline and, as a result, it "demands that the viewer bring a lot to the interpretation."[39] Like the koan, however, standard forms of interpretation yield little fruit and the point seems to lie in the confusion itself, which can be experienced as either frustrating or enlightening. The end result is determined by the individual viewer, but it is provoked by strategies that parallel the perlocutionary tactics of the koan.[40]

I have been referring to *Bodhi*'s narrative (or lack thereof) simply in terms of characters, plot and sequential time. It will be useful, however, to move to an exact definition of narrative that distinguishes it from other literary genres such as the lyric and drama (both of which also utilize character, plot, and sequence). In addition to a story (events or persons that are narrated), the most telling quality of narrative has been defined as its "magisterial voice."[41] In literary form, this entails a storyteller or narrator "who possesses (and implicitly promises) magisterial overview, the ability to see persons and events comprehensively, cohesively, intelligibly, and with minimal instability. . . ."[42] In the literary medium, the third person voice offers the most unalloyed of narrative perspectives. Its omniscient and distancing posture contrasts sharply with the first person, subjective and intimate voice of the lyric; and the multiple, limited, and competing voices of the drama.

I delineate these genre distinctions in order to draw a limited comparison to film—to suggest that the *experience* of viewing film (as opposed to actual film genres) is often akin to the narrative voice of literature. This is so because film is a visual medium. The power of images—which is more immediate than the abstract code of language—creates the experience of presence, and therefore the presumption of reality. As film theorists have noted, the cinematic image seduces with its directness and hides the fact that visual apprehension can also be a form of manipulation. The ideological mode of film criticism is concerned to point out that the verisimilitude of cinema is an illusion that communicates something more than its images, and that these images are lyrical manufactures of a specific creator. The insight of this criticism is predicated on the ability of film to reinforce the spectator's sense of omniscience by allowing her to occupy the controlling consciousness of the film.

Film can resort to actual voice-over narration, but montage is the more effective aspect of film grammar that allows the spectator this experience of mastery. When conventional montage is deployed, the spectator's ability to follow the story and the characters produces the experience of an "infallible perceptual fullness."[43] In other words, watching film reinforces our unconscious sense of intelligibility, which in turn keeps our sense of coherent and unified selfhood intact. But words and images can also be utilized to opposite purpose. "Ch'an discourse," for example, "is disruptive, first of itself and then of its reader, by overturning and undercutting any effort to hold on to it as correct vision or true belief."[44] If koans are speech acts specifically designed to violate and therefore call attention to the illusion of mastery, then *Bodhi* is a film that accomplishes the same objective in the context of its own language. The specific result of both perlocutionary texts is to throw one into confusion because the violation of normal grammar confounds one's sense of reality. While it is easy to dismiss such ungrammatical representations as bad speech or art, Chan Buddhism utilizes this very strategy as a form of soteriology that destroys illusory constructs of reality and self.

    Bodhi can be described as non-narrative in two distinct but related ways. First, its opening montage fails to establish the expected elements of story—the delineation of character, plot, and time sequence. Second, this failure impugns the viewer's expectation of mastery and demands a very different version of perceptual fullness. If the power of images can be bent to reinforcing standard constructions of intelligibility, it can also be utilized to break that construct down and scrutinize it. *Bodhi*'s montage does not respect the conventional barriers between individual selves and between the human and natural worlds, following traditional Buddhist teachings that emphasize the egalitarian emptiness of all things and the unifying dominance of movement and process. This message is the essence of Hyegok's sutra reading, and the subsequent scenes reinforce it. We see Kibong in his monk's habit chopping wood high atop the hermitage mountain range. The breathtaking landscape that Kibong pauses to contemplate is only one of many such cinematic inquiries. Here the contemplation is bracketed by Kibong's human activity, which is brought to a halt when he cuts his own hand and the blood mingles with the elements of earth and wood. The next scene features another natural setting—a stream from which Haejin emerges to stone the bird whose death and whose mate will haunt him throughout the film. The water interlude transitions back to Kibong bearing his load of chopped wood through the mountain trails, but this fragment of narrative continuity is quickly lost as the scene cuts from his deep contemplation of trees and rocks to his former, secular self in depressive contemplation in the family slum dwelling. This prolonged and jarring juxtapositioning finally cuts back to the mountain valley, this time devoid of all human presence and dominated only by the wind. The inventory of nature comes to one full circle as the scene switches to the roaring fire in the hermitage hearth, and the first dialogue of the film commences as Haejin, who is tending the fire, engages an unseen Kibong in a conversation about the world below the mountain and the mother he has never known.

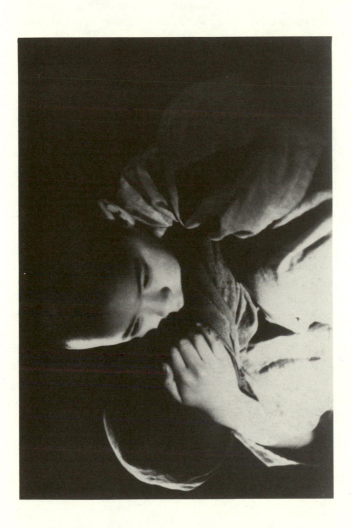

Fig. 9.3 "The indistinguishable capacity for attachment in human and animal alike underscores the Buddhist cosmological view that all things are created by the capacity of desire."
(From the film *Why has the Bodhi-Dharma Left for the East?*. Still courtesy of Milestone Film & Video, New York)

Bodhi's opening images allows for "no controlling consciousness—no human point from which the narrative is constructed which the viewer can occupy as her own."[45] The alternative, then, is the metaphysics of presence in which perceptual fullness is derived from attentiveness to what simply is, minus the usual conceits of intelligibility. Bae's use of montage in a way that destroys the expected delineations of narrative has didactic—and therefore ideological— content, but the film communicates only by virtue of the ability of the viewer to tolerate and profit by its cinematic transgressions.

Conclusion

I conclude with one significant and related ramification of the arbitrary nature of the sign in the production of cultic experience. Although Chan, as a historical entity, accumulates its own storehouse of ideological formulations, its repeated kataphatic and iconoclastic swipes insist on the point that the experience of presence itself mandates no particular content. This latter realization constantly threatens to obliterate the legitimacy and necessity of Chan itself. Bae Yong-kyun's Buddhist film, then, is Buddhist to the degree that it leaves this ideological marker behind and provokes an experience of vivid presence. This is what many film makers seek to do, although they may do it in very different ways. It is an art that Bae himself developed through the influence of Western directors such as William Wyler and Robert Bresson. The larger point here is that when Chan is understood as an inducement to cultic presence rather than as a body of ideological mandates, then it is impossible to delineate what is Chan (or religious) and what is not. This is just as the Chan masters intended, if we are to believe their own words and actions. We can take the example of Zen Master Ryōkan (1758-1831), whose poetry/calligraphy is exceptionally popular and influential to the present day. Some modern scholars argue that his poems are an expression of his Buddhism enlightenment; others, that it is evidence that he abandoned religion for art.[46] The argument is a function of the conventional opposition between religion and art, but it merely perpetuates the kind of illusory dualism that Chan aims to destroy. In Ryōkan's own words:

Delusion and enlightenment
two sides of a coin
Universal and particular
just parts of one whole
All day long I read the wordless scriptures
All night I practice no-practice meditation
On the riverbank, a bush warbler
sings in the weeping willow
In the sleeping village
a dog bays at the moon

Nothing troubles the free flow of my feelings
But how can this mind be passed on?[47]

Ryōkan's closing question is particularly apropos in the context of contemporary Buddhist aesthetic expression, and even more so when it is entangled in popular media such as film. The most interesting Buddhists, at least as defined by their continuing popularity and cultural impact, are those like Ryōkan and Zen Master Hakuin (1685-1769) before him, who freely and masterfully utilized the cultural resources available to them rather than deferring to the canons of either art or religion. Academics and scholars, however, are no less informed by the economic forces that film analysts like to bear in mind when engaging in criticism. Hence, when scholars of Buddhism analyze what makes for legitimate Buddhist expression, it is tempting to revert to the kind of narrow ideological definitions that our discourse is so well suited to make. With the rising popularity of Buddhism in the West, the proliferation of popular Buddhist icons, and their enthusiastic embrace by the gurus of mass culture, academia encourages us to draw a line of demarcation between "real" and "false" Buddhism. But we have been ensnared by this trap before. As Buddhist studies completes its movement from the embrace of doctrinal texts to the valorization of popular practices as artifacts of "real Buddhism," it is useful to guard against making the same journey through other vitiating dualisms. If we are to capture something of the historical phenomenon of religious signification, we must resist our impulse to snort at the Hollywood philistines and rock stars, and formulate theories (which is what we do so well) about specific and alternative ways in which people signify meaning.

Endnotes

1. "Chan" is the Chinese transliteration of the Sanskrit term *dhyana* (meditation) and the name of an indigenous school of Buddhism that originated around the seventh century. Most Westerners are more familiar with "Zen," which is the Japanese pronunciation. This paper deals with a Korean film, and therefore should technically use the term "Sŏn," which is the Korean version. Rather than juggle all this terminology, I uniformly employ the term Chan. From time to time, however, I refer to a specific Japanese master or tradition and revert to the use of "Zen." Because of Chan's relatively late introduction to Japan in the twelfth century, and its flourishing well into the twentieth century (particularly in the realm of the arts), Zen Buddhism has a distinct history worthy of individual mention. Also, many secondary sources usually use the Wade-Giles transliteration of "Ch'an," whereas I prefer the Pinyin system that dispenses of the apostrophe. The former version appears, however, in direct quotations of these sources in this paper.

2. "A Conversation with Bae Yong-kyun," in *Tricycle: The Buddhist Review* (Summer 1994): p. 104.

3. Ibid.

4. The strong association between Japanese Zen and the arts was propagated in the West primarily by D. T. Suzuki (see his *Zen and Japanese Culture*), as well as Hisamatsu Shin'ichi and Nishida Kitaro of the Kyoto School. The current trend in Buddhist scholarship, however, is to attack the idea that Zen is concerned with artistic expression. Much of this criticism is actually an attack on the nationalist sentiments of Suzuki, which infuse a normative and chauvinistic tone to his scholarship on Zen culture in Japan (see Robert Sharf's "The Zen of Japanese Nationalism," in *Curators of the Buddha*, Donald S. Lopez, Jr., ed., for an example of this kind of critical assessment). In my view, such attacks do not succeed in denying the historical association between Zen and the arts. Such denials are based on implicit notions about history, as well as undefended definitions of "Buddhism" as an object of study. Although these issues are too complicated to consider here, they are central to my own current research.

5. Unpublished translation of Qiu Wei's "Looking for the Hermit of West Mountain and Not Finding Him In," by Paula Versano.

6. Faure offers this analysis in the context of a larger discussion of the controversy between "sudden enlightenment" and "gradual cultivation" schools of Chan Buddhism. As Faure argues, this nomenclature is not indicative of actual conflicting factions. Rather, it sketches the elements of an internal paradox and set of concerns that were vociferously debated in the Chan tradition. In *The Rhetoric of Immediacy: A Cultural Critique of Chan/Zen Buddhism* (Princeton: Princeton University Press, 1991), p. 47.

7. Ibid. p. 45.

8. See "Im Kwon-taek: Art Cinema and Buddhism," unpublished manuscript by David E. James.

9. Cf. Maria Maisto's essay above, and Brent Plate's "Religion/Literature/Film," *Literature and Theology*, 12.1 (March, 1998).

10. Irena Makarushka offers a succinct and helpful account of the ideological reading of film in "A Picture's Worth: Teaching Religion and Film," in *Religious Studies News*, 13.2 (May 1998), p. 7. The critical reading of film not only reveals its political dimensions, it entails a rejection of an authoritative meaning behind the text and a process of reinterpretation that changes both reader and text. This form of reading, Makarushka argues, is itself a form of religious practice.

11. John Lyden groups the *theological* and *mythological* modes as allied approaches that "commend" the religious content of film, and opposes them to the *ideological*, which "critiques" the same. See "To Commend or to Critique? The Question of Religion and Film Studies," in *Journal of Religion and Film*, 1.2 (http://www.unomaha.edu/~wwwjrf). Clive Marsh's response to John Lyden in *JRF*, 2.1, draws out the category of "ideology" by insisting that it be applied to the specific religious commitments or framework of the film interpreter.

12. See Eliade's "Divinities: Art and the Divine," in *Symbolism, the Sacred and the Arts*, Diane Apostolos-Cappadona, ed. (New York: Crossroad Publishing Company, 1985), pp. 55-63.

13. My references to David Freedberg are drawn solely from his work, *The Power of Images: Studies in the History and Theory of Response* (Chicago: University of Chicago Press, 1989).

14. Bernard Faure has given much attention to this cultic context, and points out the reciprocity of power between the image and viewer. If the icon fails to respond to prayers, it can be abused and insulted, and most importantly, the cult can die, effectively withholding from the icon its source of ritual power. See *Visions of Power: Imagining Japanese Medieval Buddhism* (Princeton: Princeton University Press, 1996), pp. 262-63.

15. From the *Samguk Yusa* (Legends and Memorabilia of the Three Kingdoms), compiled by the Buddhist monk Iryon in the thirteenth century. Translation by Ha Tai-Hung and Grafton K. Mintz (Seoul: Yonsei University Press, 1972), pp. 216-17.

16. See Eliade's "The Sacred and the Modern Artist," in *Symbolism, the Sacred and the Arts*, pp. 81-85.

17. Freedberg claims, "Much of our sophisticated talk about art is simply an evasion" (*Power of Images*, p. 429). Throughout the book, the form of evasion that concerns Freedberg is sexual. Our strong erotic response to images has led to fear and embarassment that is actively repressed through aesthetic criticism. Bernard Faure argues that in the case of Buddhist art, Western aestheticization has functioned to emasculate the art's religious power. See "The Buddhist Icon and the Modern Gaze," in *Critical Inquiry*, 24.3 (Spring 1998): pp. 768-813.

18. Gregory Schopen led one of the earlier charges against the Protestant bias in his own research, and his views are articulated in "Archeology and Protestant Presuppositions in the Study of Indian Buddhism," in *History of Religions*, 31 (1991): pp. 1-23. Donald Lopez has taken up the battle more recently with his introductory essay in *Curators of the Buddha* (Chicago: University of Chicago Press, 1995), of which he is the editor, as well as through his editorship of the Princeton Readings in Religions series, which includes the volume *Buddhism in Practice*. The general thrust of these charges is that the prejudice for canonical texts and doctrine in the study of Buddhism is reflective of a narrow Christian view of religion, which also distorts the actual history of Buddhist practice throughout Asia.

19. To some, this Buddhist confession perhaps conforms the most to the sense of the term ideological. Clive Marsh argues that both commending and critiquing in film interpretation first requires full disclosure on the part of the interpreter of the theologically discrete tradition in which he or she stands. This form of self ideological disclosure is necessary, Marsh points out, because our postmodern space does not allow for the possibility of a Promethean standpoint (p. 5). I agree, and wish to further emphasize the distinction between the interpretive community out of which one speaks (Marsh's ideology), and the interpretive system *of* which one speaks (my sense of ideological reading). See Marsh's response to John Lyden, referenced in footnote #11.

20. Bernard Faure makes this argument most strongly in "The Buddhist Icon and the Modern Gaze" (see footnote 17), where he indicts Western interpretations of Buddhist art for the violence of its gaze. This form of violence desecrates and strips the icons of their ritual context and cultic power. Faure devotes much discussion to these original ritual elements in his discussion of Buddhist icons in *Visions of Power: Imagining Medieval Japanese Buddhism* (Princeton: Princeton University Press, 1996), and in his discussion of Buddhist relics in *The Rhetoric of Immediacy*.

21. See Faure, *Visions of Power*, p. 269.

22. Jan Fontein and Money L. Hicksman, *Zen Painting and Calligraphy* (Museum of Fine Arts, Boston, Massachusetts, 1970), p. xxiv.

23. See Richard Lynn's survey of Song poetry criticism, "The Sudden and the Gradual in Chinese Poetry Criticism: An Examination of the Ch'an-Poetry Analogy," in *Sudden and Gradual: Approaches to Enlightenment in Chinese Thought*, edited by Peter Gregory (Honolulu: University of Hawaii Press, 1987): pp. 381-427. Although a great deal of Lynn's analysis is concerned with the Chan "sudden" and "gradual" breakdown that is reflected in the poetry criticism, this detail merely reinforces the point of the thorough going nature of the Chan-poetry association.

24. James Cahill, "Tung Ch'i-ch'ang's 'Southern and Northern Schools' in the History and Theory of Painting: A Reconsideration," in *Sudden and Gradual*, op.cit., p. 433.

25. Ibid., p. 439.

26. Richard Lynn, "Orthodoxy and Enlightenment: Wang Shih-chen's Theory of Poetry and Its Antecedents," in *The Unfolding of Neo-Confucianism*, Wm. Theodore De Bary, ed. (New York: Columbia University Press, 1975), p. 222.

27. See Gregory's introductory essay in *Sudden and Gradual*, pp. 1-12.

28. Lynn, "Orthodoxy and Enlightenment," p. 255.

29. To quote Cahill, "I believe . . . that Neo-Confucian ideas, especially those of Wang Yang-ming and his late Ming followers, make up a much more pertinent intellectual setting for Tung (Ch'i-ch'ang)'s beliefs" ("Southern and Northern Schools," p. 438). From Lynn, "This tradition of poetry . . . owes much to Ch'an as a source of inspiration (or stimulation), ideas, and terminology, but in the final analysis its ultimate aims lie entirely within the boundaries of Neo-Confucian discipline and aspirations" ("Orthodoxy and Enlightenment," p. 236). The mandarin bias that all Chinese culture is the product of Confucian thought is also clearly echoed in Western scholarship on Chinese literature, which I have spent some effort to question in my past scholarship.

30. See Susan Bush, *The Chinese Literati on Painting: Su Shih (1037-1101 to Tung C'hi-ch'ang (1555-1636)* Harvard-Yenching Institute Studies 27 (Cambridge: Harvard University Press, 1971), for a discussion of Song literati theories of painting. Bush confirms the free use of Chan and Daoist tropes in literati criticism, and the fact that these literati were little concerned with the technical differences between religious traditions (p. 65). The relevant point is that the language of spiritual experience is appropriate to and almost indistinguishable from the description of artistic process.

31. Lynn, "The Sudden and the Gradual," p. 406.

32. Malcolm David Eckel offers a study of the problem of the Buddha's absence as probed by the Mahayana philosophical tradition. See, *To See the Buddha: A Philosopher's Quest for the Meaning of Emptiness* (New York: HarperCollins, 1992), especially pages 65-72.

33. Koan #3 in the *Mumonkan* (The Gateless Gate). See *Two Zen Classics*, trans. Katsuki Sekida (New York: Weatherhill, 1977).

34. Here I draw upon Bernard Faure's use of "perlocutionary speech acts" to describe Chan language. See his chapter on "Chan and Language: Fair and Unfair Games," in *Chan Insights and Oversights* (Princeton: Princeton University Press, 1993), as well as "Fair and Unfair Language Games in Chan/Zen," in *Mysticism and Language*, Nathan Katz, ed. (New York: Oxford University Press, 1992).

35. See Freedberg, chapter 8 ("*Invisibilia per visibilia*: Meditation and the Uses of Theory"), for his discussion of the Christian medieval practice of meditation upon religious images. Freedberg expounds upon the well-wrought theories of theologians that recognized the power of such meditation to excite religious emotion, and to move from sensual material form to spiritual attainment. The theory can be applied wholesale to Buddhist meditation, which also uses a host of visual aids.

36. Not surprisingly, much of this criticism comes from ethnic Asian scholars of Asian cinema. See for example, Yingjin Zhang's "Chinese Cinema and Transnational Cultural Politics: Reflections on Film Festivals, Film Productions, and Film Studies," in *Journal of Modern Literature in Chinese*, 2.1 (Spring 1998), and Rey Chow's *Primitive Passions: Visuality, Sexuality, Ethnography, and Contemporary Chinese Cinema* (New York: Columbia University Press, 1995).

37. Linda Ehrich's review of *Bodhi* in *Film Quarterly*, 48.1 (Fall, 1994), p. 27.

38. Ibid. p. 31.

39. See Michael Gillespie's, "Picturing the Way in Bae Yong-kyun's *Why Has Bodhidharma Left for the East?*" In *Journal of Religion and Film*, 1.1.

40. For a discussion of koan strategies, see Dale Wright's "The Discourse of Awakening: Rhetorical Practice in Classical Ch'an Buddhism," in *Journal of the American Academy of Religion*, 61.1 (Spring 1993): pp. 23-40. Wright describes koans as rhetorical practices that work against the concept of persuasion that is central to classical Greek rhetoric. Successful persuasion means that the "discourse will seek to conform to the conventions of the addressee" (p. 26). Koan rhetoric, on the other hand, deliberately thwarts the conventions of speech, particularly the expectation that it be representational—that is, assertive of intelligible claims about the world. The specific strategy that Wright describes as "direct pointing" suggests the resonance between koan discourse and film. Direct pointing is the use of non-verbal signs, which, "like spoken words, can become events of signification" (p. 29). These non-verbal signs are comprised of the actions and gestures of Chan masters, which, like film, communicates through a visual medium.

41. I take this point from Frederick Ruf's *Entangled Voices: Genre and the Religious Construction of the Self* (New York: Oxford, 1997). Ruf attempts a concise and differentiating definition of narrative, lyric, and drama, arguing that each of these genres lead to different experiences of reality, and to different forms of coherence and intelligibility. This argument, especially when applied to film as an extension of narrative, is extremely consonant with my analysis here.

42. Ibid. p. 62.

43. I borrow the phrase "infallible perceptual fullness" from David James, at the School of Cinema, University of Southern California, who has been invaluable in providing me with some fundamental bearings in the world of film analysis. This phrase arose in the context of our conversation of September 1, 1998, about montage and the French New Wave school of film theory, represented by figures such as Jean-Luc Godard.

44. Wright, "Discourse of Awakening," p. 33.

45. David James, in specific reference to *Bodhi*, from the same conversation referenced in footnote 43.

46. For further description of scholastic interpretations of Ryōkan, see Ryūichi Abe's essay, "A Poetics of Mendicancy: Nondualist Philosophy and Ryōkan's Figurative Strategy," in *Great Fool Zen Master Ryōkan: Poems, Letter, and Other Writings*, Ryūichi Abe and Peter Haskel, eds. (Honolulu: University of Hawaii Press, 1996).

47. Quoted in ibid. p. 42.

Behold Thou the Behemoth:
Imaging the Unimaginable in Monster Movies

Timothy K. Beal

Can otherness be imaged, envisioned, filmed? What is the relation between otherness and the imagination in cinema? How can the camera image the unimaginable? How can one present—that is, imagine, make imaginable— otherness without reducing it to the familiar, the same? These questions, which may be read between the lines of this book's title and within many of its essays, are perennial questions for religious studies, frequently put in terms of the paradox of the sacred: How can the sacred be experienced within the order of the profane, the usual? How can the "wholly other" be revealed within the familiar, the same, the worldly?

Perhaps less obviously, these questions are equally important to ask in relation to cinematic horror, especially in relation to the monster movie, insofar as monsters are horrifying precisely because they are, paradoxically, *embodiments of otherness*; they are in this world but not of it, eliciting an irreducible combination of desire and fear, attraction and repulsion.[1]

This chapter dog-paddles in the hoary wake of a particularly well-known yet remarkably protean sea monster, Leviathan, as it swims its way from ancient mythology into the irradiated waters of Eugene Lourie's 1959 eco-horror classic *The Giant Behemoth*, in order to explore how otherness is imag(in)ed in the monster movie.[2] Make no mistake: this is not a great film by any critical standards, although it did fairly well in theaters in the wake of *It Came from Beneath the Sea* (1955) and *Godzilla* (1956), and although it has continued to draw television and video audiences to this day. In fact, I have chosen this movie as a place to explore questions concerning filmic visions of monstrous otherness precisely because it, like the ever-pervasive "B" movies of contemporary horror, keeps innovation to a minimum, thus providing ready examples of common, well-established narrative patterns, themes, acoustic and camera techniques.

In this movie, we may identify three common cinematic strategies for imag(in)ing monstrous otherness. First, the monster movie often remythologizes otherness as an embodiment of the forces of chaos that perpetually threaten the cosmos. As reenactment of the mythic battle against chaos monsters, monster movie time is a kind of sacred time. Second, within this mythic structure of the monster movie narrative, the otherness of the monster is maintained primarily by resisting visualization; likewise, its inevitable appearance on screen is linked to its ultimate objectification and destruction. The camera shot is fatal for monsters. Third, the image of the monster, as paradoxical embodiment of otherness, the other within, is presented as a conglomeration of mutually exclusive categories, working to confuse distinctions between inside and outside, this-worldly and other-worldly, and especially between self and other. Following discussions of the first two strategies, I show here how this third cinematic strategy works against the monster movie's general progression toward ultimate visualization, objectification, and annihilation, thus revealing a camera eye divided against itself.

Monster Time

The monster movie often remythologizes otherness as an embodiment of the forces of chaos that perpetually threaten the cosmos. As reenactment of the mythic battle against chaos monsters, monster movie time is a kind of sacred time.

As is well known, modern theater in the west has been patterned on the service of Christian worship—in everything from playhouse architecture to liturgy to printed program. Theater time is sacred time. The same goes for movie time. We gather together, seated in rows, necks craned, silently facing the screen of light and revelation (the source of which, we almost forget, is behind a curtain in the back); we share food uniquely blessed for movie time (popcorn, Good 'n' Plenty) in specific, movie-house-only vessels and portions; we follow a carefully patterned and widely familiar liturgical sequence, from meeting the well-dressed usher at the entrance, to the obligatory announcements of forthcoming events, to the opening reminder to be still and keep silence, to the Feature Presentation (usually of a certain length, with certain narrative expectations), to a well-marked conclusion with credits and a closing song as we file out in silence, crossing back over into the monotony and homogeneity of the ordinary world. Movie time is sacred time.

Monster movies, I suggest, often represent a particular kind of sacred time, in that they often *remythologize otherness*. Mircea Eliade and others describe sacred time as communal reenactment of myths about the creation of the world, or cosmogony.[3] By reenacting such myths during festivals and on other appropriate occasions, a community resacralizes and thereby recreates the world. Religion is, in this sense, world-recreative. As the myth is reenacted, the primordial forces of chaos that threaten the world (on cosmic, political, and personal levels) are once again pushed beyond the boundaries of creation. Significantly, in many ancient myths, the forces of primordial chaos that threaten cosmic order are embodied in the so-called chaos monster, and the world is resacralized and recreated by a creator deity who defeats the chaos monster in battle, or *Chaoskampf*. Such battles abound in ancient mythologies. For example, in the *Enuma Elish*, which was recited or reenacted as part of a new year festival in Babylon, Marduk defeats the watery chaos mother Tiamat, creating the inhabitable world from her fileted body and establishing Babylon as its center. And in ancient Ugaritic poetry, as well as in some biblical passages (Psalm 74:12-17; Isaiah 27:1; and, relatedly, the red dragon in Revelation 12), Leviathan is just such a watery chaos monster, threatening the divinely ordained creation and requiring a good head-bashing by the deity.[4]

In monster movies, otherness is often represented as a return of just such ancient mythic monstrosity, and the narrative of the monster movie itself is often patterned as a mythic battle against that monster. In fact, monster movies frequently remythologize their monsters by identifying them explicitly with mythic chaos monsters. In some cases the identification is only implied, as in *Leviathan* (1989), where the title—along with the fact that the story takes place at the bottom of the ocean—are the only obvious links between the film's monster and the Leviathan of ancient Near Eastern mythology. In many other cases, however, the identification is made explicit by one or more of the characters in the film. Often the identification is first made by the not-so-modern, not-so-cosmopolitan townsfolk, and only later acknowledged by men (yes, nearly always men) of science, suggesting that such folk are more mythically inclined and that, as such, they may be able to give name to that which modern consciousness has largely repressed. Thus, for example, the townsfolk in Dracula's neighborhood first warn Jonathan Harker that his host is a vampire; only later is the identification fully researched and confirmed by Professor Van Helsing. Likewise, in *The Giant Behemoth*, the first victim, a local fisherman, Thomas Trevethan, first gives this irradiating "it" a name—a biblical one—just before he dies: "From the sea . . . burning like fire . . . Behemoth!" Apparently Thomas knows the biblical book of Job well enough to identify this monster with a mythic biblical beast, but not well enough to avoid confusing the marshy land beast called Behemoth in Job 40 with the sea monster Leviathan in Job 41. This (mis)naming echoes, moreover, the voice of God that thunders over the movie's opening image of ocean waves: "And the Lord said, 'Behold thou the Behemoth!'" It is echoed, in turn, by the preacher's graveside homily for Thomas:

> "Man that is born of woman is a few days and full of trouble. He cometh forth like a flower and is cut down" (Job, chapter 14, the first verse). And if any man could know the sufferings of Job, it was Thomas Trevethan. Job, in his suffering, turned to God for an answer. "Then answered the Lord unto Job and said, 'Behold thou the Behemoth, which I made with thee. He moveth his tail like a cedar. Out of his mouth go burning lamps. And spouts of fire leap out from the Behemoth. He maketh the oceans to boil like a pot. His breath kindles coals and a flame goeth out of his mouth.'" (my transcription)

Leaving aside whether this is any kind of answer from God to Job *or* Thomas in their suffering, the preacher of this graveside homily provides confused scriptural backing for Thomas's confusion of Behemoth with Leviathan. In the book of Job, only the first two sentences quoted here (from "Behold" to "cedar") refer to Behemoth (Job 40:13a and 40:17a); the remaining lines refer not to Behemoth but to the mythic chaos monster Leviathan (41:19-21; "from the Behemoth" is inserted), whose description follows that of Behemoth. Nonetheless, here as elsewhere we find the local folk first mythologizing the monster. This mythic identity is then confirmed by religious authority (the preacher), and is finally acknowledged by the American marine biologist, Steve Karnes, and his more reserved British colleagues.

Indeed, the very plot of the monster movie frequently follows the pattern of a mythic *Chaoskampf*, with the scientist, more often than not, taking on the role of monster-destroying deity. As a result of human tampering (moral, biological, and/or cosmic) with the order of creation, the mythic primordial chaos monster awakens from its slumber just beyond the edge of the world as we know it, threatening to bring an end to that world. By the end of the story, after a final climactic battle, it is overcome, and the order of the cosmos is once again, at least for the time being, stable and secure. Thus in *The Giant Behemoth*, as in *Godzilla*, *It Came From Beneath the Sea*, and many others, the chaos monster is roused to action by nuclear explosions (in this case, remote off-shore nuclear bomb testing). Once roused it quickly becomes clear that the chaos monster's destructive powers threaten the very order of creation (one of the movie trailers reads, "The biggest thing since creation."). However, after charring a few people and demolishing several ships, cars, and buildings, Karnes is able, with the help of his professor and a rather goofy paleontologist, to come to a more precise "scientific" explanation of it: it is a 200-foot "electric" (like an eel) "paleosaurus" that, after taking in a few too many radioactive particles, is able to "project the radiation" at its victims. This explanation, by which he comes to know the formerly unknowable, provides the means to destroy the monster: a radium tipped torpedo that will push its radiation levels over the top, leaving it to "burn itself out." This is precisely what Karnes does, and the chaos monster is vanquished.

"The ocean is my province, gentlemen," Karnes declares in his opening lecture. And indeed, like some modern-day Marduk battling Tiamat or Anat battling Leviathan, he proves himself, in the end, a worthy opponent to the chaos monster.

Monster movie time, then, offers a ritualized context in which to encounter monstrous otherness, assured by a well-established mythic structure that, although there will be some collateral casualties along the way, in the end the monster will be vanquished and the world will be safe once more. Well, safe for the time being, anyway. For just as the *Enuma Elish* needed to be regularly reenacted every New Year, so also with the monster movie there will always be need for another ritual re-enactment, another re-release, another sequel.

Shooting the Monster

Such is the common end for the chaos monster: expelled from the cosmos with its tail between its legs or blown to bits. Indeed, by the time of the final battle, the sense of horror that was experienced previously in relation to the monster has often been replaced by the adrenaline rush of a street fight, even as the hero of *Chaoskampf* takes on a certain demonstrocizing bravado—"I got you! You son of a bitch." (*Alien*) . . . "Say aah, mother fucker!" (*Leviathan*) . . . "Smile, you son of a bitch!" (*Jaws*).

Thus in *The Giant Behemoth* as in so many other monster movies, we are aware of a shift as the narrative progresses: from horror in relation to a monstrous otherness with mysterious agency, who sees—even stalks—but is not seen, to aggression against a monstrous opponent that is fully visible, objectifiable, targeted for obliteration. In other words, as the monster movie progresses, there is a shift from monster as unknowable and unseeable *subject* to monster as known and clearly seen *object*, just as the characters (and viewers) shift from *hunted object* to *hunting subject*.

Such a shift is common in both literary and cinematic monster tales. The means of accomplishing this shift in film, however, is unique in at least one respect: *within the mythic structure of the monster movie narrative, the otherness of the monster is maintained primarily by resisting clear and steady visualization; likewise, its inevitable appearance on screen is linked to its ultimate objectification and destruction.* Therefore, the shift from monster as hunting subject to monster as hunted object takes place primarily through its gradual visualization. In the beginning, we only see traces of the monstrous other in its effects: boils on the skin, a charred corpse, wreckage; then a shadow, a rustling in the woods, a glowing eye, a tail slithering back into the sea or around the corner.[5] Yet the monster inevitably crosses over into the visible world, and once it does its days are numbered. Once caught on camera, it will not be long before it will be caught in the crosshairs and shot to pieces. The full-frame camera shot is fatal, reducing the monstrous other to nothing more than big game.

This progression toward full visualization is accomplished in *The Giant Behemoth* primarily through the film's use of two kinds of camera shot: *the solitary reaction shot* and *the shot/reverse shot formation*. To be more precise, the gradual visualization and objectification of the monster begins with a single solitary reaction shot in the first encounter, leaving the monster completely unseen, and then progresses through a series of shot/reverse shot formations toward its final full revelation and demolition.

The *solitary reaction shot* gives a close-up shot on the face of someone reacting to something, but does not provide a subsequent point-of-view shot to show us what the person is reacting to. In monster movies, the solitary reaction shot holds on the horrified face of the victim without allowing the viewer to see what the victim sees.[6] Thus, although the monster is revealed to the victim at this very moment (and then, usually, is killed), we the viewers do not see it. In fact, our point of view is more closely aligned with that of the monster than with that of the victim. At the same time, the monster remains, for us but not for the victim, beyond visualization. In *The Giant Behemoth*, the monster's attack on the first victim, Thomas Trevethan, utilizes this classic shot: as the camera holds steady on Thomas kneeling at the water's edge to gut a fish, a siren-like whining gradually overtakes the orchestral soundtrack; as the sound gains volume, he slowly looks up and his face contorts in a terrified, frozen scream as radiant light engulfs the screen (Fig. 10.1). Thus, even while we are aligned more closely with the view of the monster (the source of the radiating light) than with the victim, the monster remains unseen. It is present without being presentable, unimaginably "there." Indeed, as boil-ridden Thomas himself attests to his daughter and her friend immediately before dying, he himself did not see the monster so much as its radiant emanation: "From the sea ... burning like fire ... Behemoth!" Once given this mythic name, however, as mentioned earlier, the preacher soon follows with a biblical description. So the gradual visualization begins—elliptically at first, but soon enough it will be captured by the camera's eye, demonstrocized and gutted by a torpedo.

Fig. 10.1 The solitary reaction shot. Thomas "slowly looks up and his face contorts in a terrified, frozen scream as radiant light engulfs the screen." (From the film *The Giant Behemoth*. Allied Artists Pictures.)

Following this initial solitary reaction shot, the progressive visualization of this Behemoth is accomplished through a series of *shot/reverse shot formations*. In the shot/reverse shot formation, the camera cuts from an initial shot to a reverse shot (turned approximately 180 degrees), so that we are given the point of view of the character(s) in the initial shot. In monster movies, this formation typically opens with a shot of the face of someone reacting to the monster, and then reverses to show the monster—or part of it—as that character sees it. The effect of this shot formation is to align our point of view with that of the character in the first shot, thereby encouraging us to identify with that character's subject position and her/his reaction to whatever s/he sees. This is the key shot formation for cinematic "suture," by which the subjectivity of the viewer is identified with (i.e., sutured to) a particular subject position within a particular scene.[7] In *The Giant Behemoth*, a series of cinematic sutures take us from identification with the hunted victims of a seeing but not fully seen monstrous other to identification with the victorious hunter as he (along with the camera) targets a fully visible, easily objectifiable, over-radiated, over-rated electric eel.

There are several significant shot/reverse shot formations in the course of the film, each of which adds at least a third shot, reversing back again to the initial camera position (i.e., shot/reverse shot/shot). Interestingly, each of these shot formations is related in some sense to hunting and/or the shooting of a weapon. In the first, just after Karnes has determined to "track down this thing, find out what it is, and then destroy it," we see Karnes in a fishing schooner looking through binoculars for the monster. Like some modern-day Ahab from California, he is hot on the trail of the monstrous Leviathan. Just after hearing that the coast guard is searching for a large steam ship that has disappeared on its way to Hull, the Geiger counter on the wall begins clicking. As Karnes stares through the binoculars in edgy fascination (Fig. 10.2a), the camera gives the reverse shot, framed roughly in binocular-vision, of the monster's scaly neck and part of its head as it slips back into the churning sea (Fig. 10.2b). Completing the suture, the camera then reverses back to Karnes' face as he puts down the binoculars (Fig. 10.2c). "That's it," he tells the skipper with a fearlessly determined face, and the chase begins. It is soon over, however, as the monster quickly leaves them behind. Thus this first shot/reverse shot formation identifies the viewer with Karnes, the hunter, and yet resists visualization of that which he is just on the threshold of seeing. Indeed, insofar as this shot formation is immediately preceded by news that a steam ship has recently disappeared (we know that it has been hunted down and destroyed by the monster), this scene plays in the tension between identification with the monster-hunter (Karnes) and the monster-hunted (other victims at sea).

The second significant shot/reverse shot formation takes place when a boy and his father go outside to see why the dog is barking. The father grabs the shotgun on the way out, and the boy unchains the dog. It looks like a father-son out hunting. The dog goes around a corner, we hear a yelp, and then silence. As the boy and his father come around after the dog, they both look up in terror. The father aims his gun and fires, and then the camera reverses to catch a radiating light and part of Behemoth's hide. He has it in his gun sight, yet he, and we, cannot really see it: we are looking down the barrel at an impossible target. The camera then reverses back to show the squinting father being swallowed up by light. So also the son, leaving him burnt like the victim of a nuclear explosion. As with Karnes on the schooner, then, this scene begins with an image of the monster hunters; but whereas last time the monster escaped its

Fig. 10.2a "As Karnes stares through the binoculars in edgy fascination . . ."
(From the film *The Giant Behemoth*. Allied Artists Pictures.)

Fig. 10.2b ". . . the camera gives the reverse shot, framed roughly in binocular-vision, of the
monster's scaly neck and part of its head as it slips back into the churning sea."
(From the film *The Giant Behemoth*. Allied Artists Pictures.)

Fig. 10.2c "Completing the suture, the camera then reverses back to Karnes'
face as he puts down the binoculars."
(From the film *The Giant Behemoth*. Allied Artists Pictures.)

hunters, here the hunters suddenly become the hunted. The effect of the suture here, then, is to identify us with the hunting subject turned hunted object, face to face with something that is at most only partially imaginable. We had it in our sights for a second but we never really saw it.

Soon after, the monster emerges from the threshold of the visible world, captured on camera as it stomps through the London streets, smashing cars, chasing down herds of commuters and toasting them in their tracks. Anticipating just such a confrontation, military forces are on hand, and so the *Chaoskampf* moves rapidly toward its conclusion. As is typical in monster movies, the full appearance of the monster here leads to an immediate increase in collateral damage and casualties—from isolated attacks to a full-blown monster mash. Yet it will also lead very quickly to the monster's ultimate demise. Its appearance signals not only the peak of its power but also its inevitable disempowerment.

The next shot/reverse shot formation only delays the inevitable end of the monster, who is now fully visible from head to tail. First, we see four armed soldiers firing away at the monster in their sights; the camera reverses to show a clear view of the monster (now clearly a dinosaur) firing back; as the camera reverses back once more we see them, like the boy in the previous scene, charred by the monster's radiant beams. But it is really all down hill from here. Now that the monster has been fully captured on screen (and fully explained, demythologized, by Karnes and his scientific colleagues), its demise is not far off. Though dangerous game, it is game nonetheless.

The final shot/reverse shot formation takes place in the final scene of undersea *Chaoskampf*, in which Karnes chases down and destroys the monster by firing a radium-tipped torpedo into its body, thus giving it a taste of its own medicine. First, as the monster swims into the crosshairs, we see Karnes excitedly call out to his submate, "Fire!"; the lever is pulled, and the camera reverses to the monster, who turns to face the speeding missile and catches it straight in the mouth; as the torpedo blows it apart, the camera reverses back to the triumphant face of Karnes.

In the monster movie, the otherness of the monster is linked to its resistance to visualization. Likewise, its fixation as an object targeted for annihilation is linked to its fixation as a visual object. Isabel Cristina Pinedo rightly identifies the two most important appearances of the monster as its initial birth, transformation, or entrance, and its destruction—that is, its first and last appearances.[8] In fact, these two appearances are inextricably related. The monster's first full appearance marks the inevitability of its last. The camera shot is fatal. The camera's eye *de-monstrates* the monstrous and targets it for annihilation. For the monster, looks kill; for the viewer, seeing is disbelieving.

Paradox of the Monstrous

In other ways, however, the camera works against its own aim of revelation in the monster movie. Running counter to the gradual visualization—and thereby objectification and annihilation—of otherness in the monster movie discussed above, there are other cinematic strategies that work to image the unimaginable. *The image of the monster, as paradoxical embodiment of otherness, the other within, is presented as a conglomeration of mutually exclusive categories, working to confuse distinctions between inside and outside, this worldly and other worldly, and especially between self and other.*

This is accomplished primarily by another sort of suture, that is, by stitching the monster's body together from various pieces that do not fit together into any kind of unified, sensible whole. The resulting monster produces what Noël Carroll, drawing from Mary Douglas, calls "category jamming" in our cultural classification systems.[9] Sewn together from that which does not fit together, the monster is an embodiment of impurity and abomination.

Judith Halberstam has shown how the technology of monster-making in Gothic literature and film often involves stitching the monster together out of various representations of non-normative sexuality, race, ethnicity, and national identity.[10] Yet, insofar as the monster is, paradoxically, an embodiment of otherness—in some sense both self and other, inside and outside, the other within—the conglomerate body of the monster must also incorporate elements of self, sameness, normativity. Thus, for example, when Jonathan Harker meets Dracula he initially appears simultaneously not at all British (he has never been there, his accent is odd, etc.) and altogether *too* British (highly literate, grammatically correct, well-versed in English history and geography). Likewise, he is simultaneously a meticulous host and a wild animal. In cinematic horror, the conglomeration of otherness and sameness in the monster's body is often more a matter of appearance than behavior. In *Alien* (1979), as in its deep-freeze and deep-sea imitators *The Thing* (1982) and *Leviathan* (1989), the other first appears precisely *within* the self, either violently bursting forth from someone's body or gradually boiling up just beneath the skin. In *Leviathan*, moreover, the monster itself incorporates not only the bodies (especially faces) of its unwilling victims, but also their intelligence—using it against their own moral wills to hunt down and consume more victims.

The Giant Behemoth, like other classic eco-horror films, takes a somewhat different approach. The monster itself, of course, is a conglomeration of several mutually incompatible elements. In terms of time and age, it is the primordial-mythic within modern techno-scientific, and also the prehistoric (dinosaur) infecting/infected by twentieth-century history. Cosmologically, it is both this-worldly and other-worldly, and an envoy of the deep sea within the urban. Ecologically, it is both natural and unnatural. Beyond these conglomerations, however, certain images and dialogues further suggest ways in which modern technology and its scientists are *themselves* monstrous like Behemoth. After the opening credits, the first images are of several nuclear bomb tests, followed by images of scientists in strange leaded suits with Geiger counters, wandering through the ruins of an explosion (Fig. 10.3). These images, we soon realize, are from a film that Karnes himself is showing to a group of scientists. Here is his commentary: "And afterwards [after the bombing], these mysterious figures, faces masked with lead, these are ourselves, men, the kings of the earth, trying to measure the extent of the destruction they themselves have created" (my transcription). Here in the movie's opening lecture, "we" (modern, scientific men) are in some sense mysterious, masked monsters, who have "created" in turn an even more monstrous catastrophe, which will lead to a "radioactive conglomerate" resulting from a "biological chain reaction, a geometrical progression of deadly menace." "For all we know," he concludes, "what we have started may have already matured, and who can tell when this, this whatever it is, will rise to the surface and strike back at us." Clearly the sense is that "we" modern men of science are monsters engendering monsters.[11] The chaos monster that will soon rise to the surface (in the next scene, in fact) mirrors our very own monstrosity.

In fact, as noted earlier, the radioactive chaos monster is ultimately destroyed by a torpedo that Karnes and his colleagues, working in a dark and mysterious laboratory, wearing the same outfits as those in Karnes' film ("mysterious figures, faces masked with lead"), have tipped with radium (Fig. 10.4). The implication here is not only that fire is fought with fire, but that monsters are destroyed by monsters.[12]

In cinematic horror, therefore, the camera often works against its own aim of making perfectly visible by presenting the monster as an embodiment of the socially and conceptually impossible. Against its own objectifying, demonstrating tendencies, it presents viewers with an image of the unimaginable, "witnesses to the unpresentable."[13] In conjunction with other images that imply the self-as-other, the monster movie works to confuse commonly held distinctions between inside and outside, this-worldly and other-worldly, and especially between self and other. As such, it not only produces "category jamming" in the our conceptual frameworks, but also allows otherness to get under our skin, warning us (from Latin *monere*, "to warn") that the world can never be rid of its monsters, just as the self can never be rid of the otherness within.

Thus there is tension in the monster movie between, on the one hand, gradual visualization, objectification, and ultimately annihilation of monstrous otherness, and, on the other hand, imaging the unimaginable and witnessing to the unpresentable. This tension is, in fact, as old as cinema itself, and reflects the tension between the realist and formalist (or anti-realist) schools. From the

Fig. 10.3 "[T]he radioactive chaos monster is ultimately destroyed by a torpedo that Karnes and his colleagues, working in a dark and mysterious laboratory, wearing the same outfits as those in Karnes' film ('mysterious figures, faces masked with lead'), have tipped with radium."
(From the film *The Giant Behemoth*. Allied Artists Pictures.)

Fig. 10.4 "The implication here is not only that fire is fought with fire, but that monsters are destroyed by monsters."
(From the film *The Giant Behemoth*. Allied Artists Pictures.)

beginning, the movie camera, like the still camera, promised a new level of realism beyond that of painting or narrative. Lyotard defines the primary aim of realism in the arts as follows: "to preserve various consciousnesses from doubt . . . to stabilize the referent, to arrange it according to a point of view which endows it with a recognizable meaning, to reproduce the syntax and vocabulary which enable the addressee to decipher images quickly, and so to arrive easily at the consciousness of his own identity."[14] In short, realism builds and preserves confidence and security in the known, in a certain conception of cosmopolitical order. That which is other, unpresentable, is precisely that which would introduce doubt, interrogate widely recognized meanings, impair one's ability to decipher, and put one's sense of identity at unease. The work of realism is to make otherness known—to lay it on the table, dissect it, explain it, know it—or else, if its resistance is too great, to banish it and to forget it forever. To talk about imag(in)ing otherness in film in a way that does not reduce otherness to the familiar, then, is to ask how film can and does break free from the promise of realism—not necessarily in order to interpret the world or create an alternative world (often the aim of formalist cinema), but to open toward what might un-create our present conception of the world.

Inconclusion (The Work of Failure)

Within the mythologized sacred time of the monster movie, we are provided with a ritualized time and space to experience what H.P. Lovecraft called "cosmic fear" in relation to an unknowable, monstrous otherness that is as much within as without.[15] As others have noted, moreover, the monstrous other of horror is not purely repulsive or dreadful, but is also attractive, even fascinating. Analogous to the experience of vertigo, the otherness of the monster elicits an irreducibly ambivalent experience of both desire and fear, attraction and repulsion. Given that our focus here is on the way monster movies often mythologize otherness as chaos monster, it is interesting to note that religious experience is often described in precisely the same way: as an encounter with radical otherness, to borrow Rudolph Otto's famous phrase, a *Mysterium tremendum et fascinans*, an unknowable otherness that is simultaneously terrifying and fascinating, repulsive and alluring. Altering Otto's phrase slightly, we may consider the monster as *Monstrum tremendum et fascinans*, an envoy of sacred terror. Certainly this is the case in *The Giant Behemoth*, in which the very identity of the monster is presented as divine revelation ("And the Lord said, 'Behold thou the Behemoth!'").

Such movie-time encounters with monstrous otherness are ostensibly safe, because narrative expectation assures us that by the end of the tale the monster will have been faced and overcome. In another sense, however, the world can never be rid of monsters. As with Leviathan, Tiamat, and other ancient mythological chaos monsters, the monsters of modern horror, once conjured, always survive—"overlive"—the end designated for them within the narrative. They resist oblivion. No matter how many times we blow them up, filet them like fish, send them back to the grave, or jettison them back into deep space, they keep creeping back into our world and under our skin, revealing a radical, unknowable, unimaginable otherness within. This, too, is revealed by the camera, as we have seen.

German filmmaker Fred Keleman (*Fate*, 1994) suggests that cinematic horror is about naming otherness so as to control and/or exorcize it:

> . . . in the ancient caves of Lascaux, France, for example, the first reason for mankind to make pictures was to "bannen" [ban, banish, exorcize], to fix it, to bring out, to capture the demons, because when you name them, they'll lose their power. That was the first reason people started to paint. . . . I think that is a lot like film, because cinema is like a modern cave, people come together— that's why the darkness is so important—and you have the screen like a wall in the old caves. And the aim is to put a spell on the demons. To exorcize, if you want.[16]

Keleman's explanation of the aim of ancient cave painting here is similar to what we have characterized as one of the purposes of myths, that is, to encounter the chaos monster and ultimately to banish it. In cinema, the camera does point in this way. That is, it *points out*, naming otherness in order to exorcize it. Indeed, as we have seen, the camera points and shoots, and we viewers point and shoot along with it. But the camera also always necessarily points out its own failure to point out, to exorcize. To talk about imag(in)ing otherness in film in a way that does not reduce otherness to the familiar is to talk about the work of failure, that is, the camera's inevitable failure to present, to image, otherness. For it points with a severed finger, with a gouged eye, in a bad light, in a hall of broken mirrors.

Endnotes

1. On relations between religion, horror, and the monstrous, see my *Religion and Its Monsters: From Ancient Scripture to Contemporary Horror* (New York: Routledge, forthcoming).

2. *The Giant Behemoth*, written and directed by Eugene Lourie (Artists Alliance Limited, 1959); alternatively titled *The Beast from 20,000 Fathoms*.

3. For a summary discussion of myth and sacred time, see Mircea Eliade, *The Sacred and the Profane: The Nature of Religion*, trans. Willard R. Trask (San Diego: Harcourt Brace & Company, 1957), pp. 68-113.

4. For a discussion of these and other similar myths in Egyptian, Mesopotamian, Israelite, Vedic, and Zoroastrian tradition, see Norman Cohn, *Cosmos, Chaos and the World to Come: The Ancient Roots of Apocalyptic Faith* (New Haven: Yale University Press, 1993), pp. 1-140. Note that Leviathan in biblical literature is a highly ambivalent figure. In some texts, it

is a primordial or extraordial chaos monster that threatens God's created order (Psalm 74:12-17; Isaiah 27:1; Job 3:8). In other texts, while still in some sense monstrous and chaotic, it is aligned with God (esp. Job 41; cf. Psalm 104:26).

5. This sense of a monstrous subjectivity that sees without being seen is further heightened in many horror films by use of the unclaimed point of view shot, which identifies the viewer's point of view with that of the implied monster as it stalks its oblivious victim. The viewer looks through the eyes of a monster. On this cinematic strategy, see esp. Isabel Cristina Pinedo, *Recreational Terror: Women and the Pleasures of Horror Film Viewing* (Albany: SUNY Press, 1997), pp. 51-55.

6. See Pinedo, *Recreational Terror*, p. 52.

7. The concept of suture was first developed not in film but in psychoanalytic discourse, by Jacques-Alain Miller, a student of Jacques Lacan. For a fuller discussion of suture in psychoanalysis and film theory, see Kaja Silverman, *The Subject of Semiotics* (Oxford: Oxford University Press, 1983), pp. 199-236.

8. Pinedo, *Recreational Terror*, p. 56.

9. Noël Carroll, *The Philosophy of Horror, or Paradoxes of the Heart* (New York: Routledge, 1990), pp. 31-32, 182-86; Mary Douglas, *Purity and Danger: An Analysis of Concepts of Pollution and Taboo* (New York: Praeger, 1966), esp. pp. 41-57.

10. Judith Halberstam, *Skin Shows: Gothic Horror and the Technology of Monsters* (Durham: Duke University Press, 1995).

11. Note that the world of this film is almost completely homosocial. Indeed, what this monster destroys, or threatens to destroy, is the very fabric of patriarchal family life (first Thomas, leaving his daughter in hysterics, and then the father and son) and patriarchal techno-science (the "kings of the earth").

12. One finds a similar implication in battles against monsters in ancient mythology. Thus, for example, Marduk wields flood and storm weapons to destroy the stormy Tiamat in the Babylonian *Enuma Elish*; the wild man Enkidu is crucial in defeating the forest monster Humbaba (Huwawa) in the *Gilgamesh Epic*; and in one mythos from Egypt the formerly anomalous and chaotic Seth stands at the front of the sun-god's boat, piercing the serpent of the chaos waters and helping to preserve the cosmic order (*ma'at*). For helpful summaries, see Cohn, *Chaos, Cosmos*, pp. 1-56. Compare also early Jewish and Christian apocalyptic texts, in which it is often difficult to determine which side in the battle is more monstrous.

13. Jean-François Lyotard, *The Postmodern Condition: A Report on Knowledge*, Geoff Bennington and Brian Massumi, trans. (Minneapolis: University of Minnesota Press, 1984), pp. 81-82.

14. Lyotard, *The Postmodern Condition*, p. 74. On film and techno-realism, see Stan Brakhage, "Metaphors on Vision," *Film Culture* 30 (1963), esp. the section on "Camera Eye." Of course, Lyotard's and Brakhage's conceptions of realism and its objectives differ from those who identify with the realist school in film. For a discussion of Bazin's theory of realism as applied to *Babette's Feast*, see Maria Maisto's "Cinematic Communion?" in this volume, pp. 87-88.

15. H.P. Lovecraft, *Supernatural Horror in Literature* (New York: Dover, 1973), pp. 1-15.

16. Quoted in John Gianvito, "An Inconsolable Darkness: The Reappearance and Redefinition of Gothic in Contemporary Cinema," in Christoph Grunenberg, ed., *Gothic: Transmutations of Horror in Late Twentieth Century Art* (Cambridge: MIT Press, 1997), p. 48.

Afterword:
Otherness ad infinitum

David Jasper

In Dostoevsky's novel *The Brothers Karamazov*, Alyosha Karamazov remarks, "We are all responsible for everyone else—but I am more responsible than all the others." The excessive challenge of this statement has been picked up in the twentieth century by, among others, Emmanuel Levinas and Paul Ricoeur. In his book *Oneself as Another* (1992), Ricoeur begins with a reflection on the "modalities of identity," of which the contraries are "other," "distinct," "diverse," "unequal," "inverse." And yet his argument is that it is only in the other that we find the self—*"soi-même comme un autre."*

Such a dialectic threads its way through the various and different essays in this book, and at various and different levels. My fellow editor, Brent Plate, begins his Introduction with a reading of our title which exhibits a relationship between aesthetics and ethics. The nature of this relationship is altered by the specific and peculiar potential and demands of the modern cinema, which brings together the power of the image with the power of the word, related within movement and narrative. It is often remarked that the twentieth century has exchanged the verbal for the visual, and that this has meant the abandonment of intellectual traditions founded in the word, for a culture much more responsive to the immediacy of the senses. As the neo-plasticist artist Piet Mondrian, also a prolific writer, once put it, "Curves are too emotional." Francisca Cho in her essay draws upon David Freedberg's art historical study of the power of images, taking his thesis, with its blurring of the distinction between "low" and "high" art, and between religious and secular art, into the context of cinema. But words, too, can evoke powerful emotions, and in the cinema, the interaction of word and moving image can establish an intense place for aesthetic, ethical, intellectual, and emotional response and change.

In all of these essays, different kinds of "otherness" are proposed as challenges to our imaginations, building up through film a complex sense of our responsibility of living with others. This responsibility is not only immediate and personal (through our families or neighbors), but extends through the depths of various societies (from so-called high and low culture), along the historical narratives of traditions (linking us with others in the past and in the future), and across cultures (Eastern and Western) and across different religions. Thus we become linked with every "other" in the specific and powerful world of the film. The comment has often been made that the growing academic field of religion and film studies has tended to neglect the particular art of the cinema, and has "read" films as though they were simply written texts

213

in the more traditional sense. What is now needed, and offered by many of the essays in this book, is an informed sensitivity to the technical capabilities of the "texts" of film and cinematography (a new field of "otherness"), to draw us into a (re)vision of ethical response through an art form which can claim its own particular power and significance. Thus, Maria Maisto's study of Gabriel Axel's *Babette's Feast* indicates how the visual narrative of the film establishes a dialectical relationship with the characters and their speech—how we *see*. Babette (distant and inaccessible) contrasts with her worldliness and exoticism. The camera becomes an element in the ability of art to convey moments of transcendence, its technique a subtle instrument in establishing the viewer's perspective and response.

We have emphasized throughout this book that the art form of the cinema is culturally complex and many-sided (like all others), and that the commercial and popular cinema of Hollywood is only one of its expressions. This we have not ignored, but different cultures have developed specific and readily identifiable cinemas which reflect their particularities and characteristics, so that film has become one of the most sensitive reflectors of both the differences between societies and the complex interactions which characterize our contemporary, shrinking world. Nowhere in this collection is this better illustrated than in Ira Bhaskar's essay on Peter Brook's *Mahabharata*. This hugely popular enterprise lies "entangled . . . in a whole host of political, ideological contradictions," at the heart of which is a religious confusion as societies meet one another in the international medium of the cinema. We think we "know" India in the performance, but this is an India which has never existed in any response to the great epic classic of its religious literature. It is as constructed and as syncretistic as the India of David Lean's version of *A Passage to India*, a film which finally avoids the hesitant, divided ending of E. M. Forster's original novel. Lean, it may be, sets out with an eye to profit, to construct an exotic culture, while the film *Dead Man*, in Gregory Salyer's essay, in a "non-commercial" spirit deliberately undercuts the myth of the American "West" and, by a confusing eclecticism, leads us to encounter an otherness on the edges where most people, as Salyer puts it, "don't get it." Irena Makarushka, similarly, sees the disconcerting complexities of *Breaking the Waves* as the deconstruction of culturally constructed paradigms—cinema's constructions inviting a deconstruction that opens up profound moral, and perhaps religious, questions "that viewers will invariably need to answer for themselves."

It is precisely cinema's ability to bridge cultural gaps in a commercial and artistic packaging of difference, which can enable it to offer a new series of possibilities of living together in a world which (at least in the West) has lost its confidence in the specific claims of its religious and theological traditions, or, worse still, ossified them in various forms of religious fundamentalism. Such fundamentalism has, generally speaking, been avoided by the cinema, and precisely because of its recovery of that which is insisted upon throughout this collection—that is a sense of community. Whereas, it could be said, in the past the Church in the West has offered its liturgy as a cultural event to a participating community, religion has now in practice become the pastime of the few who build exclusive walls around their commitment and activities. The cinema and film (even in the video age) has become one of the major cultural events within our societies, binding them together through its technology and in its temples which have developed from the first picture "palaces" to the modern "multiplex." The price of admission may be assessed commercially, yet it has a freedom which is, in the end, less exclusive than the rules and doctrinal demands made by traditional religions.

> Cinema and film are both sold at the same point, at the point of sale of an admission ticket. It is not the film that is sold at this point, it is the possibility of viewing a film or film; it is not cinema as an object that is sold, but cinema as an anticipated experience.[1]

Functioning as a special event, cinema thus becomes a new form of liturgical activity, bound not by the traditional religious demand that, for example, we celebrate the eucharist as far as possible as it has always been celebrated so that we are bound in continuities through time and geography, but by difference. That is, cinema invites exotic possibilities across cultures, even though these may be transgressive. We may find a new "cinematic communion" in which we live together imaginatively and celebrate a (re)vision of sacramental otherness in what Maria Maisto calls an "aesthetics of self-expression." Different images and presences of India may thus emerge through the films of Satyajit Ray, David Lean, and Peter Brook representing the perspectives of different cultural approaches using "India" to explore universal themes such as honor, truth, family values, and religion. Individually and together they becomes means of imagining otherness and reflecting on community, both specific and universal.

I recall my own experience of watching films which I had seen in London—specifically *A Man for All Seasons* (Dir. Zinnemann, 1966), and *Girl on a Motorcycle* (Dir. Cardiff, 1968)—in an open air cinema in rural Bihar in north India in the early 1970s, and realizing that these films, in their different ways, represented the "West" to everyone else watching, and that, in a way, their conclusions as Indians about, respectively, Tudor England and the camp freedoms of the Europe of the late sixties, were probably little different from my own. What was very different, however, were the moral deductions which my Indian friends drew. But the result was that we were drawn into a community of imagined otherness in a conversation which was stimulated into something like universal conclusions. Seeing these films together took me out of my own assumptions and invited them to "see" the other as portrayed through the images of its own myths, both historical and contemporary. What emerged, perhaps, was something very like the contextual therapy described by

Patrick Caruso and Brent Plate, in which freedom and obligation exist in dynamic tension.

For similar reasons, the growing number of films about the Holocaust have offered a serious contribution to how we relate to that enormity as a community within which no-one is finally innocent and no-one, in a way, is not a victim. The ambiguities, as Jennifer Koosed explores in her essay, are grounded in paradoxes of the Bible itself—betrayal and loyalty, abandonment and rescue. Above all, the very impossibility of the images presented by the Holocaust offer to the cinema a profound challenge of "otherness." The fact that the degradations of the camps cannot be "filmed" has made the repeated attempts to do precisely that all the more powerful in pushing our imaginations at every level towards an acknowledgement that the unimaginable only becomes such in the image which cannot be born, or which admits its own triteness as an attempt to explain or even excuse. Such imaging of the unimaginable is explored in detail in Timothy Beal's essay which focuses on the ancient biblical figure of Leviathan, and from there to different heterologies of monstrous otherness in film. The "other," in Brent Plate's words at the beginning of this book, "may be divine, monstrous, or some combination of the two." Film thus, and in spite of itself, has its own sometimes terrible "real presence" beyond itself, engendered in the minds of the community, or perhaps congregation, of watchers.

Cinema occasionally acknowledges and even explores this as in Woody Allen's comedy *The Purple Rose of Cairo* (1984), which deliberately steps out of its own limitations and explores the confusion which ensues when "film" and "reality" are merged, when otherness becomes present to the dreaming watcher in the film (Mia Farrow), whom we, in turn watch. Film, like the liturgy, is a serious business when it confronts a community with the otherness that is in its midst as part of itself though often unacknowledged. Such otherness may be profoundly ambiguous—perhaps necessarily so—like Babette, at the end of Babette's Feast, remaining as an awkward presence to deconstruct the too-ready desire to interpret the film as a celebration of the eucharist, a filmic version of the Mass. Our whole argument has made the claim that cinema is precisely independent of such immediate and derivative connections.

The study of film and religion has a growing history, stretching as far back as the late 1950s, through the work of scholars like John R. May and Paul Schrader.[2] Much of it has focused on film *about* religion, such as the great Biblical epics produced in Hollywood from Cecil B. DeMille to the present day, or else the moral and ethical implications of films, particularly from art house cinema. We have expanded the religion and film discussion in two significant ways. First we have drawn upon international scholarship to consider cinema from a global perspective—North American, European, Indian, and East Asian, and from within a variety of religious traditions. Second, our theme of "otherness" situates these discussions within a major concern of contemporary theological discussion, bearing comparison with such works as Buber's classic *I and Thou* (1937), and more recently the work of Emmanuel Levinas and Paul Ricoeur, among others. In Levinas, the debate is carried forward from Heidegger's ontological concerns in *Being and Time*, to the ethical and religious consideration of the Other to which we are endlessly obligated. In Ricoeur's great work *Oneself as Another*, he explores "the ethical and moral determinations of action [which are] confirmed by a meditation grafted onto the poetics of *agapê*."[3]

Our work here develops such profound concerns in philosophy and theology through the medium of cinema, making claims for that art form which set it at the very heart of the most significant religious and theological discussions of the present time. Quite simply, the art of the cinema seriously continues that great task of art in all ages, a task which is at the same time profoundly religious, which is to draw us back to an imagining of otherness and a relearning of the business of living with the Other and living in community.

Endnotes

1. John Ellis, *Visible Fictions: Cinema, Television, Video*. (London and New York: Routledge, 1992, rev. ed.), pp. 25-26.

2. See, for example, John R. May and Ernest Ferlita, *Film Odyssey: The Art of Film as Search for Meaning* (New York: Paulist Press, 1976), and Paul Schrader, *Transcendental Style in Film: Ozu, Bresson, Dreyer* (Berkeley: University of California Press, 1972).

3. Paul Ricoeur, *Oneself as Another*. Trans. Kathleen Blamey (Chicago: University of Chicago Press, 1992), p. 25.

Contributors

S. Brent Plate teaches Religion at the University of Vermont. He has published articles on religion, literature, and the arts in the journals *Literature and Theology*, *Postmodern Culture*, and *Biblical Interpretation*, and the volume *Teaching Apocalypse* (ed., Pippin, Scholars Press) among other places. His edited volume *The Apocalyptic Imagination: Aesthetics and Ethics at the End of the World* was published by Trinity St. Mungo Press in 1999.

David Jasper is Dean of the Divinity Faculty, University of Glasgow. He has published over a dozen books and numerous articles, and has had his work translated into several languages. He is the founder of the international journal *Literature and Theology* and current co-editor of the Macmillan/St. Martins Press series, "Religion and Culture."

Gregory Salyer is Assistant Professor of Humanities at Huntingdon College in Montgomery, Alabama. He is the author of *Leslie Marmon Silko* and is the North American general editor for *Literature and Theology*. Dr. Salyer has published numerous articles on Native American literature, postmodernism, the Bible, and mythology.

Jennifer L. Koosed is a graduate student in Hebrew Bible at Vanderbilt University. She has co-authored with Tod Linafelt "How the West Was Not One: Delilah Deconstructs the Western" which appeared in *Semeia 74*.

Tod Linafelt is Assistant Professor of Biblical Studies at Georgetown University. He is co-editor of *God in the Fray* (Fortress, 1998), and author of a commentary on the book of Ruth (Liturgical Press, 1999) and *Surviving Lamentations* (University of Chicago Press, forthcoming). His articles have appeared in the journals *Semeia*, *Biblical Interpretation*, and *Horizons in Biblical Theology*, as well as in the edited volumes *Reading Bibles, Writing Bodies, A Feminist Companion to Reading the Bible*, and *Bibel und Midrasch*.

Kyle Keefer is Assistant Professor of Biblical Studies at Eckerd College.

Irena S. M. Makarushka is Associate Dean for Academic Affairs at Goucher College in Baltimore, Maryland. The primary focus of her scholarship and publications is in the area of religion and culture, particularly in contemporary film. She has also published in the field of philosophy of religion, specifically on nineteenth century thinkers including Friedrich Nietzsche, Ralph Waldo Emerson and Elizabeth Cady Stanton.

Maria Consuelo Maisto is a PhD candidate in Comparative Literature at the University of Maryland, College Park. Currently she serves as the assistant to the national coordinator of Racial Legacies and Learning: An American Dialogue, a Ford-funded initiative of the Association of American Colleges and Universities promoting campus-community dialogue about the history of race relations and the potential for racial reconciliation in the United States.

Patrick Caruso holds an M.Div from Princeton Theological Seminary, and an M.S.W. from Rutgers University. He is a clinical social worker at the Family Guidance Center in Hamilton, New Jersey. He lives with his wife and son in Princeton, New Jersey.

Ira Bhaskar is an Instructor in English Literature at Delhi University, India, and a PhD candidate at the department of Cinema Studies, Tisch School of the Arts, New York University. Her work in both film and literature deals with issues of nationalism. She has published most recently in the journal *Literature and Theology*.

Francisca Cho is Associate Professor of Buddhist Studies in the Theology Department at Georgetown University. She is the author of *Embracing Illusion: Truth and Fiction in the Dream of the Nine Clouds* (SUNY Press, 1996), and most recently, "Leaping into the Boundless: A Daoist Reading of Comparative Religious Ethics," in *Journal of Religious Ethics* (Spring 1998). She is the East Asia editor of *The Encyclopedia of Women and World Religion*, published in 1998 by Macmillan Press.

Timothy K. Beal is Harkness Associate Professor of Biblical Literature at Case Western Reserve University. He is the author of *The Book of Hiding: Gender, Ethnicity, Annihilation, and Esther* (Routledge, 1997), *Esther* (Liturgical, 1999), and *Religion and Its Monsters* (Routledge, forthcoming). He is co-editor of *Reading Bibles, Writing Bodies* (Routledge, 1996) and *God in the Fray* (Fortress, 1998).

Filmography

Aparajito (The Unvanquished)
    Director: Satyajit Ray
    Writing credits: Satyajit Ray, Bibhutibhushan Bandyopadhyay (novel: *Aparajito*)
    Producer: Satyajit Ray
    Original music: Ravi Shankar
    Cinematography: Subrata Mitra
    Editor: Dulal Dutta
    Production company: Epic Productions
    Country: India
    Language: Bengali
    Released: 1956

Babette's Feast (Babettes gæstebud)
    Director: Gabriel Axel
    Writing credits: Gabriel Axel, Isak Dinesen (novel; as Karen Blixen)
    Producers: Just Betzer, Bo Christensen
    Original music: Per Nørgaard
    Additional music: Johannes Brahms (from "Waltzes, Op. 39 No. 15"), Wolfgang Amadeus Mozart (from "Don Giovanni")
    Cinematography: Henning Kristiansen
    Editor: Finn Henriksen
    Production companies: Panorama
    Country: Denmark
    Language: Danish
    Released: 1987

Breaking the Waves
    Director: Lars von Trier
    Writing credits: Lars von Trier
    Producers: Lars Jönsson (executive), Peter Aalbæk Jensen, Vibeke Windeløv, Axel Helgeland (co-producer), Rob Langestraat (co-producer), Marianne Slot (co-producer), Peter van Vogelpoel (co-producer)
    Original music: Joachim Holbek
    Cinematography: Robby Müller
    Editor: Anders Refn

Production companies: Trust, Zentropa Entertainments, Liberator Productions, Argus Film Produktie (Distributed in the U.S. by October Films)
Country: Denmark / Netherlands / Sweden / France
Language: English
Released: 1996

Dead Man

Director: Jim Jarmusch
Writing credits: Jim Jarmusch
Producers: Demetra J. MacBride, Karen Koch (co-producer)
Original music: Neil Young
Cinematography: Robby Müller
Editor: Jay Rabinowitz
Production companies: 12-Gauge Productions/Miramax Films
Country: United States
Language: English
Released: 1995

The Giant Behemoth (AKA *Behemoth, the Sea Monster*)

Director: Douglas Hickox, Eugène Lourié
Writing credits: Alan J. Adler, Robert Abel (story; as Allen Adler), Eugène Lourié, Daniel James
Producer: David Diamond, Ted Lloyd
Original music: Edwin T. Astley
Cinematography: Desmond Davis
Editor: Lee Doig
Production companies: Aristes Alliance Limited, Diamond Pictures, Allied Artists Pictures Corporation
Country: UK
Language: English
Released: 1959

The Mahabharata

Country: India / France / UK
Language: English
Released: 1989 (as TV mini-series)
Director: Peter Brook
Writing credits: Peter Brook, Jean-Claude Carrière, Marie-Hélène Estienne
Producer: Michael Propper

Original music: Philippe Eidel, Rabindranath Tagore, Toshi Tsuchitori
Cinematography: William Lubtchansky
Editor: Nicolas Gaster
Production Design: C. Obolensky
Country: United States
Language: English
Released: 1995

A Passage to India
Director: David Lean
Writing credits: David Lean, E.M. Forster (novel)
Producer: John Heyman, Edward Sands
Original music: John Dalby
Cinematography: Ernest Day
Editor: David Lean
Production companies: EMI Films
Country: UK
Language: English
Released: 1984

The Quarrel
Director: Eli Cohen
Writing credits: David Brandes, Chaim Grade (based on: "My Quarrel
    with Hersh Rasseyner"), Joseph Telushkin (play)
Producers: David Brandes, Kim Todd, Joseph Telushkin (Associate)
Original music: William Goldstein
Cinematography: John Berrie
Editor: Havelock Gradidge
Production companies: Apple & Honey Productions/Atlantis Films
    Limited
Country: Canada
Language: English
Released: 1992

Why Has the Bodhi-Dharma Left for the East?
Director: Yong-Kyun Bae
Writing credits: Yong-Kyun Bae
Original music: Kyu-Young Chin
Cinematography: Yong-Kyun Bae
Distribution: Milestone Film and Video (US)
Country: Korea
Language: Korean
Released: 1989

You Can't Take It with You
       Director: Frank Capra
       Writing credits: Robert Riskin, George S. Kaufman and Moss Hart (play)
       Producer: Frank Capra (uncredited)
       Original music: Dimitri Tiomkin
       Cinematography: Joseph Walker
       Editor: Gene Havlick
       Production companies: Columbia Pictures
       Country: United States
       Language: English
       Released: 1938

Selected Bibliography

Listed below are books mentioned at various places in this volume, as well as additional, relevant material. The academic fields represented here encompass film studies, religious studies, religion and film, cultural studies, and philosophy. Due to the interdisciplinary nature of this volume, a full bibliography would be an impossible task. This bibliography simply provides the reader with a variety of sources that dovetail with the major themes of the volume.

More exhaustive bibliographies for "religion and film" can be found in the Marsh and Ortiz edited, *Explorations in Theology and Film*, and in the John May edited, *New Image of Religious Film*.

Bach, Alice, ed. *Semeia 74* (1996).

Bataille, Georges. *Erotism: Death and Sensuality*. Trans. Mary Dalwood. San Francisco: City Lights, 1986.

Beal, Timothy K. *Religion and Its Monsters: From Ancient Scripture to Contemporary Horror*. New York: Routledge, forthcoming.

Berkhofer, Robert. *The White Man's Indian: Images of the American Indian from Columbus to the Present*. New York: Vintage, 1978.

Bhaskar, Ira. "Allegory, nationalism and cultural change in Indian cinema: *Sant Tukaram*." *Literature and Theology* 12.1 (March, 1998): pp. 50-69.

Brakhage, Stan. "Metaphors on Vision." *Film Culture* 30 (1963).

Brooker, Peter, ed. *Modernism/Postmodernism*. New York: Longman, 1992.

Chow, Rey. *Primitive Passions: Visuality, Sexuality, Ethnography, and Contemporary Chinese Cinema*. New York: Columbia University Press, 1995.

Doane, Mary Ann. *The Desire to Desire: The Woman's Film of the 1940s*. Bloomington: Indiana University Press, 1987.

Dyer, Richard. *White*. London: Routledge, 1997.

Eck, Diana. *Darśan: Seeing the Divine Image in India*. 3rd ed. New York: Columbia University Press, 1998.

Eliade, Mircea. *The Sacred and the Profane: The Nature of Religion*. Trans. Willard R. Trask. San Diego: Harcourt Brace & Company, 1957.

Ellis, John. *Visible Fictions: Cinema, Television, Video*. London and New York: Routledge, 1992, rev. ed.

Faure, Bernard. *The Rhetoric of Immediacy: A Cultural Critique of Chan/Zen Buddhism*. Princeton: Princeton University Press, 1991.

———. *Visions of Power: Imagining Medieval Japanese Buddhism*. Princeton: Princeton University Press, 1996.

Freedberg, David. *The Power of Images: Studies in the History and Theory of Response*. Chicago: University of Chicago Press, 1989.

Guerrero, Ed. *Framing Blackness: The African American Image in Film*. Philadelphia: Temple University Press, 1992.

hooks, bell. *Black Looks: Race and Representation*. Boston: South End Press, 1992.

de Lauretis, Teresa. *Alice Doesn't: Feminism, Semiotics, Film*. Bloomington: Indiana University Press, 1982.

———. *Technologies of Gender*. Bloomington: Indiana University Press, 1987.

Douglas, Mary. *Purity and Danger: An Analysis of Concepts of Pollution and Taboo*. New York: Praeger, 1966.

Halberstam, Judith. *Skin Shows: Gothic Horror and the Technology of Monsters*. Durham: Duke University Press, 1995.

Lingis, Alphonso. *The Community of Those Who Have Nothing in Common*. Bloomington: Indiana University Press, 1994.

McLuhan, Marshall. *The Gutenberg Galaxy: The Making of Typographic Man*. Toronto: University of Toronto Press, 1962.

Marsh, Clive and Gaye Ortiz, eds., *Explorations in Theology and Film*. Oxford: Blackwell, 1997.

Martin, Joel W. and Conrad E. Ostwalt, eds., *Screening the Sacred*. Boulder: Westview Press, 1995.

May, John R. *New Image of Religious Film* London: Sheed and Ward, 1997.

May, John R. and Ernest Ferlita, *Film Odyssey: The Art of Film as Search for Meaning*. New York: Paulist Press, 1976.

Miles, Margaret. *Seeing and Believing*. Boston: Beacon Press, 1996.

Ong, Walter. *Orality and Literacy: The Technologizing of the Word*. London and New York: Methuen, 1982.

Penley, Constance, ed. *Feminism and Film Theory*. New York: Routledge, 1988.

Pinedo, Isabel Christina. *Recreational Terror: Women and the Pleasures of Horror Film Viewing*. Albany: SUNY Press, 1997.

Plate, S. Brent. "Religion/Literature/Film: Toward A Religious Visuality of Film," in *Literature & Theology* 12.1 (March 1998): 16-38

Ricoeur, Paul. *Oneself as Another*. Trans. Kathleen Blamey. Chicago: University of Chicago Press, 1992.

Robin, Diana and Ira Jaffe, eds. *Redirecting the Gaze: Gender, Theory, and Cinema in the Third World*. Albany: SUNY Press, 1999.

Schrader, Paul. *Transcendental Style in Film: Ozu, Bresson, Dreyer*. Berkeley: University of California Press, 1972.

Silk, Catherine and John Silk, *Racism and Anti-racism in American Popular Culture*. Manchester and New York: Manchester University Press, 1990.

Silverman, Kaja. *The Subject of Semiotics*. Oxford: Oxford University Press, 1983.

———. *The Threshold of the Visible World*. New York: Routledge, 1996.

Vizenor, Gerald, ed. *Narrative Chance: Postmodern Discourse on Native American Indian Literatures*. Albuquerque: University of New Mexico Press, 1989.

Gerald Vizenor, *Manifest Manners: Postindian Warriors of Survivance.* Hanover, NH: Wesleyan University Press, 1994.

Winston, Brian. *Technologies of Seeing*. London: British Film Institute, 1996.

Woll, A. L. and R. M. Miller, *Ethnic and Racial Images in American Film and Television.* New York: Garland Publishing, 1987.

Index